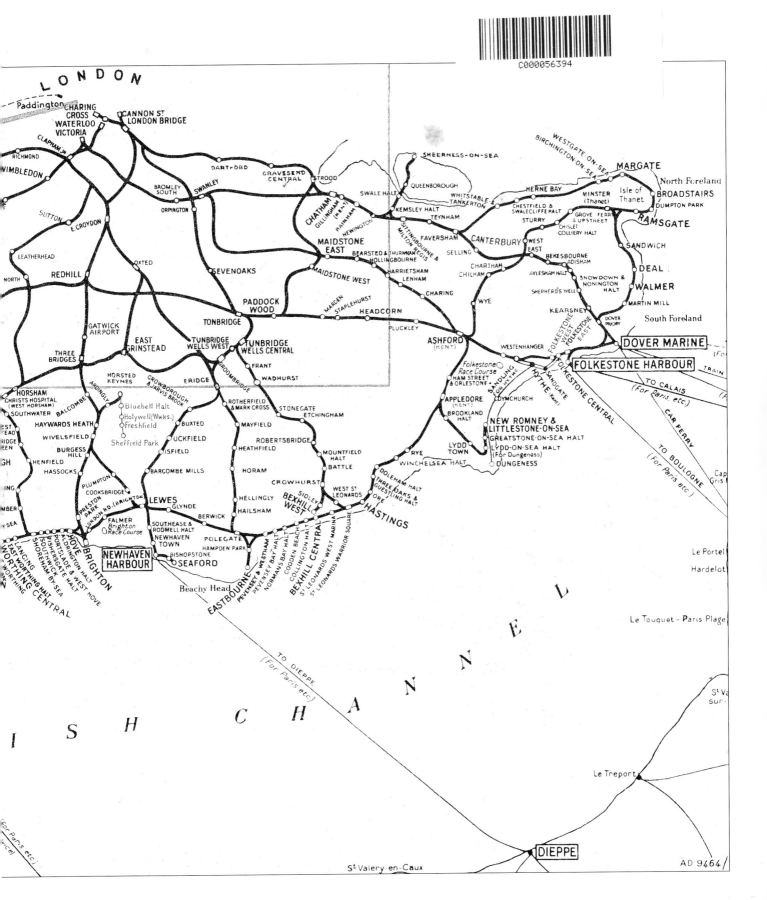

AD 9464/

SOUTHERN ELECTRIC

SOUTHERN
ELECTRIC

John Glover

Ian Allan
PUBLISHING

First published 2001

ISBN 0 7110 2807 9

© Ian Allan Publishing Ltd 2001

Published by Ian Allan Publishing

an imprint of Ian Allan Publishing Ltd, Hersham, Surrey KT12 4RG
Printed by Ian Allan Printing Ltd, Hersham, Surrey KT12 4RG

Code: 0109/B1

Bibliography

War on the Line. The Story of the Southern Railway in War-time. Bernard Darwin. The Southern Railway Company, London, 1946

British Electric Trains. Howard W. A. Linecar. Ian Allan Ltd, 1947

The Southern Railway 1923–1947: A Chronology and Record. R. A. Savill. Oakwood Press Locomotion Papers No 6, 1950

Electrification of Railways. British Transport Commission, London, 1951

The Southern Railway. R. W. Kidner, Oakwood Press Library of Railway History No 56, 1958

History of the Southern Railway. C. F. Dendy Marshall, revised R. W. Kidner. ISBN 0 7110 0059 X. Ian Allan Ltd, 1963

A Regional History of the Railways of Great Britain. Vol 2: Southern England, Vol 3: Greater London. H. P. White. David & Charles, 1964 and 1963

Sir Herbert Walker's Southern Railway. C. F. Klapper. ISBN 0 7110 0478 1. Ian Allan Ltd, 1973

On and Off the Rails. Sir John Elliot. ISBN 0 04 385089 8. George Allen & Unwin Ltd, 1982

Southern Railway Halts Survey and Gazetteer. R. W. Kidner. ISBN 0 85361 321 4. The Oakwood Press, 1985

Forgotten Railways No 6: South East England. H. P. White. ISBN 0 946537 37 2. David St John Thomas, 1987

The History of the Southern Railway. Michael R. Bonavia. ISBN 0 04 385107 X. Unwin Hyman Ltd, 1987

Going Green: The Story of the District Line. 2nd edition, Piers Connor. ISBN 185414 162 7. Capital Transport Publishing, 1994

Railway Track Diagrams 5: England South and London Underground. ISBN 1 898319 07 3. Quail Map Company, 1994.

Southern Electrics, A View from the Past. Graham Waterer. ISBN 0 7110 2621 1. Ian Allan Publishing, 1998.

abc British Railways Locomotives, Ian Allan Ltd, various editions

Locomotives and Coaching Stock, Platform 5 Publishing Ltd, various editions

Journal of the Institute of Transport

Modern Transport newspaper, weekly, 1919–65

Modern Railways, Railway World, The Railway Magazine, Rail Express

Annual Report and Accounts of the British Railways Board, its predecessors and successors. Various editions of the timetables.

Contents

Half title:

Arriving at East Grinstead is 4VEP unit No 3517 with the 12.35 Connex SouthCentral service from Victoria. This view shows how the double track from Oxted reduces to single before splitting again to the two station platforms. *Author*

Title page:

The London & South Western reached Hampton Court with electric traction on 18 June 1916. The station is seen here with one of the trains of steam stock conversions with unit No E20 at the head and about to depart for Waterloo. A second train is in the platform on the left. *Author's collection*

Above left:

A postwar build of 4SUB units had what the image makers called a streamlined appearance, as seen here. New deliveries were promised at the rate of one per week. It was stated that seating capacity had been improved, and each compartment took 12 passengers in comfort instead of 10 as before. This is unit No 4111 about to leave Orpington on its first trip on 13 May 1946, or so the information on the back of the print says. However, the train does not appear to have a conductor rail in the vicinity, and why has the driver not set up a headcode? *Author's collection*

Dedication

In memory of the late H. P. (Pat) White, Emeritus Professor of Geography at the University of Salford, but once a booking clerk at Charlton. He was my tutor at Salford during three happy years there.

Acknowledgements

The further one delves into the Southern Electric system, the more complex it becomes! I am grateful to Michael Woods for his contribution on bad-weather working at Dartford, and for his guiding me generally on the foibles of the Southern's system. Also of great help have been John Chapman and Tony Francis, for the loan of material and their knowledge of the system. Mark Horner of Seaton Tramway was most helpful, while John King provided some useful information on the abortive Lullingstone station.

The Institute of Logistics and Transport's library has been immensely helpful in making its 90-odd volumes of Modern Transport available for reference, and I have been able to draw on past issues of its Journal and its copies of *The Railway Magazine*, as well as my own volumes of *Modern Railways* and its predecessor. Other members of the Railway Studies Association and the Institution of Railway Operators have also been generous with their time, but any errors, if such there be, are my own.

Introduction

For the railways south of the Thames, with their predominantly short-distance suburban passenger traffic, electrification was an early priority, once the technical problems had been overcome. Compared with the steam railway, electric traction promised higher performance levels, lower operating costs and a much cleaner environment for the passenger. This is the story of that electrification scheme, its development and the services which have run on it over the years.

The Southern Railway was a pioneer of large scale suburban electrification. Formed as a result of the Railway Grouping in 1923, the Southern inherited two types of electric traction: the overhead system of the London, Brighton & South Coast, and the third rail system of the London & South Western. The latter prevailed.

In what was no more than a 16-year period, the Southern Railway under the guidance of its redoubtable General Manager, Sir Herbert Walker, extended vastly the coverage of electric services. By 1939, electric trains were all but universal in the suburban area, and extended along the coast from Hastings in the east to Portsmouth in the west. They also reached Reading and Alton.

The troubles of the war years bore heavily upon the Southern Railway, and it was left to its newly nationalised successor to make further additions to the electric traction coverage. Notably, the rest of Kent received electric trains between 1959 and 1962, as did Bournemouth (and also the Isle of Wight) in 1967. This left only the direct route to Hastings, where loading gauge problems inhibited previous attempts, to be completed in 1986. East Grinstead was reached in 1987, the extension beyond Bournemouth to Weymouth was completed in 1988, the Solent gap between Portsmouth and Southampton plus the branch to Eastleigh in 1990, as was the line between Redhill and Tonbridge in 1994.

By this stage, given also the effects of the line closures which had taken place in the 1950s and 1960s, electrification of the Southern system was all but complete. The West of England main line was the only route of substance to escape the third rail. But further change was afoot. The opening of the Channel Tunnel in 1994 introduced a new breed of three-system Eurostar trains, which only the most unkind would describe as an electric multiple-unit. Similarly, the vogue for cross-London services was growing, and what might once have been 'Southern' trains found themselves having to cope with alien overhead electrification systems using alternating current as far away as Bedford or Rugby. This too has resulted in trains that may use more than one electrification system.

Boundaries in today's railway are less defined than they once were. Today's Train Operating Companies are just that; they have no direct responsibilities for the infrastructure on which they run, and pay charges for their use of it. Where they operate is determined by a mixture of the terms of their obligations under their franchises, their own commercial ambitions, the suitability of their trains and the availability of track capacity. The track and its electrification are the responsibility of Railtrack, who also grant access rights to Train Operating Companies through the definition and allocation of train paths. Also, construction has started on the Channel Tunnel Rail Link.

How, then, should today's Southern Electric be defined? The author feels that readers will expect 'Southern' to encompass all lines which comprised the former Southern Railway and its British Railways successor, and which have been electrified on whatever system. Broadly, this is equivalent to Railtrack's Southern Zone. The boundaries are drawn mostly at the cessation of the third rail schemes or at some convenient point beyond. Other dc lines, such as the North London and those of London Underground, are included only as far as they shed a light on the emerging Southern picture.

The definition does however result in one surprise inclusion, which will be referred to here only as the East Devon electrification. The Waterloo & City line is omitted, as from 1994 it has been a fully fledged part of the London Underground system.

There are a number of Appendices, which it is hoped will serve as a series of useful references as to when events took place.

This book constitutes a completely rewritten, expanded and updated version of the same title, published under the authorship of G. T. Moody. This first appeared in 1957, with the fifth and most recent edition published in 1979.

John Glover
Worcester Park, Surrey
June 2001

Above:
Some of the CEP units ended their days with South West Trains, far from the Kent Coast for which they were built 40 years previously. 4CEP No 1534 approaches Vauxhall on 11 September 1998 with Big Ben and the Houses of Parliament in the background. The train is the 16.26 stopping service from Waterloo to Portsmouth & Southsea. *Author*

1. The Competition for Passengers

'That the whole (of British) society was interested in having a good system of internal communication seems to be forgotten.'

Lord Macaulay, 22 May 1846

The railways south of the River Thames have always been distinguished from their northern counterparts in the territories which each serve. The railway, let it be remembered, was first and foremost a conveyor of goods. Thus the primary purpose of the pioneering Stockton & Darlington in 1825 was to convey the products of the Durham coalfield to the River Tees for onward movement; the carriage of passengers was sub-let to coach proprietors. Such trains were horse-drawn, however, and remained so until 1833

A little later, the Liverpool & Manchester Railway of 1830 was, in the eyes of many, the first railway in a truly modern sense. Over the years, it became part of an extensive national network. This was preceded by the celebrated Rainhill trials, at which George Stephenson's Rocket locomotive produced a convincing victory for steam traction. Horse power was no longer in the running. What marked off the Liverpool & Manchester from earlier undertakings was its clear emphasis on passengers, from whom it derived around half its revenue right from the start. It was however freight from which railway fortunes were made, and this was a product, primarily, of what became the industrial Midlands, the North, central Scotland and South Wales. The coal and steel industries and their needs for the movement of both raw materials and the finished goods, were of relatively little consequence in the south east of England

Passengers were the main revenue earners of the constituents of the Southern Railway, and it was to the satisfaction of this market on which company efforts were focused. This, it transpired, meant the electrification of its services on a large scale, so large that by Nationalisation in 1948 the Southern possessed the biggest electrified suburban railway system owned by any one railway in the whole world. How this came about, and how it has developed since, is the subject of this book.

Early Construction

The growing map of railways being constructed showed the genesis of three of the four companies which were to dominate the scene south of London. The first of note and the first railway to enter London was the London & Greenwich. The first section of the line, from Deptford to a temporary terminus at Spa Road and then to London Bridge, was completed in December 1836, its $3\frac{3}{4}$ miles carried on brick arches throughout.

Soon the principle of running powers was established by Parliament, to allow the tracks of one company to be used by another on payment of a toll, or access charge. Thus, the London & Croydon Railway, incorporated in 1835, obtained powers to use the $1\frac{1}{4}$ miles of the Greenwich tracks from Corbett's Lane Junction to a London Bridge terminal of its own, alongside that of the Greenwich company. The London & Croydon completed its route via New Cross and Forest Hill to West Croydon in 1839

A third comer was the London & Brighton Railway, incorporated in 1837. The London & Brighton was to make its own junction with the London & Croydon, at a point to the south of the present Norwood Junction station. It secured running powers over the other two railways to reach the City

The situation was clearly becoming much more complex, given also that each company would wish to give priority to its own train services over those of others. However, there was yet a fourth company to enter the fray

This was the South Eastern Railway, which had obtained Parliamentary powers in 1836 to build a line from Norwood, through Oxted to Tonbridge, Ashford, Folkestone and Dover. Its trains would also use the London & Croydon's route into London Bridge. But the London & Brighton scheme of a year later offered a new opportunity to the SER. It therefore sought and was granted powers over the Brighton line northwards from what is now Redhill.

Construction of what was to have been the Brighton company's line to Redhill thus became a joint venture and, with Parliamentary sanction, ownership was then divided between the companies. Thus the London & Brighton owned the section south to Coulsdon, and the South Eastern thence to Redhill. This somewhat bizarre arrangement stemmed from a Parliamentary desire to limit the number of lines approaching London

This railway was completed to its intended Brighton terminus by 1841. The Croydon and the Brighton railways were amalgamated as the London, Brighton & South Coast Railway (LBSCR) in 1846. Two years later, and with

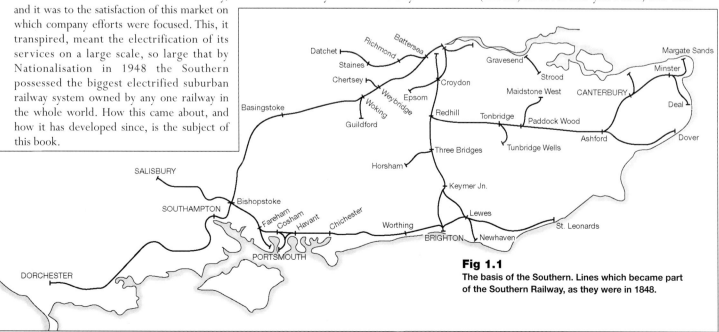

Fig 1.1
The basis of the Southern. Lines which became part of the Southern Railway, as they were in 1848.

further acquisitions, the undertaking had lines along the coast to St Leonards in the east and to Havant and Portsmouth in the west.

Other projections of the LBSCR were from Keymer Junction to Lewes and Newhaven, and from West Croydon to Epsom (both 1847), while Horsham was reached from Three Bridges in 1848, as was Cosham by an extension from Havant

To the west, the London & Southampton Railway, later the London & South Western (LSWR), was opened in stages between 1838 and 1840. The South Western promoted its branch from Eastleigh to Gosport (now closed beyond Fareham). It reached Cosham in 1848, where it met the Brighton company. The line into Portsmouth was joint LSWR and LBSCR property

Guildford gained a branch from Woking in 1845, Weybridge-Chertsey was completed in 1848, while the Richmond & West End Railway's line from Clapham Junction to Richmond was opened in 1846. It was extended by another company to Datchet in 1848, en route to Windsor; both were subsequently acquired by the LSWR. Importantly, the LSWR itself managed to extend its main line from the previous Nine Elms terminus to Waterloo on 11 July 1848

It may be added here that the South Eastern Railway's own line from Redhill which turned east and reached Ashford in almost a straight

line, was completed in 1842, and to Dover in 1844. It also spawned a branch from Paddock Wood to Maidstone West.

Tunbridge Wells was reached by the SER in 1845, while a line between Gravesend and Strood was acquired. Later, this would be the nucleus of the line to Dartford and thence to Cannon Street and Charing Cross. Further extensions took the railway from Ashford through Canterbury West to Minster, and then to both Margate in 1846 and Deal in 1847. This undertaking traded throughout as the South Eastern Railway

Another factor in all this was the topography of south east England, which was not particularly helpful to railway building. The downland ridges run broadly east-west, so they have to be penetrated by services between London and the coast. This was an expense that

the companies could do without, but it could be overcome only by the use of unacceptably steep gradients. What later became the Southern Railway has many tunnels, 10 of them being over a mile long, as Fig 1.2 shows.

Emerging Patterns

This necessarily brief description of the early days is included as a background to the later events. In particular, the following points may be noted:

- The concentration of the companies throughout was on serving the City of London; at that time the West End hardly existed. The LSWR's new terminus at Waterloo was still hardly an ideal location, while the Brighton company's line to Victoria was for the future; it was opened in 1860.

Fig 1.2: Tunnels on the Southern Electric, 1 mile or more in length		
Sevenoaks	SECR	1m 1,693yd
Polhill	SECR	1m 851yd
Lydden (Shepherds Well)	LCDR	1m 609yd
Strood	SER	1m 569yd
Oxted	SER/LBSCR Jt	1m 501yd
Clayton	LBSCR	1m 499yd
Penge	LCDR	1m 381yd
Quarry	LBSCR	1m 353yd
Abbotscliffe (Dover)	SER	1m 182yd
Merstham	SER	1m 71yd

- It is not possible for one terminal to serve adequately both the City and the West End, from whichever part of the area south of the Thames passengers originate.
- Originally, the South Eastern's only access to London Bridge was via Redhill, which resulted in circuitous and thus lengthy journeys from Kent.
- The railway companies were effective monopolies in most of their territories.
- Two separate routes to Portsmouth by the LBSCR and the LSWR, both of which were somewhat circuitous, would lead to conflict between the companies when the Direct line (from Guildford) was promoted subsequently.
- Suburban traffic, as it is known today, was a later phenomenon.

While much of the network remained to be constructed, the bare bones were there. It was, though, the South Eastern whose

Fig 1.3: The Companies and their London Termini

Company	City Terminus	West End Terminus
LSWR	none	Waterloo
LBSCR	London Bridge	Victoria (Brighton side)
LCDR	Holborn Viaduct, Blackfriars	Victoria (Chatham side)
SER	Cannon Street (via London Bridge)	Charing Cross

network map might be described as seriously deficient. The way in which this was corrected may be put down to competitive pressures and the emergence of a predator. The East Kent Railway, whose original section of line between Chatham and Faversham of 1858 expanded very quickly, may be cast in this role. What became the London, Chatham & Dover Railway (LCDR) reached Dover in 1861 and was completed via Swanley to the new Victoria in 1862.

One welcome consequence was the construction by the SER of its own line from London to Tonbridge via Sevenoaks, opened in 1868 and incorporating well over three miles of tunnelling. This reduced its journey to Kent via Redhill by 12½ miles and also avoided the growing congestion on what might more naturally be thought of as the Brighton's line. Further railway building with more than half an eye on the competition saw both companies' networks expanded. The Chatham's railway took in the Thanet coast to Margate, and a link from Swanley to Sevenoaks and also to Maidstone East and Ashford. At the London end, the Chatham secured powers for, and built, a link northwards from Herne Hill to Blackfriars and, indeed, to Farringdon.

In another attempt to ease congestion and to create its own independent route, the Brighton company opened the Quarry avoiding line between Coulsdon and Earlswood in 1900. This had the incidental side-effect of bypassing Redhill, to that town's lasting disadvantage.

The situation towards the end of the 19th century was that the London terminals were as shown in Fig 1.3.

To reach the City from Waterloo, the eventual result was the construction of the underground Waterloo & City Railway, which was opened in 1898. It was tailored to perform that function for the LSWR, and little else.

Suburban Railways

In addition, there were of course the suburban lines, opened at various stages and worked universally by steam traction. The conventional railway is a bulk mover, but it tends to shine over the longer distances for which there are a number of contributory factors:

- First, the need for relatively shallow gradients and large radius curvature often makes it difficult to site railway tracks

Left:
Hastings was one of the places served by both the South Eastern and Brighton companies, although for more than half a century the only electrified route was the slower Brighton one via Lewes. 4CIG unit No 7323 leaves the station on 16 October 1978 for Victoria. *Author*

Below:
Portsmouth could also be reached from London by the Brighton route along the coast, or by the South Western's routes via either Guildford or Eastleigh and Fareham. Both the routes via Havant, seen here, were electrified in the 1930s; this time it was the line via Fareham which had to wait. 4COR No 3158 calls at Havant with a train for Portsmouth. *Ian Allan Library*

close to traffic generating points, especially if much of the area has already been built up.

- Railways require a large capital outlay, and the general purpose railway wants to maximise its longer distance traffic in order to maximise its revenue. Correspondingly, short distance traffic is less attractive.
- Urban and suburban operations generally require closely spaced stations. Steam traction is not the preferred means of propulsion where high acceleration rates and swift turnrounds are required to keep journey times reasonably short and operating costs down.

The railway can make a worthwhile contribution to transport needs for journeys of (say) five miles or more, with successive stations a mile or so apart. This is the essence of suburban traffic as we know it today. The railway is however of less benefit in the true urban situation.

This is perhaps of limited consequence when there are few alternatives other than walking, but in the late Victorian era a real competitor emerged. This was the electric tramcar, replacing the horse-drawn trams. These featured tight geometry, which allowed the trams to negotiate most street junctions and so penetrate cities very successfully. With fast, clean and frequent services, with stops on the street perhaps 250yd apart, the remote steam railway and its smoky atmosphere

quickly took on the air of yesterday's technology. Passengers deserted the railway for the electric tramcars in droves, which left the railway companies with severely diminishing traffic. What was to be done?

The answer, which was already being exploited by the Underground companies and the Metropolitan Railway, was of course the use of electric traction. But before proceeding to look at its early applications on what became the Southern Railway, it is perhaps worth considering the whole problem of mixing fast and stopping (or slow) trains on one pair of tracks.

If a stopping train follows a fast one, the gap between the trains opens up as the second train drops further and further behind. This can easily be the equivalent of three minutes for each and every stop, given also the limited ability to reach the line speed in between successive stations and the time spent slowing down and starting away again. There is also the time spent stationary.

A secondary effect is that another fast train following the slow will need to leave a large time margin before it sets off, if it is to avoid signal checks from the train in front as it is caught up.

This problem may be overcome to some extent by the installation of passing loops, and often the routes of the trains diverge at the various junctions. However, the basic problem is caused by running trains of varying performance characteristics and different stopping patterns over one set of tracks. The

most satisfactory way of overcoming this is to double the two-track railway, with separate lines for fast and slow traffic. This enables like to be kept with like, and the throughput in terms of trains per hour may be much increased as a result. Inevitably, the issue of prioritisation between different traffics becomes an issue, between freight and passenger, between international, longer distance 10-coach trains and local two coach trains, between regular and occasional services, and so on. For each winner there is likely to be a loser, and the result does not necessarily make the best use of the track capacity available.

Four-track widening is not a panacea for all ills, and it does not represent a cheap option. Junction conflicts may, for instance, remain. The main alternative is to ensure that all trains using a given line have more or less the same stopping patterns; this is the basis on which London Underground usually works. As traffic built up on the Southern Railway as a result of the many electrification schemes, line capacity became a frequent issue to be addressed. Readers are invited to bear the foregoing in mind when considering the management options available in many of the situations which will be met.

Below:
Even Beckenham Junction, a Chatham stronghold, had the Brighton trains creeping in via the branch from Crystal Palace. This is the station entrance, seen here on 30 September 2000. *Author*

2. The 'Elevated Electric'

'The annual bookings at Peckham Rye were doubled in the first year of the electric trains.'

Cecil J. Allen

In the 40 years or so before 1900, there were several schemes for a line to Brighton in competition with the London, Brighton & South Coast Railway, but none of them ever reached the construction stage. All these schemes were for railways of the conventional type, but in 1900 a Bill was deposited with Parliament for a London & Brighton Electric Railway. The main features were what the promoters called 'an airline route', by which they meant that it had a minimum of intermediate stations. Naturally, the trains would be high speed, and of course fares would be cheap. The Bill failed to proceed as it did not comply with Parliamentary Standing Orders, and no more was heard of it.

It did however serve to focus public attention. The General Manager of the LBSCR, Sir William Forbes, was reported as making a commitment to electrification, subject to conditions. These were that as soon as an electric traction scheme had been devised which was capable of running a train at high speed for 50 miles and at the same time return a profit on the capital expended, his company would adopt it, whatever its origin. In the next session of Parliament, his company would seek powers to work its line by electricity. These were indeed obtained in 1903 and, as promised, covered the whole of the LBSCR system. The company, should it have so desired, thus had the powers to electrify what is now the Bluebell Railway.

The electrification of the horse tramways by the London County Council was the catalyst for the company to ask for a report by Sir Philip Dawson, the company's consulting engineer. Dawson recommended the adoption of a system of German origin, by which high-tension single-phase alternating current would be supplied to the trains from overhead wires, on the grounds that it would be suitable not only for the contemplated suburban electrification, but for its possible extension to the South Coast. The arrangements for the distribution of power were more simple than those for the direct current system, and the permanent way would be kept clear of conductor rails.

The company decided to adopt this system and, as a first step, to electrify the South London line from London Bridge to Victoria via Denmark Hill, hitherto one of its busiest suburban lines. At first it was proposed to electrify, for test purposes only, the section from Peckham Rye to Battersea Park, with a shuttle service of trains from about 09.00 to

Above:
The final batch of trains for the Brighton overhead system consisted of two sets of two passenger trailers and a separate intermediate power car, or motor van as it was called. This contained accommodation for the guard. As can be seen, the net result was the sterilisation of a considerable amount of space which could not be used for passengers. Car No 10114 was photographed at Coulsdon North. *Ian Allan Library*

17.00. Later, and seemingly more sensibly, it was decided to electrify the line throughout, and Dawson was instructed to prepare specifications and to call for tenders.

Early in 1906, a contract was let to *Allgemeine Elektrizitäts Gesellschaft* of Berlin, who subcontracted with R. W. Blackwell & Co Ltd for the supply and erection of the overhead lines. Work started in the same year, but trial running did not commence until 17 January 1909. The line was used to work out some constructional problems, for which it was very suitable, as virtually every physical feature of a railway was to be found upon it.

The LBSCR contracted with the London Electricity Supply Corporation for the supply of single-phase alternating current at 6,700V 25Hz from Deptford. This current was received at a switch cabin at Queen's Road, Peckham, and distributed through lineside cables, laid in wooden casing or earthenware ducts to switch cabins at each station. These were used to supply the overhead wires. The latter were made of round section copper, suspended every 10ft from double catenary wires. These were carried above the track by insulators on lattice girders, mounted on steel towers and normally 220ft apart. The conductor wires were 16ft above rail level on line and 19ft 6in at the terminals, but the headway under the bridges was so low that short sections had to be made dead. Five platforms at Victoria and six at London Bridge were equipped. As can be seen, the clearances for overhead line equipment are forever a problem in British conditions! Interestingly, no attempt seems to have been made to raise bridges.

The Trains

New trains were built by the Metropolitan Amalgamated Carriage & Wagon Co Ltd at

Birmingham, a precedent which was not followed for many subsequent electrification schemes. There were eight trains, each consisting of three loose-coupled bogie vehicles. These were:

- A third class driving motor coach
- A first class trailer
- A third class driving motor coach

Each measured 63ft 7in long and was 9ft 3in wide. Both the motor coaches contained guard's and luggage accommodation, and eight compartments with a side gangway. The first class trailers had nine compartments, also with a side gangway, the whole ensemble weighing 114 tons. While the side gangway took up some seating space, it also allowed passengers to spread themselves out along the vehicle to find seats after the doors were shut and the train had departed. As one of the attributes of the electric trams with which it was sought to compete was speed, this feature would have been helpful in reducing station stop times.

The total seating of these sets was 74 first and 144 third class, which seems unduly weighted towards the first class for such an operation. Both classes had smoking and non-smoking accommodation.

Externally, these coaches were square panelled with steel-plate underframes. The original livery was umber brown lower panels and cream upper panels. Internally, the intermediate partitions reached only to the top of the quarter-lights, over which were narrow glazed panels which could be opened for additional ventilation. Double racks were provided, the lower (and smaller) one for umbrellas. Such a facility was later limited by British Railways to first class passengers only(perhaps lower class passengers were expected to wear cloth caps).

The fittings and decorations were both lavish and ornate, and in contrast to much other Brighton suburban stock, the third class was both spacious and well upholstered. These trains were the first on the LBSCR without second class, which was abolished formally on the suburban lines on 1 June 1911.

As a means of protection from possible leakage from the current collecting bows (one for each direction of travel), the timber bodies had the sides, roof and ends covered in sheet aluminium. The double floors were packed with insulating material over aluminium sheeting, and all was earthed by connection to the underframe. Transverse ribs on the roofs were a protection against a sagging or broken conductor wire. These features were perpetuated on subsequent Brighton electric stock.

Each motor coach was equipped with four 115hp Winter Eichberg traction motors. A spindle was fitted at the driving end to show a 'head disc' (a white light) or a 'tail disc' (a red light) according to direction of travel. This could be rotated from the motorman's cab.

A carriage shed and electrical repair shop was erected at Peckham Rye. A four-wheeled petrol railmotor was used for the maintenance and repair of the overhead, and a

Below:
This classic view of the Brighton side at Victoria shows the overhead bow collectors on one of the three-car South London units as it awaits departure. The first two compartments are first class, the rest in that vehicle being third class. Close inspection will show how the width of each decreases, the space between the second and third compartments being such that the first class passenger could have his full entitlement, but the third class was the same as elsewhere.
Southern Railway/Ian Allan Library

smaller Drewry petrol-engined car was also provided. A second petrol vehicle was acquired when the system was extended.

Public services commenced on 1 September 1909. On weekdays, frequent steam trains ran from about 04.30 to 07.30, after which electric trains took over and ran about every 15 minutes until midnight. On Sundays, electric trains ran half-hourly from 07.15 to 23.15, except for the 'church interval' of two hours then usual in mid-morning. (The intention was that employees should attend church.) The journey time for the 8m 51ch, with nine intermediate stops, was 24 minutes, compared with 36 minutes by steam. Today, one might add, the journey time is 23 minutes with seven intermediate stops. A flat half-hourly service is now operated but with a later start, other than on Sundays when the service is virtually unchanged.

Coasting marks were installed to show the motorman where to cut off current before stopping at a station. These consisted of a small square blue plate, bearing a St Andrew's cross, and could be found affixed to a girder upright. Signs on station platforms to indicate where trains should come to a halt took the form of a glass panel bearing the blue figures 2, 3 or 6. These would be inserted in a convenient platform lamp. Although electric traction was introduced on a comparatively wide scale, the LBSCR retained gas lamps at stations.

Little alteration was made to the fares, but a popular innovation was the issue of weekly packets of six third class returns at a 20% discount over the daily fare. Full particulars of the train service and fares were contained in a neat pocket folder, issued free.

Thus was the birth of the 'Elevated Electric'. This marketing name was adopted due to most of the original system being carried on viaduct or embankment. It was prominent in large green and white enamelled iron signs on station frontages, lit at night by arc lamps. The signs were illuminated at London Bridge and Victoria.

Over eight million passengers were carried on the South London line in 1902, which had reduced to four million by 1909. In the first year of electric working, this rose to 7.5 million, and was still increasing. Immediately before the 1923 Grouping, the total had risen to 12 million. The General Manager Forbes claimed that a return of 10% on the capital outlay had been achieved. The whole of the service on this line was worked by electric traction from 1 June 1912.

Before long, the make-up of the South London line trains was found to be unsatisfactory. They were too short for the busy hours, too long for the slack hours, and included too much first class. The company took the relatively drastic step of removing the first class centre trailers, equipping them with lavatories, fitting them for steam-hauled operation, and putting them to work on the main line to Brighton. One driving motor in each unit was retained, but the other was removed to form part of a second unit. They were replaced by conversions of 57ft 7in bogie suburban vehicles to driving trailers. At a mere 8ft wide, these were appreciably narrower than the vehicles they superseded. Internally, they had two first and six third class compartments, but no space for guard or luggage. There was also accommodation for

the motorman. Now two-car units, these trains ran singly in the slack hours, or as a total of up to three units in the peaks and offered a better balance of 16 first class and 132 third class seats per unit.

The Crystal Palace Lines

Success breeds success, and further extensions of electrification were soon considered. In 1910, the prospect of competition for the valuable residential traffic from the Sutton area arose, when a line from Wimbledon to Sutton was proposed. This was to be operated by the District Railway. In January 1910 a South London line train was steam hauled from London Bridge to test clearances, but as the Wimbledon-Sutton scheme made no progress after securing its Act, attention was switched to the lines to Crystal Palace.

The work was carried out rapidly and electric trains began to run from Victoria to Crystal Palace, via Streatham Hill, on 12 May 1911. This was the day on which King George V opened the Festival of Empire held at the Crystal Palace to celebrate his Coronation year. The electrical equipment was continued to Norwood Junction and Selhurst to reach workshops and extensive sidings which had

been laid out between these locations. The connecting section from Peckham Rye had to await the installation of an additional generating station by the power company. Eventually, the opening date was fixed for 1 June 1912, but as the country was in the throes of a coalminers' strike that year, electric trains began to run on 1 March as a means of economising on locomotive coal.

The electrical equipment followed closely that of the pioneer installation, but the switch cabins were more widely spaced and large distribution centres were built at Peckham Rye and Tulse Hill. The overhead lattice girders were of lighter section than those on the South London line, and the supports for the overhead wires also included a number of cantilevers.

Loading gauge restrictions through Crystal Palace Tunnel prevented the use of wide coaches as previously, so ordinary compartment stock was provided. Thirty motor coaches and 30 driving trailers were built by Metropolitan Amalgamated C&W, and a further 30 driving trailers by the company's own workshops at Lancing. Both types were 57ft 7in long, with bodies 8ft wide. The three-car loose-coupled sets provided 48 first class and 170 third class seats, within an all-up weight of 103 tons. Peak hour services consisted of two sets, but a few were made up to eight coaches by adding a motor coach and a driving trailer to a six-coach train.

Internally, these coaches lacked the ornate decorations of the side-gangwayed stock, but were nevertheless comfortable and well lit, with two lights to each compartment. In their later years, many of the compartments had large pictorial advertisements affixed to the upper part of the partitions. One showed an LBSCR steamer on its way from Newhaven to Dieppe; the other was a view of Old Shoreham Bridge. Later still, enamelled iron advertising plates were fitted to the lower inner panels of the doors. The electrical equipment was similar to that of the South London stock, but the traction motors were 150hp versions from the same manufacturer.

Service frequencies in the early days seem to have been quite generous by today's standards, with three trains an hour increasing to four or perhaps five during the peaks. Numbered headcodes were used on these services, a plate with white figures on a black background being illuminated at night by lights under a hood. These headcodes were:

1 Victoria-Crystal Palace
2 Victoria-Streatham Hill
3 Victoria-Norwood Junction
4 London Bridge-Crystal Palace
5 London Bridge-Streatham Hill or Victoria
6 London Bridge-Norwood Junction

In addition, a white light was carried on the off side at night.

It was claimed that passenger numbers were increased by 70% following electrification to Crystal Palace, and the financial results were said to be satisfactory.

Remaining Years of the Brighton

In 1913, the company decided to electrify its other suburban routes as far as Coulsdon & Smitham Downs (later Coulsdon North), and to Cheam via Sutton. This excluded the lines from Streatham South Junction to Wimbledon, West Croydon to Wimbledon, and Sutton to Epsom Downs. A good deal of work was done, including the erection of many overhead supports, but work came to a halt with the outbreak of war in August 1914. Not altogether surprisingly, electrical equipment could no longer be obtained from its German makers.

The 'Elevated Electric' did not escape the restrictions imposed on train services. When the SECR withdrew its Metropolitan Extension service from Victoria to the City on 3 March 1916, South London line trains were left to deal with traffic from the stations between Victoria and Brixton. On 1 January 1917, South Bermondsey and Old Kent Road stations were closed entirely, the latter never to reopen. East Brixton and North Dulwich were closed on Sundays and the London Bridge-Crystal Palace and Streatham Hill trains withdrawn. South Bermondsey was reopened on 1 May 1919 and matters slowly returned to normal over the next five years or so.

With the end of the war in November 1918, the electrification schemes of the company

Fig 2.1: Electrification, London, Brighton & South Coast Railway ac Overhead System, Including the 1925 Work by the Southern Railway	
9 December 1909	Victoria-London Bridge, South London line
12 May 1911	Victoria-Crystal Palace LL via Streatham Hill
3 March 1912	Peckham Rye-Tulse Hill-Crystal Palace/Streatham Hill, Crystal Palace-Norwood Junction-Selhurst depot
1 April 1925	Balham-Selhurst-East Croydon-Coulsdon North, Selhurst-West Croydon-Sutton, Tulse Hill-Streatham Common

were revived. The Board approved electrification to Brighton and Eastbourne in principle, but no steps towards construction were taken. In 1922, however, the outstanding suburban schemes were resurrected, but these were still incomplete at the Grouping of the Railways on 1 January 1923.

The Brighton company's electrical traction engineer gave a valedictory account to the Institution of Civil Engineers that January. He said that the electrified sections had given

Below:
London, Brighton & South Coast Railway ac electrification as at 1 April 1925.

useful service in relatively unfavourable wartime conditions, which were not expected to last for so long. The overhead network had not inconvenienced permanent way operations, and the yearly number of traffic delays of 15 minutes or over due to overhead wiring defects ranged between only one and eight. On sections not used by steam trains, renewal of catenary and dropper wires due to corrosion was only 10% of that on sections carrying heavy steam traffic.

The electrical equipment on the trains had given satisfactory service. In 1921, the train service amounted to nearly six million vehicle miles, with an average of 1.14 miles between stations, an average running speed of 24.4mph and a scheduled speed of 22.1mph including stops.

Fig 2.1 summarises the progress of overhead electrification by the company, which is shown also in diagram form in Fig 2.2.

Southern Extensions

It is perhaps opportune to consider here the further development of the Elevated Electric, although this was undertaken under Southern Railway auspices. While committing themselves to the dc system for future use, the Southern's Board decided that the ac work which was already partly complete should be continued. The reasons for this decision are discussed further in Chapter 5.

The ac extension to Coulsdon North and Sutton was expected to be ready for 1 March 1925, although it was deferred to 1 April owing to power supply problems. Power was purchased in bulk from the London Electricity Supply Corporation and supplied to New Cross Gate. The overhead equipment followed previous practice except at Sutton, where trussed beams were used instead of lattice girders.

Twenty-one motor vans, 60 driving trailers (of two designs) and 20 trailers were built for use on these extensions. The 'motor vans' were really electric locomotives and were built by Metropolitan Cammell at their Birmingham works. These were 42ft long overall and weighed 62 tons. The motorman's cab at each end had a space behind it for electrical apparatus and in the centre was a guard's and luggage compartment. The GEC electrical equipment included four 250hp motors. There were two roof-mounted bow collectors at each end, raised and lowered by compressed air.

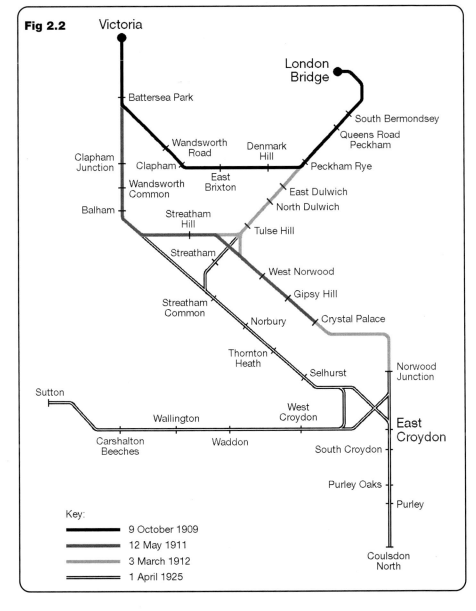

Fig 2.2

Key:
— 9 October 1909
— 12 May 1911
— 3 March 1912
— 1 April 1925

The trains were made up into loose-coupled units consisting of:

- Third class driving trailer
- Composite driving trailer
- Motor van
- Composite non-driving trailer
- Third class driving trailer

This gave a total seating capacity of 64 first class and 240 third class, within an overall length of 254ft 4in. This is very similar in length to a four-car inner-suburban 4EPB or Class 455 train. These units ran singly in slack hours and in pairs during the peaks. Before the extensions to Sutton and Coulsdon North were opened, the trains were run in on Sunday trains between London Bridge and Crystal Palace.

Barring three vehicles built by the Metropolitan Carriage Wagon & Finance Co in 1923, all the remaining coaching stock was built at the Brighton's Lancing Works. Owing to the uncertainties caused first by the war and then future policy, construction took place over a considerable period. Some vehicles were used temporarily as steam-hauled stock, while others never entered service as part of the Elevated Electric but found themselves later as part of dc trailer sets. All construction was complete by the end of 1924.

Some of these coaches were painted in Southern olive green; others had the former Brighton umber brown livery. The interiors were similar to the Crystal Palace stock, but the compartments in the third class driving trailers were very straight backed as the distance between the partitions was only 5ft 5in.

Destination boards were carried on the fronts of trains, consisting of white letters on a black ground. These were introduced on all services, except the South London line. The Southern distinguished the three varieties of stock as SL, CP and CW (the last for the motor van sets). A number of new headcodes were also introduced:

SL Victoria-London Bridge via South
    London line
7   Victoria-Selhurst
8   Victoria-West Croydon via Crystal Palace
9   Victoria-Sutton via Selhurst
10 Victoria-East Croydon via Crystal Palace
11 Victoria-Coulsdon North via Selhurst
12 Victoria-Coulsdon North via Crystal Palace

The incidental works for the new electrification were modest, the principal ones being the upgrading of Beeches Halt to Carshalton Beeches station, and track alterations at Sutton. Here, the new services used the Epsom Downs platforms (today's Nos 3 and 4).

On weekdays, the new services ran every 20 minutes for most of the day on each of the new routes, but were reduced to half hourly on Mondays to Fridays between 11.00 and 13.00, and after 21.00. The pattern was similar on Saturdays, except that the 20-minute service ran through to 16.00, at which point it became every 30 minutes. The first services left Victoria at 6am and the last at 00.10. Sunday services were half-hourly all day.

While the Brighton had a partly electrified suburban network, and all credit to the company for that, services elsewhere were generally leisurely and operated with antiquated rolling stock. The suburban services which remained steam hauled were less than satisfactory, and while the 'Southern Belle' Pullman showed what the company could achieve, many long distance services had little merit. The Brighton's routes to both Hastings and Portsmouth were much longer than those of the opposition, but there was plenty of scope for development.

Abandonment

At the annual meeting in February 1925, before the ac extensions were even open, the Chairman of the Southern Railway made a statement to the effect that one electrification system was enough and that the Brighton system was not interchangeable in any sense with those being adopted for the Western and Eastern Sections. A classic remark to the effect that 'experts were studying the problem and that he was confident that they would find a satisfactory solution' must have fooled few people.

Abandonment of the ac was announced in August 1926. The first to go were the services from London Bridge to Victoria via the South London line, Streatham Hill and Crystal Palace, on 17 June 1928. Other services via Crystal Palace followed on 3 March 1929, and the final rites were enacted on Sunday 22 September 1929. This saw the arrival at Coulsdon North of a five-car train of CW stock on the 00.10 service from Victoria.

The overhead wires between Battersea Park and Peckham Rye were kept live for a time to allow ac stock to be worked to Peckham Rye shops to be stripped of electrical equipment before being converted for dc working. After stripping, the still almost new motor cars stood derelict for nearly four years in Streatham Hill sidings, before being taken to Eastleigh and converted into 27-ton bogie goods brake vans. Known as the 'Queen Mary' brakes, because of their size, these vehicles lasted until quite recent times.

Although the overhead wires were removed soon after they ceased to be used, the supporting girders were not taken down until 1930–2. A few were kept as signal gantries and various uses were found for others. Some lattice girders were used for roofing the locomotive shed at Ryde, Isle of Wight, and some of the brackets became lighting standards in carriage sidings at Dorking North.

The suspense account for the replacement of ac by dc traction was reduced annually. It was closed finally in 1942, by the write-off of £205,473.

Left:
East Brixton station was an original Brighton station on the South London line, but it was closed due to low usage on 6 January 1976. This undated photograph from BR days shows the uninviting state which was shared by so many of these stations, and who can blame people for not using them? *Author's collection*

3. The South Western's Third Rail

'People don't like timetables, make it easy for them.'

Sir Herbert Walker

Like the Brighton company, the London & South Western Railway also found that it was the constituents of London Transport which were making the running. This time it was London United Tramways in Kingston and elsewhere, but this was in association with the electrification of the District Railway and the coming of the motor bus. As early as 1903, the South Western's chief engineer suggested that an intensive electric service could be run over two of the four lines between Waterloo and Hampton Court Junction at no greater cost than that of the existing steam trains.

The first electric trains to work over South Western lines, however, were those of the District Railway. By way of explanation, it might be added that this stemmed from an 1869 branch of the LSWR which ran from Richmond to Addison Road (now Kensington Olympia) on the West London line. The District, eager to find a route westwards at minimal cost, undertook some horse trading with the South Western. In this, the Underground interests dropped a proposed extension to Barnes in exchange for running powers over what was then part of the LSWR from Studland Road Junction, Hammersmith. This was just to the east of Ravenscourt Park. By this means, the District reached Turnham Green and Richmond.

The District also gained access to Wimbledon over the 1889 branch built by the South Western, with an end-on junction at Putney Bridge. This time, the threat was that the District was aiming at Norbiton and Surbiton. In exchange, the South Western gained running powers to High Street Kensington and South Kensington, but never used them. It might be added also that the District Railway's 1883 line to Hounslow, now part of the Piccadilly Line, was in a good position to abstract traffic from the stations on the South Western's Hounslow Loop. The less than harmonious relationship between the undertakings was to arise again between their successors, as will be seen later.

The District laid the conductor rails to Richmond and to Wimbledon. The company also provided the power, from their generating plant at Lots Road, Chelsea. District electric trains started running in this area during 1905, reaching Hounslow West on 13 June, Richmond on 1 August and Wimbledon on 27 August. It should be noted that the short sections of the South Western towards South Acton were electrified for the benefit of the North London line trains of the London & North Western Railway, whose electric services started to run on 1 October 1916.

Salvation from Electricity

Public dissatisfaction with the facilities provided by the South Western in the Thames Valley came to a head in 1912, when the Central London Railway (today's Central Line) proposed to extend its line to Richmond. A deputation from local authorities met the Central London directors, who said they were in sympathy with a suggestion that the extension should be continued into the Thames Valley – possible in the direction of Chertsey. The deputation also met the newly appointed general manager of the London & South Western Railway, Mr (later Sir) Herbert Walker. He told them that his company realised its services could be improved, and that in the next two or three years steps would be taken to provide better facilities. This might be by electrification, for which a scheme was being prepared. No more was heard of the CLR being extended to Chertsey, although the company obtained powers for a Richmond extension in 1913. These were never exercised.

Early in that same year, the South Western announced its intention to undertake a comprehensive electrification scheme. This was to cover:

- Waterloo to Wimbledon via East Putney
- The Kingston Roundabout
- The Hounslow Loop
- The Shepperton branch
- The Hampton Court branch
- Waterloo to Guildford, via Woking, via Cobham and via Epsom.

At the half-yearly meeting, the chairman (Sir Hugh Drummond) told the shareholders that in the past six years traffic worth over £100,000 a year had been lost on the sections to be electrified, and in the last six months local passengers around London had decreased in numbers by 1,250,000. The Board had come to the conclusion that electrification was the only means by which the company could regain its position.

Which system to adopt? Technical experience of the alternatives was beginning to grow, and the South Western had a neighbour on the east which had opted for ac overhead, while some of its own lines sported fourth rail dc. The company's electrical engineer, Herbert Jones, was dispatched to the United States to make enquiries, and Kennedy & Donkin were consulted. The South Western decided to adopt the 600V dc third rail system, with running rail return. Jones assured Walker that there were no difficulties expected with a running rail return. Power would be obtained from the company's own generating station, which would be built at Durnsford Road, Wimbledon.

The LSWR did not rely on an Act of Parliament to authorise electrification of its lines. Instead, a Board of Trade order was obtained under the Railways (Electrical Powers) Act, 1903. This authorised railways to use electricity in addition to, or in substitution for, other forms of motive power.

Implementation

Work commenced immediately, with the ground broken for the erection of the power station in July 1913. The rate of progress was slowed by the outbreak of World War 1 in August 1914, but the first electric trains started running on 25 October 1915. This was a regular 20-minute service between Waterloo and Wimbledon via East Putney, replacing an irregular steam service. Kingston Roundabout and Shepperton trains were advertised to start six weeks later, but this had to be postponed until 30 January 1916. This was to accommodate the Post Office, who alleged that the operation of the substation machinery was interfering with the working of long distance telephone lines.

Hounslow Loop services commenced on 12 March 1916, and those to Hampton Court on 18 June. Electric trains served the short section from Hampton Court Junction to Claygate from Waterloo on 20 November 1916. Here, the electric trains connected with an hourly steam push-pull service to Guildford. Thus the whole project, from the first public announcement to seeing trains running in public service on a substantial group of lines, took less than four years. Even more remarkably, for two and a half of those years, the country was fighting one of the bloodiest conflicts ever.

The openings which took place under LSWR auspices are summarised in Fig 3.1. See also Fig 3.2 for a map of the lines concerned.

Durnsford Road power station was a red-brick building situated on the up side of the line. The high-tension current was transmitted to nine substations through lineside cables. Their equipment included static transformers and rotary converters, with the requisite switchgear, all supplied by British Thomson-Houston Co Ltd (BTH).

The conductor rails were of special high-conductivity steel, weighing 100lb/yd, copper bonded and laid on porcelain insulators 16in from the side of the running rail and 3in above it. The running rails were bonded for the return current with two copper bonds under the fishplates, and cross-bonded at intervals. This set the standards for all future applications. Track circuits, which detect the presence of a train for signalling purposes through a low voltage current in the running rails, were converted from dc to ac. This ensured that electrical interference by traction currents did not result in spurious indications.

Infrastructure works included a widening to eight running lines at Vauxhall and a flyover to carry the down Hampton Court branch over the main line. A station at Barnes Bridge was opened with the Hounslow Loop electrification. This ended the curious situation that although the line ran through Barnes itself, the station was about three-quarters of a mile away, across the Common.

Coasting markers consisted of a white diamond. Blue enamelled plates, bearing white figures, indicated the stopping points on platforms, Nos 3 and 6, and later 8, being displayed as appropriate. A feature of the electrified lines were the glass station nameboards, on which the station name was shown in white block letters on a blue panel with a white margin. At night, it was lit from above.

Rolling Stock

The electric units provided consisted of 84 three-coach close-coupled trains, numbered E1-E84. Each consisted of two driving motor coaches and an intervening trailer, weighing about 95 tons in total. They were converted at Eastleigh Works from four-coach bogie block trains built for steam suburban working from 1904 onwards. Only first and third class accommodation was provided, this being the first time the South Western had not offered second class. The number of seats varied according to the actual vehicles used. The total ranged from 172 to 190, with about one quarter being first class.

Electrical equipment was by Westinghouse. Each motor coach had two 275hp motors, and the trains gained access to the traction current by means of cast-steel pick-up shoes bearing on the conductor rail. The shoes were mounted on hardwood shoe beams, which were attached to the axleboxes of the bogies at the outer ends of each of the driving motor cars. This allowed the current to be collected at more than one point and minimised the problem of a train becoming stranded with none of the shoes in contact with the third rail. Cables along the roof connected the pick-up shoes, so that power was available to all the traction motors in the unit at all times. Quick-acting Westinghouse brakes were fitted, with compressors under each coach.

The motor coaches were made distinctive by their torpedo, or cigar shaped, outer ends. Underframes were of timber; central buffer couplers were fitted between the coaches with ordinary round buffers and screw couplings at the ends. Internally, first class compartments were trimmed in dark blue cloth, with side and three intermediate armrests allowing eight seats to be provided. In some of the units, part of the first class accommodation was arranged as a saloon. Third class compartments were upholstered in red and black tapestry with full back cushions, and flat woven wire framed seats. Each compartment had two lights, with opal glass bowls. The livery was dark green, lined out in black and yellow, with underframes and bogies painted black. The initials LSWR, vehicle number, '1st' and '3rd' were inscribed on the waist panels.

No destination boards were used, an omission which did not begin to be rectified until 1980, but a white stencil plate bearing a letter route code was mounted prominently on the front of the train. This was in front of an opal glass panel, illuminated at night. These headcodes featured in the posters and publicity advertising the new services. It was indeed these headcodes, chosen because of their distinctiveness at a distance, which could be put together to read HOVIS. This was much welcomed by the publicity department of the purveyors of that famous brown loaf, the outcome of which was an advertisement featuring a fan of five approaching trains, bearing the name. 'The route to health', we were told, 'has HOVIS at the end.'

Cleaning and inspection sheds for the electric trains, with electrical repair shops, were erected on a site south of the Durnsford Road power house. Later, the steam shed at Strawberry Hill was converted for use as an electric depot.

Fig 3.1: Electrification, Third Rail, London & South Western Railway	
June/August 1905	District Railway electrified fourth rail to Richmond and Wimbledon over LSWR tracks
25 October 1915	Waterloo-Clapham Junction-East Putney
30 January 1916	Waterloo and Kingston Loop, Shepperton branch
12 March 1916	Hounslow Loop
18 June 1916	New Malden-Surbiton-Hampton Court
20 November 1916	Surbiton-Claygate

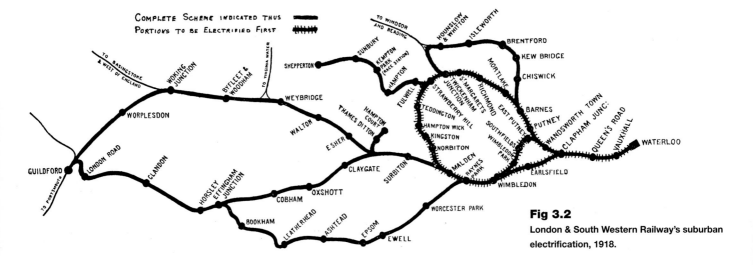

Fig 3.2
London & South Western Railway's suburban electrification, 1918.

Left:
Headcodes have the purpose of informing both passengers and staff of the route of the train. They thus have a similar function to route numbers on buses. However, destination plates or blinds were much rarer, and on the railway the headcode had to do. It was therefore incumbent upon the railway to let everybody know its system, and this poster appeared on the South Western in 1916. *Author's collection*

Service Provision

Walker had strict ideas on how a timetable should be organised, adopting the benefits of a mathematical basis. Study of early timetables for the South Western electric services shows that his principles might be summarised as follows:

- The basic hour's service should provide for even intervals between successive services on the same route.
- The timetable should be repetitive from one hour to the next.
- That where higher carrying capacity was needed, as in the peak hours, this should if possible be met by running longer trains to the same timetable.

Fig 3.3 (overleaf) shows a typical weekday hour of the service introduced in late 1916 when the Claygate line was opened. Malden, it might be noted, 9¾ miles from Waterloo, refers to the station which is now New Malden.

The timetable is far from being above criticism, demonstrating as it does the difficulty of combining a two trains per hour service (Shepperton, headcode S) with a four trains per hour service (Kingston Roundabout, headcode V). These routes are common for the first 13½ miles. Had it not been decided to run the Shepperton semi-fast in the earlier part of the journey, a regular 10-minute headway from Waterloo might have been possible. Also, the V service ends up running on the section via Twickenham with a

Right:
This illustration shows a pair of the LSWR's three-car electric sets converted from steam stock in 1914–17, the first of which is numbered E40. It is seen here passing the long since vanished Cromer Road signalbox with a train from Waterloo. East Putney Tunnel is in the background, and the train will shortly be approaching Southfields. *Ian Allan Library*

10/20/10/20-minute service interval. This too is less than ideal, but that gives an opportunity to integrate it with the 30/30 interval service on the Hounslow Loop. That is exactly what happened, as Table 3.4 (overleaf) demonstrates. This shows the equivalent position in the down direction on the Windsor lines.

The situation here is if anything trickier, in that a three trains per hour (tph) service, as in the Wimbledons, (headcode P) mixes uncomfortably with either 4tph or 2tph on the other services. The longest common route on the services shown is to Twickenham via the main line (11¼ miles), which does indeed benefit from a train departing from Waterloo at even 10-minute intervals.

It is perhaps worth mentioning that roundabout services do have their problems, in that the time that the train sets off from its

Waterloo origin effectively determines the time it gets back again. It can only be held at an intermediate point for timing purposes at the expense of irritating the passengers. End-to-end operation, as with the Hampton Court branch, is that much simpler, as the return departure time can be chosen by the timetable clerk to fit in with other requirements. There is also a chance to build in some modest allowance to recover from any operational delays which might be experienced. Not all railways run absolutely perfectly, all of the time!

Rush hour electric extras to Hounslow via Brentford left Waterloo at 17.12, 17.42, 18.12 and 18.42, with steam extras to Shepperton (fast to Mortlake, not St Margarets) at 17.05 and 18.45. As has been shown, the basic Shepperton service ran, and still runs, via New Malden and Kingston. It is a sobering thought that these peak services of 1916 via Twickenham are still in existence today, 85 years later. Departures from Waterloo are now at 17.17, 17.47 and 18.17, headcode 47, but they call all stations. They are no longer steam hauled. Brentford and Hounslow also achieve some additional services, from stops in Reading trains which are routed via the Hounslow Loop.

Services started with the first electric train leaving Waterloo at 03.53 for Teddington via Malden, with the last as late as 00.45 for Twickenham via Richmond. On a comparable basis, today's equivalents are the 05.03 Shepperton and the 00.40 to Strawberry Hill, both via New Malden. Sunday services were

Fig 3.3 South Western Main Line Interval Services, 20 November 1916

Waterloo depart*	Head-code	Route	Notes
03	V	Waterloo-Malden-Kingston-Twickenham-Waterloo	
10	I	Waterloo-Malden-Claygate	Not Vauxhall, Earlsfield, Raynes Park
13	V	Waterloo-Malden-Kingston-Twickenham-Waterloo	
18	H	Waterloo-Malden-Hampton Court	
26	S	Waterloo-Malden-Kingston-Shepperton	Fast to Wimbledon, not Raynes Park
28	H	Waterloo-Malden-Hampton Court	
33	V	Waterloo-Malden-Kingston-Twickenham-Waterloo	
40	I	Waterloo-Malden-Claygate, connection to Guildford	Not Vauxhall, Earlsfield, Raynes Park
43	V	Waterloo-Malden-Kingston-Twickenham-Waterloo	
48	H	Waterloo-Malden-Hampton Court	
56	S	Waterloo-Malden-Kingston-Shepperton	Fast to Wimbledon, not Raynes Park
58	H	Waterloo-Malden-Hampton Court	

* Minutes past the hour.

Fig 3.4 South Western Windsor Lines Interval Services, 20 November 1916

Waterloo depart*	Head-code	Route	Notes
08	V̄	Waterloo-Twickenham-Kingston-Malden-Waterloo	Not Queen's Road, Wandsworth Town
14	P̄	Waterloo-Putney-East Putney-Wimbledon	
18	V̄	Waterloo-Twickenham-Kingston-Malden-Waterloo	Fast to Clapham Junction
22	O	Waterloo-Brentford-Hounslow-Twickenham-Waterloo	
28	Ō	Waterloo-Twickenham-Hounslow-Brentford-Waterloo	Not Queen's Road, Wandsworth Town
34	P̄	Waterloo-Putney-East Putney-Wimbledon	
38	V̄	Waterloo-Twickenham-Kingston-Malden-Waterloo	Not Queen's Road, Wandsworth Town
48	V̄	Waterloo-Twickenham-Kingston-Malden-Waterloo	Fast to Clapham Junction
52	O	Waterloo-Brentford-Hounslow-Twickenham-Waterloo	
54	P̄	Waterloo-Putney-East Putney-Wimbledon	
58	Ō	Waterloo-Twickenham-Hounslow-Brentford-Waterloo	Not Queen's Road, Wandsworth Town

* Minutes past the hour.

half-hourly, except on the Hounslow Loop where they were hourly. The 1916 timings showed a decrease of about one third on those of the superseded steam trains. The electric sets proved to be very lively runners, attaining a speed of 50mph or so with ease.

In July 1919, the services needed altering to cope with additional traffic. However, success appears to have been partial, as the Claygate electric trains were withdrawn and the Waterloo to Wimbledon via Putney trains cut back to operating only during rush hours. This enabled the rolling stock which was freed up to be used elsewhere. Generally, the amount of non-stopping at selected stations was also reduced.

In the following year, 24 two-coach third class trailer sets were provided to work between two of the motor units. Traction power must indeed have been ample. These sets were converted by Eastleigh from steam stock and each consisted of one eight- and one nine-compartment vehicle, close-coupled. The overall width was 8ft 10½in and the weight 46 tons. While the concept of non-powered coaching vehicles is of no consequence to those used to locomotive-hauled trains, the nuisance value of such vehicles must have been considerable. After all, they had no driving positions, or traction motors, or even forward visibility, and they

Right:
Sir Herbert Walker, who made it all possible, is commemorated in a plaque at Waterloo station. This reads, in part: 'This station, the development of the docks at Southampton & the electrification of the Southern Railway, to which he gave his genius & leadership, are his memorial.' *Author*

were working in an all multiple-unit environment.

The heavy traffic to and from Kempton Park race-course on the Shepperton branch was worked by electric trains, and the return specials were marshalled in close order on the up line between the terminus and Sunbury. They were then worked forward as required. The ordinary trains between these points used the down line in both directions, controlled by electric tablet instruments, which were specially provided for race day workings.

In the last prewar and all steam year of 1913, about 25 million passengers were carried on the lines later electrified. By 1915, this number had fallen to 23.2 million, but in 1916 with new electric services commencing

during the year, this had risen to 29.4 million. In 1920, 52.6 million were carried. This last result was inflated by the conditions which followed World War 1, but even allowing for this it was evident that the traffic had increased far beyond the original expectations. The South Western was never one of the fastest lines in Britain, but at least it had made a good start on electrification.

4. South Eastern Electric

'The South Eastern & Chatham had rather more ideas than money with which to carry them out.'

Michael Bonavia

The electric tramway competition which so severely depleted the traffic over the Brighton's South London line soon began to affect the suburban services of the South Eastern & Chatham Railway (SECR), as the two warring undertakings (SER and LCDR) had become in 1899. They were, in fact, still two financially independent railways run by a managing committee, but for the present purposes they can be considered as one.

In 1903, the SECR obtained an Act of Parliament, which included power to electrify its suburban lines, to use land for generating stations, and to hold patent rights relating to electric power. This cleared the legal hurdles out of the way, but there was no progress. Six years later, the neighbouring LBSCR inaugurated the first stage of its overhead electrification, but it was not until 1912 that the Managing Committee approached Messrs Merz & McLellan, consulting engineers. Their report was presented in the following year, which recommended the conversion by stages of the whole of the suburban lines and the main lines to Hastings, Dover and Ramsgate, as well as the two Maidstone lines, the branches

from Redhill to Reading and Tonbridge, and the Oxted line to Edenbridge. The estimated cost of conversion was £5,599,000, but a saving in operating costs of £350,000 a year was anticipated. The scheme budgeted for an all-round improvement of 20% in speed and frequency of train service, and it was expected to increase revenue in the suburban area by 50%. This would have amounted to a return of 20% on the capital outlay.

The 1,500V dc system was considered the most suitable for conditions on the SECR. Both third rail and overhead wire current collection were to be employed, but the principal means would have been third rail. The traction units' collecting shoes were to make contact with the underside of the conductor rail, the top of which was to be protected. The overhead wire was to be used in goods sorting sidings and carriage yards. All the 166 locomotives and 666 EMU coaches were to be fitted with dual equipment. Estimates showed that although £700,000 could be saved by installing 6,000V single-phase ac power distribution, the rolling stock equipment would have cost

Below:

The South Eastern & Chatham Railway's electrification never took place as planned, but this was the intention in 1921 as interpreted by *Modern Transport.* **Reference to Section A is the inner-suburban services, to be completed first, and Section B the outer-suburban as then defined. The third stage was to bring in all longer-distance services, including freight, which would be electrically hauled when within the whole area. Of the routes shown, that west of Reigate has yet to acquire third rail, while the branch from Nunhead to Greenwich was closed first. The line from Fawkham Junction to Gravesend West was likewise never electrified and underwent what seemed like a slow death, but in practice the southern end of it is now being revived as part of the Channel Tunnel Rail Link.** *Author's collection*

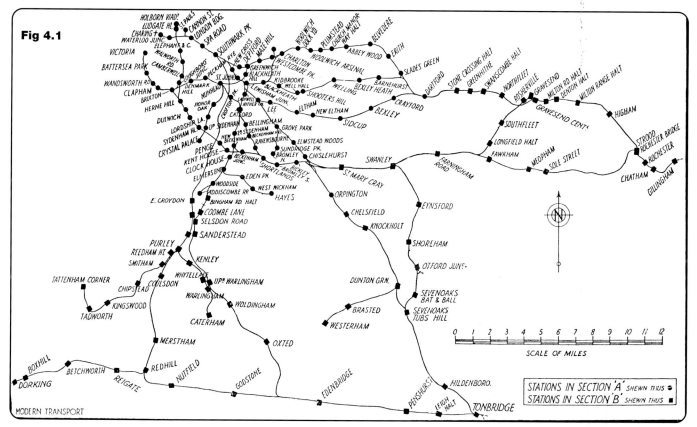

Fig 4.1

STATIONS IN SECTION 'A' SHEWN THUS ●
STATIONS IN SECTION 'B' SHEWN THUS ■

SCALE OF MILES

MODERN TRANSPORT

Above:
The train is a Holborn Viaduct to West Croydon service, seen here passing the now defunct Camberwell box between Elephant & Castle and Loughborough Junction. This is a 4SUB unit, No 4342. It was built new for the Eastern section in 1925 as a three-car unit, and was augmented to this form immediately following World War 2.
R. C. Riley/Ian Allan Library

£1,900,000 more than for the dc installation. Moreover, adoption of the ac method would have added another £72,000 to the annual working expenses.

The use of electric locomotives for main line work was calculated to show several advantages, chiefly a lower cost of renewals and maintenance and a longer actual life in service. The type of passenger locomotive proposed had four driving wheels and a four-wheeled bogie; for heavy trains two could be coupled to make up a 2-Bo+Bo-2 unit. For freight work, an eight-wheeled machine was to be built. The suburban stock was to be composed of two-car sets with one motor coach to each unit.

At the half-yearly meeting held early in 1913, the Chairman H. Cosmo Bonsor told the shareholders that it was not thought opportune to incur heavy capital expenditure to compete with trams and buses. On account of their complicated suburban network, with its many junctions and six London termini, the cost of electrification was bound to be heavy, and the Committee considered that it would be most unwise to ask the shareholders for powers for such a large capital expenditure.

The outbreak of war naturally postponed any further proposals, although wartime restrictions caused the removal of some of the complications mentioned by the Chairman.

During the years 1915 to 1917 a number of suburban services were closed and several suburban train services withdrawn. This included those over the Metropolitan Extension towards Farringdon, and the Greenwich Park and Crystal Palace branches. SECR trains ceased to work over the Metropolitan Railway to Moorgate, and the practice of running trains into Charing Cross via Cannon Street was given up for good in 1917. Services to Moorgate and to Greenwich Park were never reinstated, and that which became Thameslink had to wait until recent times.

In 1919, Alfred Raworth, electrical engineer of the SECR, prepared a fresh report on electrification, as the rise in the cost of materials and labour since the original proposals had revised the economics of main line conversion. It was now proposed to make Gillingham and Tonbridge the limits of haulage by electric locomotives of main line passenger and goods trains. A total of 36 passenger locomotives was proposed at an estimated cost of £7,000 each. For goods trains, 50 locomotives would have been required, at £4,200 each. The cost of converting the suburban area, including the provision of locomotives and power distribution, was now estimated at £13,241,000 – more than double the prewar assessment. Yet, in spite of the large capital outlay, the calculations indicated that £422,000 could be saved annually by the electrification, and if the receipts in the suburban area increased by 50% the net annual gain would be £1,250,000. Perhaps it is unnecessary to say that all costs are contemporary!

The conversion was to be tackled in three stages, as follows:

- Stage 1 comprised the Orpington, Bromley North, North Kent, Mid-Kent, Catford Loop and Crystal Palace lines. Services during both rush and slack periods were to be three trains per hour.
- Stage 2 envisaged extensions to Tonbridge, Caterham, Tadworth, Dorking and Edenbridge via Croydon, and Gillingham via Swanley and via Gravesend. Other lines of which electrification was contemplated were the Westerham and Gravesend West branches and the Redhill-Tonbridge line.
- Stage 3 was to effect the working of

through passenger and goods trains by electric locomotives to the limits of the electrified area, where trains were to be handed over to steam locomotives.

On all the lines in Stage 2, it was proposed to run two trains an hour in peak periods, with an hourly service during the day. A schedule of 58 minutes from Charing Cross to Gillingham via Gravesend, with nine intermediate stops, was contemplated, and from Victoria via Swanley the run was to be made in 62 minutes with 10 stops. Edenbridge would have been reached in 47 minutes from Charing Cross with seven intermediate stops.

Under the modified scheme, the suburban trains were to be formed from 193 three-car units, having two third class driving motor coaches each equipped with two 200hp motors, and an intermediate first class trailer. Each motor coach was to have seated 96 passengers, arranged six-a-side, and the first class coach was to have 64 seats in eight compartments. A nine-coach train would thus have seats for 768 passengers. The coaches were to have been 9ft wide and 57ft long.

The trade depression of the early 1920s resulted in Parliament passing the Trade Facilities Act, which provided for a system of State-aided credits to enable works held up by the financial and industrial position to be resumed and so relieve unemployment.

The SECR's reawakened interest in electrification proposed to take advantage of this. State aid was forthcoming as a guarantee for 25 years of the principal and interest of £6.5 million. Of this, £1.5 million was intended for the generating plant. Owing to the peculiar make-up of the SECR, a subsidiary SECR Construction & Power Company was formed to undertake the scheme and then lease the works and equipment to the railway.

In 1922, the SECR sought permission from the Electricity Commissioners to build a generating station on the riverside at Angerstein's Wharf, Charlton. The Commissioners refused, as they considered that power should be bought from an existing electricity supply company. The railway then asserted that it could not make such an arrangement, but the Commissioners held their ground and this was eventually accepted by the railway.

Raworth's remit was to encompass a very wide area and to provide for the elimination of steam. Therefore, to cover the distances involved with the minimum number of substations, he proposed a third and fourth rail system to give 3,000V across the trains. This would have meant no short to earth greater than 1,500V. Conductor rail placing at junctions would have been decidedly problematic, as it would have required one conductor rail to be fed at 1,500V above ground potential and one

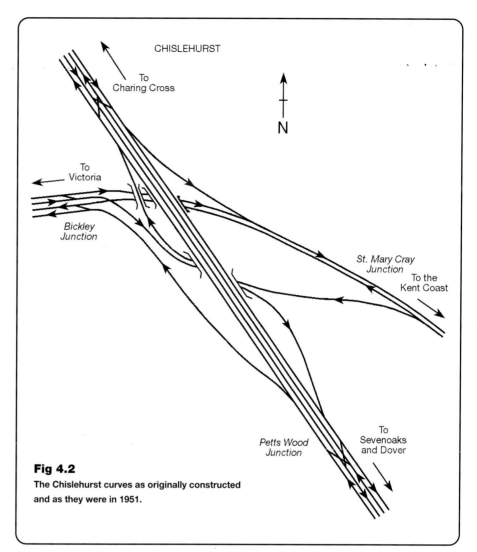

CHISLEHURST

To Charing Cross

N

To Victoria

Bickley Junction

St. Mary Cray Junction

To the Kent Coast

To Sevenoaks and Dover

Petts Wood Junction

Fig 4.2

The Chislehurst curves as originally constructed and as they were in 1951.

at 1,500V below, with an earthed return through the running rails.

The four substations were to be erected at Lewisham Junction, Rochester Bridge, Redhill and Tonbridge. The conductor rails were to be protected by timber to minimise the chance of accidental contact, and the running rails were to be bonded for the return current. The system proposed was believed to have been best suited to the needs of suburban and main line working and it could have been further extended to cover all main lines and link up with the Channel Tunnel, if that were constructed. Again, overhead wires were proposed for use in sidings.

In 1920, Raworth gave evidence for the South Eastern & Chatham to the Electrification of Railways Advisory Committee of the Ministry of Transport. Eventually, the Committee recommended 1,500V dc delivered through a third rail and the SECR felt that it was not far away from this proposed standard.

However, the LBSCR was going to be allowed to retain and extend its own ac overhead system. This would have made for a considerable amount of duplicated equipment from London Bridge right through to Redhill, to say nothing of the route via Oxted, over both of which the South Eastern had access, as discussed previously.

The result was a classic situation in which 'do nothing' for the time being was the only tenable answer. That something needed to be done was not disputed. The South Eastern & Chatham's steam suburban services were provided by elderly rolling stock, and suffered from both overcrowding and unpunctuality. As a result, they were unpopular with the public, and deservedly so. The public would welcome any improvement

One area in which the SECR had made useful progress was the establishment of the loops, or junctions, a little to the east of Chislehurst. Neither the Chatham nor the South Eastern had any four-track routes into London, and thus all had to be shared between express and local trains.

At Chislehurst, the South Eastern main line crosses above the Chatham's main line. With the use of grade separation to avoid conflicts, connections were laid first between Bickley on the Chatham to Orpington on the South Eastern. This work was completed in 1902. Two years later, the link was completed between Chislehurst on the South Eastern to St Mary Cray on the Chatham. The purpose was to make it possible to run from any SECR terminus to either the Chatham or the South Eastern. Fig 4.2 (above) shows the layout, as established initially. While such work was not an essential preliminary to electrification, it was nevertheless a very useful way of adding flexibility and the availability of alternative routes to the network.

Here, the story of the South Eastern Electric ends, for on 1 January 1923, the London & South Western Railway, the London, Brighton & South Coast Railway and the South Eastern & Chatham Railway were merged as the Southern Railway. The lines of these constituent companies were shortly afterwards distinguished as the Western, Central and Eastern sections of the new system.

This is, perhaps, a suitable point at which to review the progress made so far with electrification on a national scale. By the time of the Grouping, the South Western and the Brighton had both made a substantial start on electrification, as shown in the accompanying table. Dated 1921, it was compiled by J. P. Thomas of the Underground companies. The combined electrified route mileage of what was to become the Southern Railway was 82m 60ch, representing 22.8% of the then national total. The expansion which took electrification for passenger operation out of the urban and suburban environments had yet to come. Meanwhile, the prowess of the Lancashire & Yorkshire is of note, as was that of the LNWR's London area. The North Eastern's electric services were the passenger operations around Tyneside, but also the relatively short-lived freight installation at Shildon on Teesside.

Fig 4.3: Electrification of Railways in Britain, 1921

Name of Railway Company	Route Mileage m ch	% Total
London & South Western (i/c Waterloo & City)	57 53	15.9
Lancashire & Yorkshire	50 78	14.0
North Eastern	49 17	13.6
London & North Western and associated companies	32 06	8.8
London, Brighton & South Coast	25 07	6.9
Midland (i/c LT&S east of Bow)	21 68	6.0
Mersey Railway	4 62	1.3
Metropolitan (i/c Met & GC Joint)	30 03	8.3
Metropolitan & District Joint, City lines and extensions, i/c Metropolitan District and Whitechapel and Bow and City lines)	28 74	8.0
London Electric	24 61	6.8
City & South London	7 26	2.0
Central London	6 66	1.9
East London	4 02	1.1
Great Western (i/c Hammersmith & City)	3 67	1.1
Liverpool Overhead	9 00	2.5
Great Central (Grimsby-Immingham)	6 73	1.9
Total	363 28	100

Source: Modern Transport, 26 November 1921.

Below:
The Class 365s are dual voltage units, but those leased by Connex SouthEastern are equipped only with third rail capability. No 365501 is at the head of an eight-car formation as it hurries through Herne Hill on 30 September 2000 with a Victoria-Ramsgate service. *Author*

5. Suburban Electrification Completed

The companies merged by the Act of 1921 to form the Southern Railway brought with them a number of organisational and philosophical barriers. These included:

- Two if not quite three electrification systems, each of which had its own adherents.
- The results of more or less independent companies each trying to reach both City and West End destinations.
- The physical layouts at boundary locations inherited from the past, which cried out for rationalisation.

One of the latter was between Margate and Ramsgate in Thanet, where the separate railways of the Chatham and South Eastern had never been sorted out; this was an essential preliminary to the electrification which, in the event, was still 40 years away.

Also in need of resolution was the situation at Epsom and at Leatherhead, where the Brighton and South Western each maintained their own separate stations, despite sharing the 3¼ miles of track between the two points.

These were however small matters compared with different corporate approaches and the personal and inter-company frictions between the main participants. Suffice to say for present purposes that, after an aimless six months or so, the Southern Railway Board decided to appoint Sir Herbert Walker KCB as General Manager, with effect from 1 January 1924. It was the right choice for the Southern. Public esteem of the company and its mixed bag of constituent railways was not of the highest. Walker provided the leadership that was needed, and a highly progressive outlook. Securing the full backing of his Board, Walker embarked on a continuous and all-embracing programme of electrification, on a scale which few others might have even contemplated. It stimulated both traffic and receipts on a huge scale. The Southern Railway rose from the ashes to be second to none, with the world's largest suburban electrified system.

Right:
This advertisement appeared in the issue of *Modern Transport* dated 25 July 1925, so the events concerned had already taken place!
Author's collection

Making Ready for July 12

One of the New Southern Electric Trains.

Interior of a First Class Compartment.

FOR the past twelve months the carriage works of the Southern Railway at Ashford, Brighton and Lancing have been at full pressure building the trains for the new Electric Services to be opened next month and in December.

WHEN, on **July 12th**, the "Electrics" start to run from Holborn, St. Paul's, and Victoria to Orpington and Crystal Palace, and from Waterloo to Guildford and Dorking, many of the older steam trains now filling the gap will be withdrawn.

The travelling public has appreciated the fact that it takes time to construct 850 vehicles; next month they will have concrete evidence—and what could be better?—that the line with the greatest suburban traffic has been, and is, hard at work on its reconstruction; and will be hard at work until the "change over" is complete.

The new South-Eastern portion has cost £1,600,000 and that from Waterloo £833,000— a total of £2,433,000

SOUTHERN ELECTRIC
New Coaches
More Trains — H. A. WALKER, General Manager.

E. 21/6/5.

Above:
The busy South Eastern line east of London Bridge, seen here on 27 April 1990, is built continuously on brick arches. There are three trains in sight; the South Eastern tracks are on the far side, and the Brighton tracks are nearer. On the SER is a blue and grey 4EPB unit, while centre is a 2x4CEP formation in Network SouthEast and London & South East liveries. The other EPB is in NSE colours. *Author*

In the opinion of Sir John Elliot, the Southern's last General Manager, Walker was 'the outstanding British railway manager of the century'.

After the Great War

In a new era, railway electrification was to be encouraged, according to the Government's White Paper Cm 654 on Ministry of Transport estimates 1920/1. Or, more precisely, 'The policy of the Ministry is to encourage the different railway companies to spend their own capital on electrification schemes wherever a well-considered scheme can be produced, more especially with suburban traffic.' Any form of financial assistance from the Exchequer was not on the table at this stage.

Poor housing conditions were giving rise to a debate about where people should live. It was becoming common ground that additional houses should be constructed some distance away from the overcrowded towns and cities. If this was to be a reality, some form of transport would be needed for those living there, to take them to work daily. Government saw the railway as a substantial part of the answer, and electrification was a means of harnessing that advantage. 'In solving the suburban traffic problem,' said *Modern Transport*, 'the railways will be performing a national service. To enable men and women to quit the tenements of the city and live in the pure air of the country is a

means of building up the stamina of the people and producing a virile population.'

In addition, for the railways, there were the two problems then seen as being associated with suburban traffic:

- How best to deal with existing traffic, but also cater for further development and still continue the effective operation of other train services.
- How to counter tramway competition.

It was thought that the problems of all-stations trains occupying line capacity could be dealt with by:

- Using longer trains, to increase the number of passengers moved by each train.
- Shortening block sections, to allow closer headways between successive trains.
- Higher speeds, by use of larger and thus more powerful locomotives.
- The building of additional running lines, to further separate expresses from stopping services.
- Electrification.

Or some combination of any or all of these. Nevertheless, it was recognised that the costs of electrification could not be justified for infrequent services. Also, electric trains would still have the problems of stock and train crew utilisation outside the peak hours.

When it came to tram competition winning the short-distance traffic, there was a school of thought that, quite simply, railways would do well to get out of providing for markets where passenger journeys were less than four or five miles in length. If railways were increasingly being asked to cater for longer distance suburban traffic, to stop trains at stations which are close in to the terminus for a dwindling patronage results in a less than ideal use of line capacity. This can be illustrated in the cases of three Dartford line stations on the South Eastern. Deptford was closed during World War 1, but rebuilt and reopened with electrification. This was completed for St John's on 28 February 1926 and for Deptford and Greenwich on 19 July 1926.

Electrification, as can be seen from Fig 5.1, did little to restore these stations' fortunes. But worse was to come with the South London line from Victoria to London Bridge via Peckham Rye, the scene of the pioneer Brighton electrification scheme of 1909. By

Fig 5.1: Patronage Trends in Terms of Passengers Booked at Inner-suburban Stations

Distance From London Bridge	Station	September 1902	Before Electrification		After Electrification 1		After Electrification 2	
3m 06ch	Deptford	75,755	station closed		4,324	9/26	4,141	1/28
3m 46ch	Greenwich	78,621	10,370	4/26	12,499	9/26	9,697	1/28
3m 57ch	St John's	51,976	17,615	12/25	19,612	4/26	13,706	1/28

1928, the electric service on this line was conveying fewer passengers per train than any other in the suburban area of the Southern Railway. This unpalatable finding was put down wholly to each station being within the London tram and bus area. In other words, the railway had tasted competition and had lost, at least for the time being.

Yet the Southern's enthusiasm for electrification continued unabated. This reflected the growth in the longer-distance traffic, which perhaps made the subsequent extensions to Brighton and elsewhere inevitable. This was illustrated by a comparison of the number of journeys made on the electrified network as a whole over the years 1924 to 1927. Passenger journeys by electrified services in this period increased by 4.6%. So far, so good. However, this masked a difference between those lines electrified pre-1923, which had seen a fall of 9.1% in passenger journeys, and the more recent post-1923 schemes which showed a healthy growth of 17.6% in the space of three years.

While this division is only broadly on the lines of inner and outer areas of London, as may be seen by comparing the dates in Appendix 1 at which the various schemes were completed, the areas more distant from central London appeared to show a much more satisfactory result.

The main concern of the company was to improve services with electrification, leading to more traffic and lower operating costs. Little was done about labour productivity and ceasing marginal activities – the latter might have included some of the branches, particularly on the former Brighton lines. However, traffic costing was not then developed in the sense that the impact of infrastructure costs on routes with low traffic volumes was not fully appreciated, while less labour would nearly always mean more capital investment.

A Growing Market

One of the problems confronting the new directors of the Southern Railway was the operation of the heavy suburban traffic. From 1913 to 1923, the number of passengers carried by the three Southern lines rose by a little more than a quarter. However, the shortening of working hours after World War 1 resulted in the morning and evening peak traffic having to be carried in one and a half hours less than it had been in 1913. Steam operation under these conditions became increasingly difficult, with considerable congestion in the London termini and on their approaches. Line widening was out of the question owing both to cost and the time needed for construction, and the only realistic solution was to press on with the electrification schemes already developed or proposed.

Clearly, though, it would be foolhardy and perhaps impractical to have three different systems of electrification on the new company's lines. The first step, therefore, was to decide which of the three systems should be adopted as the future standard. A Departmental Committee was set up, presided over by E. C. Cox, the chief operating superintendent and an ex-SECR man. After taking expert advice, including that from Philip Gibb of the Pennsylvania Railroad, the Committee recommended adoption of the direct current, 600V, third rail system as used by the LSWR. Their grounds were the ease of installation, and low cost of construction and maintenance.

The Board accepted this recommendation, with the proviso that as the extension of the LBSCR high-tension ac system was so far advanced, it should be completed and brought into service. Kidner suggests that this was little more than a ploy to quell Parliamentary unrest about the standards of service currently being provided by the Southern in that area, and that further ac electrification was an initiative by which the company could be seen to be responding.

At the company's first annual meeting in March 1924, Chairman Sir Hugh Drummond said that the decision of the SECR Managing Committee to proceed with the

Left:
New Eltham is on the route via Sidcup, and a pair of Networkers cross in this view of 27 January 2001 looking towards London. Both are ABB units with Brush traction motors. *Author*

Fig 5.2: Assessment of ac Overhead and dc Third Rail Electrification Systems

ac Advantages	ac Disadvantages
Availability to draw extra power for acceleration.	High cost of overhead support systems.
No interference with permanent way maintenance.	Interference with signalling visibility, leading to need for signal resiting.
Lower electricity distribution costs, as fewer substations.	ac motors used by LBSCR rather low power, so poor acceleration.

dc Advantages	dc Disadvantages
Simple system.	Limits to current which can be taken in a single section.
Low first cost.	Close spacing of costly substations.
Low maintenance requirement.	Icing of conductor rail in winter.
	Interference with track maintenance.
	Safety of permanent way staff and others.

electrification of its suburban lines was entirely approved and supported by the Board. It had also been decided to extend the Western Section electrification from Claygate to Effingham Junction and Guildford, Raynes Park to Epsom, Leatherhead and Effingham Junction, and Leatherhead to Dorking. On the Eastern Section, the suburban area within a 15-mile radius of central London was being electrified. Extraordinary progress had been made and the whole was anticipated as being in operation by April 1926.

South Western Suburbs

The first additions to the South Western system took in Epsom, Leatherhead and then the separate routes to Dorking (then Dorking North) and to Effingham Junction and Guildford. The opportunity was also taken to extend electrification from the somewhat curious previous choice of Claygate as a terminus through to Effingham Junction, and thus complete the third rail to Guildford over two routes. The scheme of 67 single-track miles was authorised by the Board on 6 December 1923, and was operational 1 year

Below:
By 1926, the Southern had become a sizeable electric suburban operation, as this map shows. There are some gaps; Sutton can be reached by electric train only via West Croydon, and the extension to Epsom has yet to receive the third rail. Elsewhere, Dartford is a terminus as is Orpington, while Guildford is reached only via Cobham. The Hounslow Loop also shows no signs of its continuation to Staines and beyond. All these would be addressed before the outbreak of war, still 13 years away. *Author's collection*

7 months and 5 days later, opening to the public on 12 July 1925.

Included in this was the construction of a new island platform station at Motspur Park, with an additional bay platform on the down side at Guildford (which is still used for its original purpose) and at Dorking. All of these were to what became a standard length of 520ft, to accommodate an eight-car electric train.

Other work, which was common to all schemes, included:

- Signalling and track layout alterations, also work on station premises, where necessary to accommodate a greatly increased train service and patronage.
- Platform extensions where needed.
- The provision of additional refuges in confined spaces such as tunnels or viaducts for those working on the track.
- Protecting signal wires from the live rails.
- Moving any fixtures such as detonator placers, which might foul current collection shoes.
- Providing coasting marks (a white diamond mounted on a short post) where needed.
- Providing stopping marks (a square blue plate bearing white figures 3, 6 or 8) fixed on station platforms.
- Removal of redundant facilities.

Carriage sheds were erected at Effingham Junction. Power for the extensions was supplied from the Southern's own sources at Durnsford Road and transmitted to the seven

substations built for the purpose and used to convert the power to 600V dc. Four of these were equipped with two 1,259kW rotary converters, but the other three each had one converter only and were unattended and remotely controlled. Thus those at Leatherhead and Clandon were controlled from Effingham Junction, and that at Oxshott from the existing installation at Hampton Court Junction. The removal of the need to staff substations would become an important consideration in the economics of low voltage dc systems, as will be seen later.

Operationally, the new services resulted in 15 electric trains in a standard hour on the local lines via Wimbledon. The total service was not dissimilar to that presently provided, but the balance has shifted away from the inner areas. Thus the Kingston Loop then enjoyed trains leaving Waterloo at 03, 13, 33 and 43 minutes past the hour, the times at 23 and 53 being for Shepperton services. In 2001, that becomes 03 Shepperton, 18 Kingston Loop, 33 Shepperton and 48 Kingston loop. The principle of even intervals remains.

A major reconstruction took place at Epsom, where the opportunity was taken to end the peculiar arrangement which had existed there for many years. Both the Brighton and South Western lines had their own station; the Brighton station, Epsom Town, had a large goods yard and engine shed. The South Western station was situated on the Ashtead (western) side of the junction of the two lines; its platforms could only be used by trains to and from Waterloo, with the Brighton trains having to run through on the

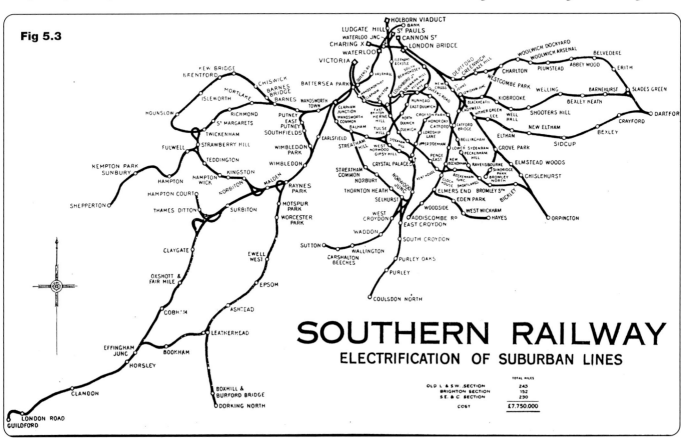

North Sheen station is an island platform, opened on 6 July 1930. The construction required the up and down lines to be separated, and a path with a concrete fence built to the bridge from which this photograph was taken. Approaching is 4VEP unit No 3154 with a Waterloo to Reading semi-fast service in March 1990. *Author*

middle roads. This station also had a goods yard, closed on 2 January 1928 when all goods traffic was concentrated on the Brighton yard.

At Leatherhead, there were separate stations for the former LSWR line from Effingham Junction and the former LBSCR route to Dorking. There was a signalbox at each station as well as at the junction of the two lines. A spur was built from the Effingham Junction line so that all trains could use the LBSCR station, and the signalling was concentrated in one cabin. The South Western station was closed, but the lines through it kept as sidings. This work was completed on 10 July 1927.

The new Epsom station, opened on 3 March 1929, was on approximately the same site as the former South Western station. It was a large and spacious edifice in the new Southern concrete style, with two 650ft island platforms each 30ft wide and reached from a subway. Signalling was controlled from a box located above the platforms. Berthing sidings were provided on each side of the line at the Ashtead end. The former Brighton premises were closed on electrification.

Other stations were opened on the South Western suburban area, mostly to serve the developing housing estates. These were at Sunnymeads in 1927, Hinchley Wood, North Sheen and Whitton in 1930, Syon Lane in 1931, Stoneleigh in 1932 and Berrylands in 1933.

Work Starts on the South Eastern

The first part of the Eastern Section to be electrified comprised the following:

- Victoria-Herne Hill-Beckenham Junction-Orpington
- Holborn Viaduct-Herne Hill
- Brixton/Loughborough Junction-Nunhead-Catford-Shortlands
- Nunhead-Crystal Palace HL

Apart from the last couple of miles into Orpington, this was all former Chatham territory. Extensive incidental works were undertaken. The disused and dilapidated stations between Victoria and Elephant & Castle were taken down in 1924. Lengthening the up and down main line platforms at Brixton involved rebuilding an underbridge and substantial lengths of platform on steel and concrete cantilevers owing to site restrictions. At Herne Hill, the platforms and track layout survived from the time when practically every train ran to or from both Victoria and the City. Consequently, it stopped there to divide or combine. A new island platform was provided for up trains and an existing one lengthened for down trains. The track layout was simplified and the curves through the station eased.

The Catford Loop platforms at Loughborough Junction were closed, as site difficulties prevented their extension. The main line side was rebuilt as a single island platform. At the London end, and with further alterations at Blackfriars, the track layout was altered to allow parallel working. This enabled a greater range of what would otherwise be conflicting movements to be made simultaneously. Thus trains from the Catford Loop could continue on the fast lines through to the terminal platforms at Blackfriars at the same time as those from Herne Hill could use the slow lines to

Above:
Hastings station is a good standard Southern design, with a high ceiling inside the ticket hall. There is space in the forecourt for buses as well as taxis. It was photographed on a foggy 1 February 2001. *Author*

Holborn Viaduct. The technique was later applied elsewhere. Track and signalling alterations were made at Shortlands so that trains from the Catford Loop could be terminated in the down local platform and return without interfering with the main line. A station was built at Nunhead, opened on a new site on 3 May 1925.

Alternating current was received at Lewisham distribution switch room and transmitted to the trackside substations for conversion to dc. The track circuits, control functions and signal lighting came from a supply at 3,300V ac from Lewisham, transformed locally as required. The point machines were operated by direct current originating from the conductor rail.

Public services began on 12 July 1925, after periods of trial running. There were services each at 20-minute intervals from both Victoria and Holborn Viaduct, via Herne Hill to Orpington. However, there were only two lines over the six miles between Herne Hill and Orpington, and five intermediate stations as well as the long Penge Tunnel. These trains therefore had to be timed to leave as many paths as possible for main line and Continental boat trains. This was achieved by running the electric services five minutes apart, leaving a 15-minute window for the steam-hauled services. Additional electric

services at peak omitted two of the intermediate stations, to minimise their running times over the crucial section.

A similar technique was used for the trains from Blackfriars running every 20 minutes to each of Shortlands and Crystal Palace High Level. This was designed to give an opportunity to run main line trains via the Catford Loop on occasion. Services on all routes were reduced to half-hourly on Sundays.

The launch of the new services did not go well, with blown fuses on the trains and sticking brakes, while one set of traction motors burnt out. It was perhaps as well that press advertisements had warned the public that work of this magnitude was likely to produce some problems in the first week or so, as everything was new both to passengers and staff.

The second stage two concentrated on the South Eastern lines:

- Charing Cross/Cannon Street-London Bridge-Ladywell-Elmers End-Addiscombe/Hayes
- New Cross-Grove Park-Orpington
- Grove Park-Bromley North
- New Beckenham-Beckenham Junction
- Charing Cross/Cannon Street-Dartford via all four routes (Greenwich, North Kent, Bexleyheath, and Dartford Loop)

The principal task was the complete rearrangement of the lines, and hence signalling, between Charing Cross and Cannon Street. The layout on the Cannon Street bridge over the Thames was designed

to suit the practice of working trains to Charing Cross via Cannon Street, with reversal there – quite an undertaking with steam traction. The new set-up placed suburban trains in Platforms 1 to 3 at Charing Cross, and main line trains in Nos 4 to 6, as is still approximately the situation now.

Services between Elmers End and Hayes began on 21 September 1925 for crew training purposes, but the main scheme commenced on 28 February 1926. The services are discussed after details of the next stage to be completed.

The next task was the complete reconstruction of Cannon Street and its approaches, the station being closed completely for 23 days from 5 to 28 June. A workforce of 1,000 removed the old platforms, track and signalling, and installed the new. The track, including conductor rails, cabling and point machines, was laid out on spare ground at New Cross Gate, thoroughly tested and numbered, so it could be taken to Cannon Street and laid down section by section. The number of point ends was reduced from 101 to 77.

While Cannon Street was closed, traffic had to be handled at London Bridge and Charing Cross. Temporary electric services were run on all four routes to Dartford from 6 June, to ease the handling problems. During the three-hour morning peak, 81 trains arrived at London Bridge, of which 23 terminated there and 58 went on to Charing Cross. London Bridge had the task of dealing with 26,000 rush hour passengers, $2\frac{1}{2}$ times the normal number.

The new layout at Cannon Street comprised eight platforms of varying lengths; the three longer platforms did not have conductor rails, being intended for main line steam services. Four-aspect signalling north of Borough Market Junction was introduced on 27 June 1926, controlled from boxes at Charing Cross (107 levers) and Cannon Street (143 levers). The section through London Bridge and beyond to Spa Road was brought under the control of the existing box at Borough Market Junction (35 levers) and a new one at London Bridge (312 levers) on 17 June 1928. This box also controlled the Brighton lines, by then being converted to dc. Further extensions on the South Eastern side took place in 1929 and 1930.

Electric power was supplied from Lewisham through lineside cables to 19 rotary converter substations. These had up to three machines in them. At Upper Sydenham, the substation served both the Crystal Palace branch and the main line, the latter by means of cables led down a shaft into Penge Tunnel below. Owing to the then movable bridge, a special submarine cable had to be laid across Deptford Creek.

Cleaning and inspection sheds were erected at Orpington and Addiscombe, while the former engine shed at Slade Green was rebuilt to serve as a depot. A new building was added for use as repair shops. Other works included a new station at Bromley North.

The full Dartford lines service started on 19 July 1926, and the rebuilt station at Deptford opened the same day.

Noticeably, the peak service augmentation was almost entirely from Cannon Street. The West End still did not match the City in volumes for travel to work. In any event,

housing development in many of the areas served by the new services was still in the future. Trains to Orpington appear relatively infrequent, but these were supplemented by main line steam services.

New stations opened in the Eastern Section in the ensuing period up to 1939 were: Petts Wood 1928, New Hythe 1929, Swanscombe 1930, Albany Park 1935, and Falconwood 1936.

The Suburban Electric Units

In 1923, the Southern Railway took over 434 vehicles for use in electric trains, made up as shown in Fig 5.5.

As already discussed, the rolling stock situation in the early days was somewhat fluid. Conversion of old steam stock, with the use of new underframes, was later matched by the use of old underframes and new bodies. Also, the bodies reclaimed from steam stock were not necessarily the same length as the underframes on which they were positioned. As an example, some of the units used for the Eastern Section electrification of 1925–6 had bodywork converted from ex-SECR six-wheelers and from four-wheeled close-coupled sets. No doubt some careful panelling was able to hide the join, although this would become more difficult if the roof profiles differed. Ashford did the main work, but Brighton undertook the finishing, including the upholstery and the painting. Not all the vehicles in the pool to be converted would have been identical, and any generalisations on detailed matters with these vehicles are fraught with difficulty. Others have tackled this problem, and the enquiring reader will find references in the bibliography.

In general, the Southern followed LSWR practice of a motor unit-trailer-motor unit for the new trains. This gave three possible formations:

- A single three-car motor unit.
- Two three-car motor units, coupled.
- Two three-car units, with an intervening trailer unit.

All the trailer units were third class only.

The three-car motor units were all close-coupled, with side buffers and screw couplings at the ends. Underframes were rolled steel. The motor bogies had two nose-suspended 275hp traction motors, geared 59/21 to steel wheels of 3ft 7in diameter. With a conductor rail voltage of 600V dc, an eight-coach train on level track could reach a free running speed of 54mph. The electromagnetic control gear was mounted at the back of the motorman's compartment and the control cables ran along the roofs. The motorman was located on the near side. He was provided with a seat and the window in front of him with a windscreen wiper. The master controller had a deadman's handle. The Westinghouse brake was fitted and had a compressor on each motor coach and two pipe lines – one for the train lines and the other to equalise the pressure in the air reservoirs.

First class compartments were upholstered in floral tapestry and thirds in velvet with 'half back' cushions. They had the usual glazed panels of the period for displays of scenery, notices and advertisements.

The livery was the standard olive green, lined out in black and yellow, with window mouldings and droplight frames in light brown. The coach number and 'SOUTHERN RAILWAY' were inscribed on the top panels in block figures and letters in gold, black shaded. Class was indicated by a large block '1' or '3' in gold, black shaded, midway on the lower door panels. The doors of the guard's compartment were lettered 'GUARD' and 'LUGGAGE' respectively. Stepboards, frames, etc were painted black. Many original features from converted coaches were retained, including the door and commode handles.

The use of the LSWR system of head end indicators was continued, a stencil plate being shown on the leading end in front of an opal glass panel, lit from behind at night. The tail lamp was carried on the near side, above the buffer.

Until 1934, compartments in which smoking was allowed were indicated by the word 'SMOKING' etched on the quarter-light glasses. From that month, window labels were applied – 'NON SMOKING' in green and 'SMOKING' in red. From December 1938, smoking was permitted in any compartment not specifically labelled 'NON SMOKING'. This was a reversion to the practice initiated by the SECR in 1920.

Fig 5.4: Eastern Section Electric Services Each Hour, From 19 July 1926

All trains call at London Bridge, and Charing Cross trains call additionally at Waterloo East

Destination	From Charing Cross		From Cannon Street	
	Peak	Off-peak	Peak	Off-peak
Plumstead via Greenwich	1	1	2¹	1
Dartford via Blackheath and Woolwich	1	1	2	1
Dartford via Bexleyheath	1	1	2	1
Dartford via Sidcup	1	1	2	1
Orpington	1	1	1	1
Bromley North	1	1	2	1
Beckenham Junction	1	1	2	1
Hayes	1	1		
Addiscombe	1	1²	3	1²

¹ Not beyond Woolwich Arsenal
² Connection at Elmers End for Hayes

Fig 5.5: Electric Rolling Stock, 1923

Company	Description	Sets	No Vehicles	No Series
LBSCR	South London line stock		30	
LBSCR	Crystal Palace stock		104	
LSWR	Three-coach motor sets	84 x 3-car	252	1201-84
LSWR	Two-coach trailer sets	24 x 2-car	48	1001-24

On 6 May 1956, a four-car train of 1925 stock, later 4SUB, leaves Tulse Hill for London Bridge on a circular working via Forest Hill and Crystal Palace. To the right is 'Battle of Britain' Pacific No 34087 *145 Squadron*, which embarrassingly has stalled on the 1 in 66 climb from Herne Hill with the empty stock of the 'Bournemouth Belle'. The train was routed this way because of engineering work at Battersea, and was to gain Waterloo via Wimbledon and reversal. Eventually, 'N' class 2-6-0 No 31411 came to the rescue.
R. C. Riley/Ian Allan Library

2NOL and 4SUB

This economical approach to rolling stock provision did not prevent new stock from being acquired, but this was an intermittent luxury. Rebuilding old vehicles is fine, but it does prevent much in the way of technical advance. Even if some vehicles are built completely new, they will still have to be compatible with others in the same set. The use of new vehicles only really got under way with the Brighton and subsequent main line electrification schemes, as described later. The last of the 'conversions' was that of the 2NOL units (the telegraphic code names came into general use around the early 1930s). These two-car close-coupled units, numbered 1813 to 1890, were converted from LSWR steam stock at Eastleigh from 1934 to 1936. The motor coaches contained motorman's, guard's, coupé third and seven third class compartments. The driving trailers contained three first, six third and motorman's compartment. The overall length was 129ft

6in, with 24 first and 135 third class seats. These sets had a varied career in that they undertook main line and suburban work with equal success. When the bodies wore out in the late 1950s, the underframes were reused, as will be shown later.

The earlier three-car units, latterly acquiring the all-embracing 3SUB categorisation, were pressed to carry some of the growing crowds travelling, and an extra trailer vehicle would later be found for many of them to become 4SUBs. During the 1939–45 war, 10 examples of early versions of a new all-steel four-car suburban set were produced, Nos 4101-4110, these having electro-pneumatic control gear. Originally to cater for first class as well, the design was revamped when it became clear that this luxury had disappeared for good, and some versions then had open saloons substituted for straight compartments. Importantly, these were the first to seat six persons per side in third class compartments, adding materially to their capacity.

As a class of vehicles they were far from uniform, but only those in the know were able to distinguish the origins of the vehicles from outside with any certainty. This could have its benefits when travelling; those built to really restrictive dimensions of compartment pitch were of the unpopular interlocking knees variety. Then there were the ordinary ones, but the prize was to travel in the would-be first class vehicles, the ballroom dancing type, since the space between the seats opposite each other was allegedly sufficient so to do!

Mass production started following the war, and continued in British Railways days until 1951.

The Brighton on Third Rail

In the case of the Brighton or Central Section lines, the announcement that conversion to third rail would take place was made in August 1926. Further sections would also be electrified. The additional sections would be as follows:

- London Bridge-Norwood Junction
- Sydenham-Crystal Palace LL
- Crystal Palace LL-Beckenham Junction
- Purley-Caterham/Tattenham Corner
- Herne Hill-Tulse Hill-Haydons Road-Wimbledon
- Streatham North Junction-Sutton-Epsom
- Sutton-Epsom Downs

The most important of the incidental works was the resignalling and the revised track layout in the London Bridge area. This was in part three lines only, and even with one of them reversible was not enough for the electric services envisaged. Rearrangement would offer separate pairs of lines for the South London and the main lines to Croydon. One result was that South Bermondsey station had to be resited, having lost one of its platforms.

At Tulse Hill, there were separate platforms for London Bridge and Holborn Viaduct trains, but all had to use the same two tracks on the bridge across Norwood Road before diverging towards West Norwood, Streatham and Streatham Hill respectively. A second bridge over the road was built, which allowed all movements between London Bridge and West Norwood to be carried out at the same time as movements between Holborn Viaduct and Streatham or Streatham Hill. Elsewhere, platform lengthening at North Dulwich required the signalbox to be demolished and the points to be converted to motorised, so that they could be controlled remotely. At Tattenham Corner, hitherto a race-days-only station, the tracks were rearranged. Tattenham Corner has the unique distinction for a terminus well south of the Thames but less than 20 miles from London, where an arriving train finds itself facing almost due north! A further station on this branch at Woodmansterne was added in 1932.

The new train services were introduced on 17 June 1928, although some had been running to steam timings since 25 March. The basis was two services making round trips out from London Bridge and back again. The routes were via Sydenham, Crystal Palace and Tulse Hill, or for a longer ride via Norwood Junction, Selhurst and Streatham. All services operated half-hourly in each direction, every 20 minutes at peak times. Other services from London Bridge with the same frequencies were those to Epsom

Downs, to Streatham Hill and to Victoria via Denmark Hill. This last had become a commercial disaster area, especially since the Southern's services had been withdrawn for four months during the coalminers' strike in 1926, and the rebuilt and extended Northern Line had started running that same year. There was also a peak-hours-only service to Coulsdon North.

Then there were the services to Purley and the branches thence to Caterham and Tattenham Corner. South Eastern services they may have been technically, but running them to Charing Cross was fraught with problems. These centred around the need to cross between the Brighton and South Eastern lines on the London Bridge approaches, which gave them a good chance of halting a host of other services while the manoeuvre took place. They also appropriated South Eastern line capacity. The decision to cut back the peak operations (only) and terminate them at London Bridge's Brighton side platforms was eminently reasonable from an operator's standpoint, although it did meet with some protests from the local authorities affected. The new services were designed to run in portions, joining or splitting at Purley.

As an aside it may be of interest to note that today, over 70 years later, you still travel from

Charing Cross to Tattenham Corner, but only off peak. Many peak services start from London Bridge and divide at Purley.

The rest of the Central Section scheme was brought into operation on 3 March 1929, when dc electric services began over the following routes:

- London Bridge to Dorking or Effingham Junction via Tulse Hill and Mitcham Junction
- Victoria to Epsom via Mitcham Junction
- Holborn Viaduct to Wimbledon via Tulse Hill and Haydons Road

The ac service from Victoria to Crystal Palace was extended, alternately to West Croydon and Beckenham Junction, while the London Bridge to Streatham Hill services were extended to Victoria in peak hours.

The line from Crystal Palace (Bromley Junction) to Beckenham Junction had not

Below:
This curious contraption swings across the running lines at Brockenhurst to allow parcels barrows to reach the north side island platform from the station forecourt. Although suitable for wheelchair access to one of the two platforms, it is no longer in regular use. It was photographed on 6 February 2001. *Author*

been used by regular passenger trains since 1915, and required substantial work as follows:

- Lifting the Chatham main lines between Kent House and Beckenham Junction to improve the gradients.
- Raising the Mid-Kent line north of Clock House, where it passed below both the other lines, in what proved to be a not very successful attempt to reduce its liability to flooding in times of heavy rain.
- Widening the formation of the Brighton line as it approached Beckenham Junction, so that the Crystal Palace trains could run into their own platform to terminate, while keeping clear of the main line.

On 2 March 1930 a new station was opened on the branch at Birkbeck.

Power was supplied by the London Electric Supply Corporation to Lewisham, from which a series of cables led to the nine new substations.

Signalling Revolution

The Southern found that signalling enhancement was a key requirement to obtain the full benefits from electric traction. At a number of places, the signalling sections were divided by the provision of intermediate home signals, but the greatest advantages to track capacity were obtained by the introduction of colour-light signalling on the busiest portions of the line. This system of signalling was first introduced at Holborn

Viaduct in 1926 and proved so successful that by 1937 it had been extended to the whole railway between Charing Cross and Blackheath. It was also provided between Coulsdon North and Brighton (described in the next chapter), and between Waterloo and Hampton Court Junction – a total of 258 track miles.

The colour-light signalling from Holborn Viaduct to Elephant & Castle was brought into use on 21 March 1926 and was the first installation of four-aspect signalling in the world. The running signals were of two patterns: those with the aspects arranged vertically, which has since become standard, and those with the aspects being arranged in a cluster. The latter was used if necessary to overcome sighting difficulties by drivers. Route indicators were provided liberally.

Seven manual signalboxes were abolished and replaced with a new box at Blackfriars and a new power frame fitted into the existing cabin at Holborn Viaduct.

What did the Southern see as the chief advantages of closely spaced four-aspect colour-light signals, which the company pioneered? Compared with semaphores:

- The saving of time previously taken in transmitting block signals from one signalbox to the next, especially where automatic signals were installed.
- The centralised working of crossings, junctions and signals, combined with exact knowledge of the whereabouts of the

various trains as seen on the illuminated diagram, enabling traffic to be better regulated.
- No unnecessary delays from the operation of safety rules involving the checking of trains at a signal where the signal next ahead is at danger.
- Drivers are able to run at confidence and hence at higher speeds, as the signals are easily sighted and always give a clear and definite indication. This can refer not only to their own position but also to the signal immediately ahead and, with four-aspect signals, the one beyond that.
- The indication is the same, both by day and by night.
- A greater measure of safety is assured by the track circuits detecting the presence of trains and their control of points and signals.
- All the foregoing are more pronounced in foggy weather inasmuch as drivers can more readily sight the signals, while signalmen are kept fully acquainted by the diagram with the actual state of the various lines.
- There are no moving parts to go wrong.

A New Railway

The Wimbledon & Sutton was sanctioned by an Act of 1910 to run from a junction at Wimbledon with the LSWR line from Putney Bridge, through Merton, Morden and Lower Cheam to a terminus at Sutton. It would be worked by the District Railway. There had however been no progress by the outbreak of war.

Above:

Above:
Waddon Marsh on the Wimbledon-West Croydon line was also opened on 6 July 1930. Seen here on 1 March 1979 from the bridge on the A23 Purley Way, the station then still had a passing loop, and the signalman issued tickets from the box. 2EPB No 5658 is leaving with a Wimbledon-bound train. *Author*

Next, the Underground group promoted a Bill for the extension of what is now the Northern Line from Clapham Common to Morden, and its continuation to Sutton over the line already authorised. The Southern Railway opposed this and a compromise was reached. The tube extension was to stop at Morden, while the Southern would reopen the Streatham to Wimbledon line, closed since 1917, and take over the Wimbledon & Sutton scheme. The reopening was effective from 27 August 1923 and the Wimbledon & Sutton was taken over by an Act of 1924. The Northern Line opened to Morden on 13 December 1926, and the group quickly provided bus services to the outlying areas from the station forecourt, which had been laid out for the purpose. Those places included Sutton.

From Wimbledon, the Sutton line ran parallel to the South Western before diverging to the south. The first section to Wimbledon

Left:
The new line from Wimbledon to Sutton was opened in two stages in 1929 and 1930. On the right is the final climb to the junction at Sutton, the station being behind the photographer on the other side of the overbridge. Ahead is the line to Epsom. On a misty day, work would appear to be largely complete; there is no mistaking the sharp rise of the new route from West Sutton over what became known as the 'Wall of Death'.
Author's collection

Chase and South Merton (1¾ miles) was built by the railway's Engineers' Department, and opened as a single line on 7 July 1929. It was worked by train staff, with services provided by an extension of the Holborn Viaduct-Wimbledon service.

The remaining four miles to Sutton West Junction included stations at Morden South, St Helier, Sutton Common and West Sutton which were built by McAlpine. The London County Council was building its large housing estate at St Helier and secured a station at its own cost. The works were heavy and included the excavation of 500,000 tons of soil and the building of 24 over- and underbridges. The overbridges were of reinforced concrete and the underbridges of steel with concrete floors. The line was built for electric traction and the gradients were severe. From South Merton to Sutton West Junction was an unbroken ascent, with stretches of 1 in 69 or steeper. This culminated in a curvaceous climb of ½ mile at 1 in 44 from West Sutton station to the junction, which quickly became known as the 'Wall of Death'.

The concrete stations had passimeter booking offices, in which the clerk sat in a freestanding wooden box with glazing all round him, and could both issue tickets from one side and collect them at the other. The only goods yard and signal cabin on the line

were situated at St Helier. All the signals were upper quadrant and made from old rails, then a novel idea. Current was supplied from the existing substations at Raynes Park and Sutton.

Double line throughout was opened on 5 January 1930, with the train service further extended from South Merton to Sutton and West Croydon. After a pause to provide connections with a train to London Bridge, they continued via Crystal Palace to Victoria. So began the service on what has always been a difficult line to operate, although few could then have foreseen that it would one day be worked by trains originating from Midland Railway territory!

6 July 1930: All Systems Go!

The 1933 electrification to Brighton was perhaps the most noteworthy single event in the electrification agenda of the Southern, but on other occasions the company somehow had managed to keep several schemes progressing simultaneously. Take, for instance, the events of 6 July 1930. On that day, the Southern Railway:

- Extended electric services from Whitton and Hounslow Junctions to Staines and Windsor & Eton Riverside.
- Opened new stations at North Sheen and at Whitton on the Windsor lines.
- Commenced electric services on the Wimbledon-West Croydon via Mitcham line.
- Opened a new station on that line at Waddon Marsh.
- Extended electric services from Dartford to Gravesend.
- Opened a station at Swanscombe on the Gravesend line, rebuilt on a new site.
- Opened a station at Chestfield & Swalecliffe, between Whitstable and Herne Bay.
- Restored Sunday services to Cannon Street.

Rather neatly, these schemes were spread between all three of the Southern's Sections and none was of huge proportions. Thus the total track mileage electrified was 49½. Nevertheless, these schemes did mark the completion of the electrification of the suburban area.

The 6¼-mile Wimbledon-West Croydon line was an unusual candidate for electrification in that it was mostly single track but with extensive freight use. Away from the terminals, double track was provided only between Mitcham and Mitcham Junction. However, the sidings on the section from Croydon as far as Beddington Lane were joined up to make an independent running line for freight, keeping these trains clear of the passenger traffic. Latterly, this became merely a loop at Waddon Marsh.

This line is in the awkward category, since an end-to-end running time of 17 minutes or thereabouts makes running a 20-minute frequency with two trains tight, but a 30-minute frequency is downright wasteful of resources. Punctuality also depends on avoiding conflicts on the single line sections. The Southern's initial service ran every 20 minutes in the peaks and otherwise half-hourly.

By the 1990s, its BR successors had decided that a one-train service was all that they could justify, and this resulted in a decidedly user-unfriendly operation of a train every 45 minutes. The line was closed on 31 May 1997, but with the express purpose of conversion for use as part of Croydon Tramlink.

Station Reconstruction

Railway stations tend to last, although there are good reasons for major reconstructions. One might be to accommodate more traffic,

Right:
This subway between the platforms is at Leatherhead. It was photographed on 9 December 2000 from the down platform, and there is an entrance, right, from the street. It is not easy to make subways pleasant to use. *Author*

as seen for instance in the rebuilding of Waterloo, completed in 1922. Another is to correct a thoroughly unsatisfactory situation such as Epsom, as already related, and a third is to make room for the works of another party. Thus Eltham station was completely reconstructed on a new site in 1985 at the expense of the Department of Transport, as part of a new road scheme.

Of the constituent companies, the Brighton were much in favour of subways between platforms in preference to footbridges, as can still be seen at a number of locations. While the passenger probably traverses fewer steps in total, subways can be easy victims to flooding from rainwater. On the other hand, the Brighton company also produced some wide and spacious stations, those at Streatham Common and Horley being good examples.

Right:
The north end of Platforms 1 and 2 at Guildford are seen here, CCTV screens supplying train departure information. Class 455 No 5907 will depart as the 14.54 to West Croydon, a South West Trains service on 9 December 2000. *Author*

Below right:
This magnificent building doubles as London Road station, Brighton, although little is in railway use today. After the climb up the steps to the ticket office, those travelling towards Lewes still need to use the subway to reach the platform. The photograph was taken on 1 February 2001. *Author*

On the Chatham, the approach often seems to be economical and somewhat sombre, Chatham station itself at platform level being one example and Gillingham another. The South Eastern's approach might also be summed up as undistinguished. The South

Above:
At weekends, all trains on the Waterloo-Reading services are made up of Class 455 units. No 5750, whose motor saloon is named *Wimbledon Train Care*, with reference to BS5750, arrives at Wokingham with a down service on 9 December 2000. This station is a 1960s reconstruction using CLASP products which can be configured to meet site needs. *Author*

Western was perhaps generally of a good but unexciting standard.

There were always exceptions to the general rule, and notable structures remaining today from the pre-Grouping era include Wateringbury, Eastbourne, Brighton, Portsmouth & Southsea, and Windsor & Eton Riverside.

Where the Southern Railway made its mark was with precast concrete, which it seemed to use for every conceivable purpose. Produced from its works at Exmouth Junction, this extended to new platforms, platform extensions, lamp posts, fencing, cable supports and small prefabricated buildings. Concrete was often a major ingredient of footbridges and the main station buildings themselves. Thus platform extensions were carried out with ferro-concrete slabs resting on footings of similar material. Southern concrete was efficient for

Top left:
Bromley North's imposing exterior dates from 1925, although it is vastly in excess of today's needs. This photograph was taken on 25 February 1981. *Author*

Left:
Stations on double track rarely come smaller than Normans Bay, once known as Pevensey Sluice. There are standard concrete platforms, although the shelters and lighting have both been renewed. The exit is via the crossing at the east end of the platforms. This station too has an hourly service; it was photographed on 1 February 2001. *Author*

its purpose, although some might claim that the resulting stations were not distinguished. They were adequate and contemporary, rather in the way of the Odeon cinemas of the same period.

There were many major station reconstructions during the interwar period, although they have not necessarily worn well in the intervening years. Some of the most striking ones perhaps are Bromley North 1925, Margate 1926, Hastings 1931, Haywards Heath 1932, Surbiton 1937, Richmond 1937, and Horsham 1938.

The station at Surbiton had become quite inadequate, and a revised track layout was installed with two new island platforms, which had all the usual offices. These were joined by a wide overbridge, having exits to the street and to ticket offices on both sides of the line. The main entrance on the north side of the railway was built with a spacious and airy booking hall, with seats in the centre and an enquiry office at one side. The building work was of concrete throughout, and surmounted by a clock tower. A taxi rank was provided immediately outside.

Modest works can also be rewarding. In 1929, equipment replacement at Durnsford Road power station gave the opportunity to replace some station lighting. A number of stations in the outer parts of the electrified area were lit by oil, as no public gas or electricity supplies were available. Since it was considered out of place for electric trains

to serve oil-lit stations, arrangements were made to supply station lighting from the conductor rails. The system was installed originally at Ashtead, Effingham Junction, Banstead and Epsom Downs, and although it had disadvantages such as no lighting when the traction current was switched off, it was generally so much better that its use was extended.

The large London terminal of Victoria was built as two separate stations, although they were side by side. The whole was in fact owned by the Victoria Station & Pimlico Railway Company, but there any commonality of approach between the Chatham tenant on the eastern side and the Brighton tenant on the west ceased. A solid wall divided the two. It was only with the creation of the Southern Railway which absorbed all three parties under the 1921 Grouping Act that a single stationmaster was appointed for the whole and the wall cut through in 1924. This was not as simple an operation as it sounds, as railway tracks formed a physical barrier as well.

Finance

The industrial depression of the 1920s was of minimal concern to the Southern, although as a company it was vulnerable to the reduced spending power of the population and to road competition. Some capital requirements were funded from renewal funds built up from revenues.

Walker, as General Manager, was a sound judge of financial propositions. At his insistence, any frills which were not essential to the electrification project itself were to be eliminated. He thus exercised stringent cost control. This was *not* the same as saying that additional works would not be carried out; Walker required them to be justified on their own merits and not swept into a list of ancillary works which 'needed' to be undertaken as part of the electrification project. Electrification was thus kept distinct from general modernisation of the railway. Many costs met from renewal funds, for instance funds set aside for the replacement of

a class of steam locomotive, would be earmarked for the new electric multiple-units which were to replace them. Capital account expenditure was therefore minimised.

A further element was the strict monitoring of results, which in due course led to his being able to demonstrate that traffic increases followed electrification everywhere. Much later, this became knows as 'the sparks effect'.

The emphasis of undertaking necessary work only, and reusing existing assets wherever possible, led to the Southern's schemes acquiring a well-used air about them. The principal cause was perhaps the use of second-hand but serviceable bodies from steam stock on new underframes and bogies, to the extent that few of the units constructed during the 1920s for the suburban work (as then defined) were completely new. Some vehicles, indeed, were rebuilt more than once. The first occasion was for the Brighton ac electrification, and then again after its abolition for use on the dc. This economical approach did have its downsides, one of which was that rolling stock undergoing reconstruction was not available at all for traffic purposes during this period, and that

led to some resourcing problems in service provision. It also stored up difficulties for the future, when renewal became due but not for all parts of the vehicle at the same time.

As far as ancillary schemes are concerned, station platforms would be lengthened for longer trains, but not reconstructed. Somewhat incongruously, gas lighting on stations might therefore exist alongside electric traction for trains, and semaphores might also remain in use. Their conversion to multiple-aspect signalling (mas) had to be approved as a separate project. This might well be forthcoming, especially if substantial track alterations were to take place, or line capacity might prove inadequate to operate the new service levels planned. Nevertheless, pockets of semaphores remain even today, the coastal town of Hastings being one.

Later, and in a wish to counter unemployment, some Government assistance became available. The Development (Loan Guarantees and Grants) Act of 1929 enabled the Southern (and other railways) to carry out some capital improvements on the basis of the Government making grants for a maximum period of 15 years to cover the interest charges on the approved works.

6. To Brighton On the Hour, In the Hour, At the Hour

There is nothing like a little financial encouragement from the Government to get things done, although the Southern Railway, as we have seen, was not one to drag its feet. The occasion was the 1929 Budget speech by the then Chancellor of the Exchequer, Mr Winston Churchill, that Railway Passenger Duty would be abolished.

This was a tax, going back to stage-coach days (note the hyphen!), which had first been imposed in 1832. In 1842, it was established as a charge of 5% upon the gross passenger receipts, except that after 1844 the Parliamentary trains for third class passengers were exempt. It was in effect a sort of luxury tax on travel in first and second class, and became an anachronism. In the way of governments, a *quid pro quo* was extracted as a condition. This was that the railways would capitalise the amount paid in tax at 5%, and then spend 90% of this notional amount on approved new works. The Government's purpose was to relieve unemployment.

At the company's annual meeting in 1930, the Chairman said that the Southern's share of the duty was just over £2 million, and that it had been resolved to spend that amount on electrifying the lines to Brighton and West

> 'Electrification of railways is carried out not to save money, but to make more.'
>
> *Sir John Aspinall, Lancashire & Yorkshire Railway (attrib)*

Worthing. After careful consideration, it had been decided to use the 660V dc third rail system, which by then was in use on over 800 miles of its lines.

The use of one of the higher voltages to be prescribed in a forthcoming Order by the Minister would confer no benefit, and adoption of the existing system would enable suburban stock to be used for weekend and excursion traffic. Train mileage would increase by about 150% and the new services would include hourly nonstop ones between London and Brighton. In view of the character of the new services, it had been decided to work them by multiple-unit trains,

Below:
6PAN set No 3036 heads a 12-car PAN/PUL formation past St Leonards West Marina, with the shed in the background, in October 1959. This is a Victoria-Hastings service, and demonstrates well the limitations caused by the length of platforms. *D. Stubbs*

and it was hoped to continue the use of Pullman cars.

South of Coulsdon, the current would be obtained from the National Grid at a tariff fixed under the Electricity Acts. The line between Purley and Brighton would be resignalled throughout. The total cost of the whole scheme was estimated at £2.7 million. To meet the cost of the additional train mileage, depreciation and interest on capital, an increase of 6% in receipts would be required.

Signalling the Brighton Line

The new signalling was to be three-aspect, automatic or semi-automatic colour lights. Semi-automatic signals are those which can be controlled by the signalman to authorise what are relatively unusual (but wholly permissible) moves. In the normal course of events they operate automatically, and the signalman does not intervene. The signals are controlled through the occupation of the

Above:
Chelsfield station gained electric services on 6 January 1935, and this picture features unit No 1418 with a London-bound service in the very early days. This unit was a 1925/26 conversion from SECR steam stock, and most became four-car units from 1946 onwards until final withdrawal.
R. S. Carpenter/A. W. V. Mace collection

track circuits, which register the trains occupying each section of line.

The first section of the new signalling over the 17 route miles from Coulsdon North to Balcombe Tunnel Junction via the Quarry line, was brought into use on 4/5 June 1932. It was to be controlled from Three Bridges Central box. To give some idea of the scope of such work, this required a total engineering possession from 02.00 to 08.00, and 257 trained and thoroughly briefed men stationed at various predetermined points throughout the area. A huge amount of preplanning was essential. The jobs undertaken were:

- Locking alterations made in nine signalboxes.
- Seven signalboxes, which had been working the previous day's traffic, abolished.
- One entirely new 130-lever frame at Three Bridges in a cabin only 12ft wide, taking over the work of three other boxes. All power working for the box connected up.
- 141 semaphore signals disconnected and arms removed.
- 91 new colour-light signals brought into use.
- Electric track circuiting installed throughout.

It might be added that this turned out to be a dark night with steady rain falling, followed by a bright and sunny morning.

Included in the Brighton scheme was the complete reconstruction of Haywards Heath station, with two island platforms each 800ft long. This gave about a 5% margin on the combined length of a 6PUL+6PAN formation, which was to be the standard train formation found there for the ensuing 30 years or so. The lines north from the station were quadrupled as far as Copyhold Junction, for the Horsted Keynes line. When these alterations were made on 11/12 June, colour-light signals were brought into use to save altering existing signals and boxes. A new cabin with a 60-lever mechanical frame was provided at Haywards Heath and this replaced three existing boxes.

On 17 July 1932, electric trains started to run as far as Three Bridges and from Redhill to Reigate. On the same date, Salfords station was brought into public use (it had previously been a halt used by workers at the Monotype factory) and Earlswood station was opened on Sundays.

The next stage was the conversion of the section from Balcombe Tunnel Junction to Copyhold Junction to colour lights on 6 October. This is a short and uncomplicated section of just under five miles, but to read that 'this was achieved on a weekday morning during a 15-minute interval between trains' gives some idea of the pace at which the Southern was driving its projects forward. What resignalling scheme of any sort can be carried out in such timescales today? If the answer is that it all requires proper testing, it is worth recording emphatically that the Southern did not run an unsafe system.

This was followed by the section from Haywards Heath to Preston Park (11 miles) on 9 October. Meanwhile, work had been going on at Brighton, where the central four platforms Nos 3-6, were lengthened to 800ft. A short bay was abolished, and the yard layout simplified. Again, some idea of the scope for what in later years went by the name of rationalisation was the ability to remove no fewer than 17 crossovers, although steam working remained in force for a further few months. (Why were they there in the first place?)

A new signalbox was built into the side of the works building. In general, the new signalling followed previous practice and the apparatus was provided by Westinghouse. The new cabin contained an electrically interlocked frame of 225 levers in three sections, and controlled the three separate

Left:
The 4LAV units, represented here by No 2925, were the workhorses of the Brighton main line following the 1933 electrification. Sadly, the photographer has been economical in the extreme with information, and there is no hint of time, date or place provided. It must however have been towards the end of these units' career, with the yellow warning panel applied.
Ian Allan Library

routes to Preston Park, Hove and London Road. The new installation was brought into use during a five-hour period early on the morning of Sunday, 16 October 1932, in spite of pouring rain. The new signalbox, with eight signalmen and five signal lads displaced six manual boxes with a total of 582 levers, 26 signalmen and three lads. Such are the savings which can be achieved through a comprehensive resignalling exercise.

At the time it was completed, the 36 miles from Coulsdon North to Brighton was the longest continuous stretch of colour-light signalling in Britain. The block sections were about 1,400-1,500yd long, except for Quarry and Clayton tunnels, each of which was a single block. To advise signalmen, train describers were installed showing the destinations of the next three trains approaching. This allowed a degree of regulation to take place if appropriate, for instance to try to recover out-of-course delays. No fewer than 22 manual boxes were abolished and nine others retained for occasional use only. Normally, only seven signalboxes were in use south of Coulsdon North No 2 via the Quarry line.

Other major works included the conversion of the former paint shop on the up side at Brighton into a 12-road cleaning and inspection shed for the electric stock, with a mechanical carriage washer in the adjacent sidings. At West Worthing a carriage shed was erected, containing three roads 800ft long. Track alterations were made at Redhill and a new signal cabin with 85 levers was erected at the London end of the station. Platforms 14 and 15 at London Bridge were extended to 800ft.

Alternating current was taken from the National Grid at Croydon, Three Bridges and Fishergate (Brighton), and transmitted via lineside cables to 18 substations. Each consisted of outside switchgear and a static transformer, with a brick building containing a mercury-arc rectifier to convert the ac to dc. This was fed at 660V to the conductor rail.

Between each pair of substations there was a track-paralleling hut containing switchgear, which closed if a fault developed in one of the adjacent substations. The substations were designed so that any two of them could cover the work of three. They were unattended, but supervised from a control room at Three Bridges.

Rolling Stock

Four types of multiple-unit rolling stock were constructed for the Brighton services. As constructed, these were as follows. In each case, the unit numbers quoted are those carried after the January 1937 renumbering, which numbers they carried for most of their lives.

4LAV, 2921-53

The 4LAVs had a total of 70 first class seats and 204 third class, or an average of 69 seats per car. This four-car compartment stock was built in 1931/2 at Eastleigh Works for use on the semi-fast and slow trains to Brighton and Worthing. In three vehicles there were individual compartments, but the fourth, and intermediate trailer composite, had a side corridor. The purpose of this was to give access to the two lavatories, one at each end. The end vehicles were the driving motors, each with seven third class compartments seating 10 per compartment or 70 in total. The differences were in the trailers. That without the lavatories had five first class compartments seating eight in each, plus four third class, each with 10; total 80. The gangwayed version had the same number of first class compartments, but each sat only six, while the three (only) third class compartments were similarly reduced from

10 to 8. The total seats available were thus reduced to 54. Passengers who were not in the one vehicle so equipped were denied access to lavatories; hard luck if that part of the train was full.

This would appear to demonstrate two things. First, the curious attitude which the Southern Railway seems to have had towards the provision of lavatories, but also the ordinary accommodation which is lost as a result. It can certainly be argued that offering lavatories in this case cut vehicle seating capacity by 26, or very nearly one third. To that must be added the additional maintenance and cleaning costs that lavatories bring. On the other hand, not to provide them where journey lengths can easily be of an hour or more may produce its own disadvantages.

The trains had steel underframes and the bodies were steel panels on a hardwood framing. The cars were close-coupled, with elliptical side buffers and screw couplings at the ends. The electrical equipment was of standard suburban type, supplied by MetroVick, and each motor coach had two 275hp motors.

The guard's compartment, with space for one ton of luggage, had a periscope lookout and an armchair seat. The arrangements for the headcode indications were the same as for the suburban stock. These units did yeoman service between London and Brighton, and

proved capable of working 60-minute nonstop service when required. Their use on other electrified main line sections was infrequent.

Two additional units, Nos 2954 and 2955, were built in 1939. In the 1950s, two first class compartments in the non-corridor vehicle were downgraded to third class.

6PUL, 3001-20

Following experiments, orders were placed for the trains for the express services between London, Brighton and Worthing. Delivered in 1932, these consisted of 20 six-car corridor units, each including a composite Pullman car. The maximum permitted speed was 75mph. These were the flagship trains for the route as a whole, gangwayed within, but not between, units. The order for the 46 driving motors was divided equally between Metropolitan Cammell and Birmingham RCW. Eastleigh had to content itself with the trailers.

Below:
This classic view of 6PUL set No 3002 on an Eastbourne and Hastings train was taken on the Quarry line, shortly after the train had emerged from Quarry Tunnel. Above is Rockshaw Road bridge. Today, the cutting sides are completely overgrown, and the telegraph poles have long since gone. The train carries a destination board on the side of the driving motor coach, supplementing the headcode.
O. J. Morris/Ian Allan Library

The six vehicles comprised two identical all-steel driving motor brakes, containing a third class open saloon with 52 seats. Tables were not installed, but could be fitted from a supply kept in the guard's compartment. Lighting was by 29 lamps, all but nine of which were under passenger control. The side windows had patent balances, locked in position by a handle at the bottom. They were made to open 7in, an amount considered to be sufficient for adequate ventilation. Each of the two bogies was powered by two 225hp motors in each of the two driving vehicles, with the electro-pneumatic control gear provided by BTH, and mounted below the underframe. A 5kW motor generator provided current at 70V for lighting throughout the train and for control purposes. Emergency lighting batteries were installed in steel compartments between the motorman and the guard's areas. These were designed to supply train lights for 30 minutes in case of the main current failing.

The trailers in the rake all had compartments, each with double (rather than single) sliding doors to gain access from the corridor. Two were composites, each with five first and three third class compartments, while the last comprised one with eight third class compartments and a coupé for four persons. All had end lavatories.

The 15.00 down 'Brighton Belle' approaches Haywards Heath on the sunny afternoon of 8 August 1955. The lead 5BEL unit is No 3051. This wholly distinctive train may not have had the best riding rolling stock, but it certainly held the affections of its regular clientele. Above all else, it had class. In 1956, the single fare from Victoria to Brighton was 12s 0d first class, plus 3s 0d Pullman supplement, or 8s 0d second class plus 2s 0d supplement. Afternoon tea would have set you back a further 2s 6d plus, of course, a tip. *Ian Allan Library*

The 23 all-steel Pullman cars for the 6PUL and the 6CITY units (to be described) were built by Metro-Cammell in Birmingham, and each was 68ft 8¾in long. They were complete with end vestibules and kitchens. A small pantry was followed by a third class section with 16 seats, a lavatory, a first class compartment for four, a first class section with eight seats, pantry and kitchen. The interior decoration was in various Empire timbers and the metal work was finished in 'satin silver'. All-electric cooking appliances were supplied at 110V from a dynamo mounted on the underframe.

The 6PULs had a total capacity of 72 first class and 236 third class seats, of which 12 first and 16 third were in the Pullman car. This equates to a modest average of 51 seats per vehicle.

6CITY, 3041-3

This small class of three units was aimed at City season ticket traffic, and ran between Brighton and London Bridge. The history of the 'City Limited' can be traced back to 1841, and until 1919 only first class passengers were carried. The 6CITY units were similar to the 6PUL sets, except that all three intermediate trailers were first class only. This had the effect of increasing the first class seating to 138, while third class was down to 108. The average seats per car fell to 38. After the war, some downgrading took place so that they became interchangeable with the 6PUL sets.

5BEL, 3051-3

These three trains really were the pride of the line, providing first the 'Southern Belle' all-Pullman service and then, after it was renamed on 29 June 1934 by the Mayor of Brighton, the 'Brighton Belle'. These were the first all-electric Pullman trains in the world, and so far remain the only electric multiple-unit Pullman trains in Britain. Service was provided with the customary panache.

Their construction was as already described, and they were comprised as follows. Seating in third class was arranged 2+2 and in first class 1+1.

- Driving motor third brake, with guard's compartment, 48 seats
- Trailing third class parlour car, 56 seats
- Trailing first class car with kitchen and pantry, 20 seats
- Trailing first class car with kitchen and pantry, 20 seats
- Driving motor third brake, with guard's compartment, 48 seats

The overall weight was 249 tons, with 40 first and 152 third class seats.

To illustrate what in the 1930s was considered to be luxury accommodation, the following description of the lighting is taken from the *Modern Transport* trade journal:

'In the first class cars, the lighting consists of strip lighting on either side throughout the length of each saloon, mounted in and forming part of the ceiling. The general effect is extremely good, and the diffusion is such that it is possible to read in comfort at any position. The ends of the first class passenger saloons have been so designed as to form small alcoves, thus providing additional comfort for passengers occupying seats in the vicinity of the doorways. Advantage has been taken of this plan to introduce a delightful concealed lighting effect on the end saloon panel work.

'In the third class accommodation, there are semi-recessed ceiling lights with tulip shades and panel-type bracket lights with decorated glass, and all the tables are equipped with table lights. There is also a special system of bells which, by means of coloured light indicators operated by the bell pushes, enables the attendants immediately to identify the passenger requiring attention.'

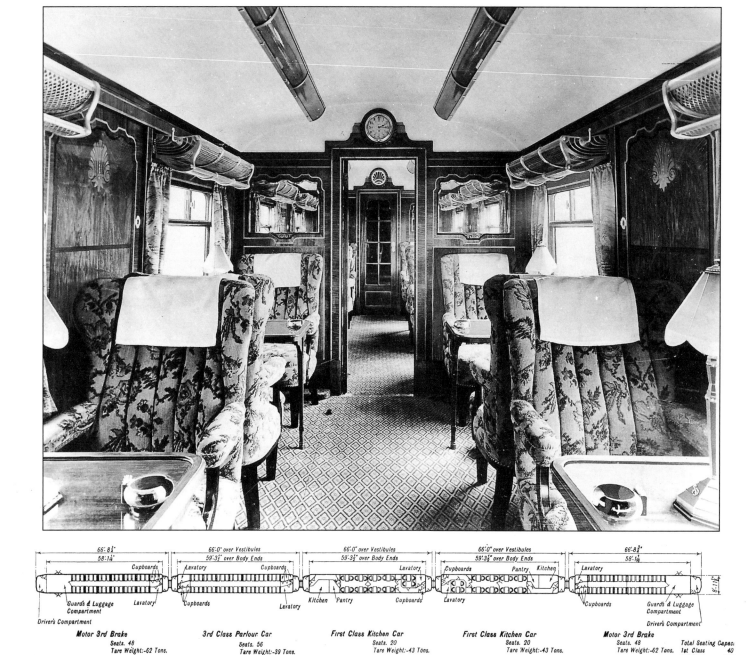

Motor 3rd Brake	3rd Class Parlour Car	First Class Kitchen Car	First Class Kitchen Car	Motor 3rd Brake	Total Seating Capacity
Seats. 48	Seats. 56	Seats. 20	Seats. 20	Seats. 48	1st Class 40
Tare Weight:-62 Tons.	Tare Weight:-39 Tons.	Tare Weight:-43 Tons.	Tare Weight:-43 Tons.	Tare Weight:-62 Tons.	3rd Class 152
				Total Tare Weight:-249 Tons.	Total 192

All the Pullman cars were equipped with heavy, self-contained buffers, couplings and gangways to Southern standards. The customary Pullman livery of chocolate lower and fascia panels, with cream intermediate panels, was used, lined out in red and gold and carrying the Pullman Car Company's coat of arms. In accordance with Pullman practice, all the first class cars were given girls' names, those for the 'Brighton Belle' sets being:

3051   Hazel, Dora
3052   Vera, Audrey
3053   Mona, Gwen

Service Provision

The new services were inaugurated on 30 December 1932 when the Lord Mayor and Sheriffs of London, with the directors and senior officers of the Southern, travelled to Worthing on a 6CITY unit to meet the Mayor

of Worthing. They then went on to Brighton to meet the Mayor and partake of an inaugural lunch at the Royal Pavilion. Examples of the new trains were exhibited at Victoria and at Brighton, and the interest was such that 11,000 people visited them in the first three days.

Public services, on a lavish scale, began on Sunday, 1 January 1933. They offered 'six trains per hour all day – comfort and frequency – you won't need a timetable', to quote from contemporary press advertising. Services were as in Fig 6.1.

The trains leaving Victoria at 11.00, 15.00 and 19.00 were made up of the 'Southern Belle' sets, and semi-fast sets were used for the 16.00 departure, which completed the journey in 63 minutes nonstop. The last train was the midnight nonstop service to Brighton from Victoria.

Peak services were equally well provided. In the 65 minutes between 07.40 and 08.45,

Top:
The interior of the 'Brighton Belle' first class cars was not to contemporary tastes. This undated but pre-1948 photograph shows the spacious seating of 1+1 each side of the gangway, which meant that a five-car 5BEL set was only able to seat 40 first class and 152 second class passengers. The latter had to make do with 2+2 seating.
Ian Allan Library

Above:
The internal layout of the 5BEL units, as built, is shown in this diagram. The kitchen in the centre seems to have pulled the short straw, with an extra 56 seats to serve from the same amount of kitchen space. *Author's collection*

five fast up trains left Brighton, two for London Bridge and three for Victoria. Two were nonstop, the others had two stops each, and all with Pullman cars.

West Worthing's services were enhanced by the local services to Brighton which ran every 15 minutes, alternate services not calling at

Fig 6.1: Hourly Pattern of London to Brighton Services – 1933 Inaugural Timetable		
From Victoria		
xx00	Brighton, nonstop	Pullman car 60min
xx25	East Croydon, Haywards Heath, Hove, Shoreham-by-Sea, Worthing Central, West Worthing	Pullman car 85min
xx28	Clapham Junction, East Croydon, Redhill, Haywards Heath, Preston Park, Brighton	79min
xx46	Clapham Junction, East Croydon, Purley and all stations to Brighton via Redhill, portion for Reigate detached at Redhill	98min to Brighton
From London Bridge		
xx00	New Cross Gate, East Croydon, Horley, Three Bridges, Haywards Heath, Preston Park, Brighton	74min
xx16	New Cross Gate, East Croydon, Purley and all stations to Brighton via Redhill, portion for Reigate detached at Redhill	98min to Brighton

the intermediate halts. Three-car suburban sets from the Western Section were used for these trains. The 'Brighton Belle' also left Victoria at 11.00, 15.00 and 19.00, and from Brighton at 13.25, 17.25 and 21.15, these schedules remaining unchanged for most of the train's existence.

Numeric headcodes were introduced, which indicated the route and whether it was nonstop, fast or slow. Odd numbers were for trains to and from London Bridge and even ones for Victoria. It was then that the prestigious headcode 4 was first used to indicate Victoria and Brighton, nonstop via the Quarry line.

What of the passenger reactions? Although the weather did not encourage seaside trips, traffic to and from Brighton and Worthing in January 1933 showed an additional 73,000 trips and a 5% gain in receipts – an encouraging start. Over the Easter Holiday period, the 150,000 tickets collected at Brighton were 78% up on 1932, while the number of passengers to Brighton on Easter Monday more than doubled the figure of the previous year. Train services were suitably enhanced. The electrification scheme as a whole attracted 2,213,000 extra passengers in its first full year, and 520,000 of these had been carried between London and Brighton alone. This amounted to additional revenue of £150,000, a very sizeable sum at contemporary prices. Indeed, it was sufficient for the Chairman in March 1934 to tell the annual meeting that their Board felt fully justified in extending electrification to Seaford, Eastbourne and Hastings via Lewes.

On 30 September 1935, a new station was opened at Tinsley Green, and this was renamed Gatwick Airport on 1 June 1936. It was closed on 27 May 1958 when the present Gatwick Airport station opened.

London Transport

On 1 July 1933, the London Passenger Transport Board (LPTB) was established, and took over all tube and sub-surface lines of the Underground group and the Metropolitan Railway, as well as the trams and buses in an area of 2,000sq miles around the capital. By statute, a Standing Joint Committee consisting of four representatives of London Transport and the General Managers of the four main line railways was set up to co-ordinate services in the LPTB area. The receipts from the provision of services in that area, less operating expenses, were to be pooled and divided pro rata between the Board and the main line railways.

The importance of this scheme to the Southern Railway was shown by the size of its share of the pool. This was as much as 25½%, and compared with London Transport's share of 62% and that of the three other main line railways together of 12½%. In theory at least, this much reduced the competitive pressures which had earlier induced first the Brighton and then the other Southern companies to embark upon suburban electrification.

Sevenoaks

The countryside east of Bickley Junction and south of Orpington, the then extent of electrified services, on the Chatham and the South Eastern's main lines respectively, was ripe for development. It was also just the type of territory where a responsive railway company would provide an electric service before the residents arrived.

Work started early in 1934 on this 23 route mile scheme for extensions to Sevenoaks, both direct and via Swanley Junction. By 1 May work was advanced sufficiently to allow the opening to St Mary Cray, and services were provided by extending the Holborn Viaduct to Shortlands operation. The principal incidental work was the remodelling of the station at Sevenoaks Tubs Hill and the installation of automatic upper-quadrant semaphores between St Mary Cray and Swanley Junction. This enabled an intermediate box to be closed.

On 6 January 1935 services began, with trains from Charing Cross to Sevenoaks every half-hour or 20 minutes at peaks, and with the former St Mary Cray terminators from Holborn Viaduct continuing to Sevenoaks via Swanley Junction. However, when eight-car trains were being operated, only the leading three cars went beyond Orpington or Swanley Junction, as appropriate. Sevenoaks thus received a liberal and comprehensive service, replacing a sparse and irregular steam operation.

Although it was to be a long time before the line to Tonbridge was electrified, 1934 saw some useful work done on easing the curve on the line from Sevenoaks as it

Below:
Bat & Ball was a typical wayside station, electrified on 6 January 1935 as the 'other' route to Sevenoaks. There would appear to be some quantity of freight traffic. Again, this photograph is thought to date from soon after opening.
R. S. Carpenter/A. W. V. Mace collection

approached Tonbridge. The original main line of the South Eastern of course continued to head almost due west for Redhill, and the curvature of the link north to Orpington was a direct result of this line being a 'second thought'. The railway industry often has great problems in escaping from the accidents of history.

Eastbourne and Hastings

The Southern's Board announced their intentions to build on the huge success of the Brighton line in increasing volumes and revenues at the annual meeting in March 1934. In infrastructure terms, the work needed for Eastbourne and Hastings was less extensive than the main Brighton line, and the capital cost of the scheme as a whole was put at £1.5 million. Included in this was the elimination of the sharp curve in Lewes Tunnel, at the London end of the line from Keymer Junction. This was necessary not only to remove the restrictions on the rolling stock using it but also to allow the adjacent footbridge to be rebuilt so that, in turn, the platforms used by the London trains could be lengthened. A new West signalbox was erected.

At Polegate the track layout was simplified, and at Eastbourne the two island platforms were lengthened to 820ft. A new lever frame was installed in the signalbox. Intermediate signals were provided to divide the long two-mile block section to Hampden Park. Back in the London area, sidings at New Cross Gate were electrified.

The halt at Cooden on the Pevensey-Bexhill stretch was rebuilt as a station, Cooden Beach, with platforms 420ft long. Hastings station had been reconstructed with two island platforms in 1931, but there was no room there for the necessary carriage sheds, so these were located at Ore, another mile in the direction of Ashford. Electric lighting was installed at 10 stations and halts. On the permanent way side, a difficulty was encountered with sections of line which had been relaid with steel sleepers; these had to be replaced with timber for use on electrified lines, and the problem was to be met again in subsequent work elsewhere.

The power supply was taken from the National Grid as before to rectifier substations. Most of these were operated from Three Bridges, and the rest from a new control room at Ore. At Southerham Bridge, junction for the Seaford branch where the line crosses the River Ouse, the ability to lift the bridge to allow the passage of vessels resulted in the lineside power cables being taken under the river in concrete ducts.

Below:
Eastbourne station is well situated for the town centre, and this makes for good integration with the bus routes which pass outside. This picture shows Leyland PD2 with East Lancs bodywork, fleet No 78, followed by an AEC Regent 5, again with East Lancs body, fleet No 55. The Eastbourne Corporation livery was mid-blue and white. The photograph dates from around 1965.
Author's collection

Trial running started in May 1935, followed by formal opening on 4 July with the local Mayor in attendance. Public services started on Sunday, 7 July. Services were provided by the 6PAN stock of which 16 sets were built, Nos 3021-37. These were very similar to their 6PUL predecessors, other than that the Pullman car had been replaced by a first class coach with a pantry. This served light refreshments and was also staffed by the Pullman Car Co.

Vehicle rosters were reorganised to spread the Pullman or pantry facilities across the enlarged main line electrified network. Profitability was questionable, especially if traffic was light. All-Pullman trains have a captive audience, but passengers had to come to a single car to buy refreshments and take them away, thus avoiding paying the Pullman supplement where applicable.

A little later, on 26 September 1938, a new station in Southern style was opened at Bishopstone. This replaced Bishopstone Beach Halt, although the latter did not close finally until 1 January 1942.

The new service was based on an hourly pattern all the way to Ore, leaving Victoria at 45 minutes past the hour and calling intermediately at East Croydon, Haywards Heath, Lewes, Eastbourne, Cooden Beach, Bexhill Central, St Leonards Warrior Square and Hastings. This was a 6PAN+6PUL formation, on which it was normal to detach the 6PAN set at Eastbourne with only the 6PUL continuing to Ore. It will be noted that the platform reconstruction at Cooden Beach was designed to accommodate a six-car formation as a maximum. Journey times were 86 minutes to Eastbourne and 120 minutes to Ore.

Connecting into and out of this was an hourly Horsted Keynes to Seaford service. This arrived at Haywards Heath in time for a connection to Brighton, and then waited for the train from Victoria which it then followed. This provided a connection from that train for all stations to Seaford. Other services offered were Brighton and stations to Seaford twice hourly, and Brighton and stations to Ore, twice hourly.

At peak times, services were augmented to provide trains such as the 17.04 from London Bridge which divided at Lewes for Seaford and Eastbourne, while the 17.20 departure was a combined West Worthing and Ore via Eastbourne train, dividing at Haywards Heath. The last train from Victoria at midnight had a Haywards Heath stop inserted where it detached a 6PAN set for Lewes, Polegate (connection for Bexhill Central, St Leonards Warrior Square and Hastings, arriving at 01.51), Hampden Park and Eastbourne, reached at 01.28. Summer Saturdays saw a virtually doubled level of service from Victoria for the holiday traffic, with the extra trains departing at 15 minutes past the hour.

The official reason for the extension of electrification to Horsted Keynes was to relieve congestion at Haywards Heath caused by trains reversing, although as H. P. White has observed, somewhat acidly, 'we were expected to believe that the Southern's planners had never heard of a reversing siding'. Be that as it may, the net result was that the branch became the second part of the Southern Electric system to lose its passenger service, with the closure of Horsted Keynes and Ardingly stations taking place on 28 October 1963. To be fair, the Southern did intend to electrify to Oxted and East Grinstead, and this would have been part of a necessary link in an alternative electrified route to Brighton.

Local Service Provision

As has already been discussed, the Southern's policy on suburban trains might be summed up as 'never build anything new when there is a chance of converting some existing stock'. Thus it proved with the trains first provided for the local services between Brighton and West Worthing, where the main problem was the balance between first and third class accommodation. Ten of the 84 Class 1201 units, themselves dating back to the steam stock of 1904 and converted for the first LSWR suburban electrification schemes, were earmarked; 48 first class seats became 24, and 130 third class became 160.

2NOL, 1813-90

By the end of 1934, the 1201 class had been returned to London and were replaced by the 2NOL units (the NOL being a descriptive NO Lavatory). Again, this was an LSWR steam stock conversion, carried out at Eastleigh with 48 of these units to be used for all local services on what was shortly to become a coastal operation from Ore to West Worthing, plus northwards to Horsted Keynes. They were, effectively, suburban stock, although not so classified. These straightforward compartment vehicles were specified as follows:

- Driving motor, with guard's accommodation, coupé third and seven third class compartments
- Driving trailer, with three first and six third class compartments.

2BIL, 2001-52

Early in 1935, 10 two-car close-coupled corridor sets, the 2BILs, were constructed for use on the semi-fast services to Eastbourne. The driving trailers came from Eastleigh, but the contracts for the motor coaches were again divided equally between Metro-Cammell and BRCW. There was no through gangway connection, but a side corridor within each vehicle gave lavatory access. A distinctive feature of these units when viewed from the outside on the corridor side was the height of the windows, which reached to the eaves. When compared with the 2NOLs, which had an identical overall unit length of 129ft 6in, accommodation was reduced by 30% from 24 first and 135 third (2NOL) to 24 first and 88 third (2BIL).

Electrical equipment included two 275hp English Electric traction motors, and the electromagnetic control gear was by MetroVick. It may perhaps be recorded here that the subsequent builds of these units, from No 2010 onwards, were supplied with English Electric electro-pneumatic control gear. These trains were used on both Portsmouth electrifications, and for services to Reading.

Waterloo Remodelling

A four-track railway in which the up and down fast lines are in the centre with the up slow on one side and the down slow on the other offers the maximum opportunity to swap trains between the lines. Out on the open track it is an essentially flexible arrangement. However, at termini, the slow trains have, somehow, to cross all the intervening main line tracks before the trains can return whence they came. At such locations, separate 'fast' and 'slow' sections of the station have much to commend them.

Such was the problem at Waterloo in 1935, to overcome which the Southern decided upon a complex remodelling scheme. This involved building a new flyover between the overbridges of Gap Road and Durnsford Road, east of Wimbledon, the only feasible site, and rearranging the track layout thence to the terminus. East of that point, the lines were altering to form up and down main fast, then up and down main slow (present nomenclature) to the terminus.

The flyover was constructed of steel girders, cased in concrete, and mounted on concrete columns. It is 2,174ft or getting on for half a mile long, but even so it still needs to rise at 1 in 60 from the Wimbledon end, cross the main lines on the skew, and then descends sharply at 1 in 45. This just emphasises the longitudinal distances needed to accomplish major railway works, and the flyover did not need to have clearances for overhead line equipment.

Reconstruction was required at Vauxhall, since there was no platform on what was to become the up main slow line. There was a side platform for the down main slow on the south side of the running line. This latter was demolished, the down main slow slewed across to occupy its space, and a new island platform built between what became the up and down main slow. This situation remains today, and this is why there is tight curvature on the down main slow line, while the platform itself and the stairs leading down from it are of less than generous dimensions for the volumes of passengers changing to the Victoria line.

Three-aspect colour-light signalling was installed at Waterloo, which became four-aspect at Nine Elms where freight working commenced. This latest resignalling introduced signals with small side aspects for the benefit of drivers whose trains had drawn up close to the signals. At junctions, indicators with a row of three diagonal white 'lunar' lights above the main signal head were introduced, to replace a separate signal head for each route. Ground signals consisted of a white disc with red bar, floodlit at night.

This was all controlled, as far as New Malden on the main lines and Clapham Junction on the Windsor lines, from a new cabin at Waterloo. There were three frames controlling the main slow, main fast and Windsor lines respectively. The track diagrams were shown as white lines on a black ground and the presence of a train was indicated by two red lights. Route indicators of the theatre type were provided liberally, and on each platform a starting signal repeater showed 'ON' or 'OFF'. This was for the benefit of the guard and also the station staff, the curvature of the platforms preventing them from seeing the signal itself. This replaced the celebrated 'A' box of 1892,

which spanned the tracks outside the station and contained 266 levers.

A new track layout for Waterloo was assembled at Mitcham and laid in, complete with further alterations on the Windsor side. On Sunday, 17 May 1936, all lines east of Surbiton were closed in a six-hour engineering possession, so that the Wimbledon flyover, rearranged tracks and the new signalling, apart from that at Waterloo itself, could be brought into service. The latter was delayed until Sunday 18 October when the summer holiday services had finished; the 00.35 to Hampton Court was signalled out by semaphores, while the 01.30 to Salisbury left under the control of colour lights.

The new signalling provided for a headway of two minutes on the main fast line and 2½ minutes on the main slow. Ten signalboxes were abolished and eight others adapted for colour-light working. During this period, the station at Surbiton was being rebuilt, and the new signalboxes there and at Hampton Court Junction were brought into use on 28 June 1936.

A small matter to affect Waterloo was the renaming of Waterloo Junction station on the Eastern Section, a name which stemmed from the connection over the main line concourse which was severed as part of the station rebuilding a quarter of a century earlier. On 7 July 1935 it became plain Waterloo, but was distinguished from the main line station by the platforms being lettered A, B, C and D from north to south. This remains today as

one of the few stations where the platforms are identified by letters, New Cross being another of this select group. Another change of name took place on 2 May 1977, when it became known as Waterloo East. It is good practice for each and every platform to carry some unique identification for the general benefit of passengers, but also to enable outside parties, such as the emergency services, to be able to identify specifically where a problem has arisen.

Crystal Palace

On 30 November 1936, the Crystal Palace was destroyed by a fire so spectacular that it was visible from the South Downs. The fire brigade made its headquarters in the High Level station, and part of the vast crowd of spectators invaded the sidings there and even climbed on the roofs of berthed coaching stock to get a better view of the fire. A special train to Blackfriars (then named St Paul's) left at midnight for those who had been unable to get away earlier because of the dense crowds. Although the 'Palace' had long ceased to be London's most popular resort, its destruction deprived the Southern electric services of an appreciable amount of traffic, since it was well patronised on Bank Holidays, especially if the weather was indifferent, and when special events, notably firework displays, were held. The High Level line did not long survive World War 2, and part of the Low Level station became an underused, gloomy and cavernous building.

7. Portsmouth, Chessington, Reading, Alton and Gillingham

'Electrification as a rolling programme avoids loss of momentum and the delays in regaining it.'

Michael Bonavia

Early in 1935, it was announced that the Government had come to an agreement with the four main line railway companies, by which funds for development and improvement schemes would be made available to them at lower interest rates than they could themselves obtain on the money market. These funds would be provided through a railway finance company, the principal (£30 million) and the interest (2½%) being guaranteed by the Treasury. The railways would be required to furnish schedules of works that they proposed to carry out, and to use the loan in such a way that it would help to relieve unemployment and assist economic recovery. Legislation authorising the scheme was duly passed and the Railway Finance Corporation Ltd was incorporated in December 1935.

At the Southern Railway's annual meeting in early 1936, the Chairman Mr R. Holland-Martin said that the financial results of electrification schemes to date had been very satisfactory. When estimates for the Sevenoaks scheme were prepared in 1932, it was reckoned that revenue would have to rise by 27% in order to cover working costs and interest on capital. In the first year of operation, 1935, the number of passengers went up by well over a half (55%), and receipts at 41% up were half as high again as the minimum needed. This comparison was with 1932.

Similarly, for the Eastbourne and Hastings scheme, a rise in revenue of as little as 1¼% was needed to cover the capital cost, but in the first six months the number of passengers rose by over one fifth (22%), while revenue was up by 16%.

In view of these results, the Southern Board had been persuaded that they should undertake further electrification schemes, which he then specified. These included the construction and electrification of a new line from Motspur Park to as far, initially, as Chessington South. To the 1937 annual meeting, Holland-Martin was able to give precise figures.

The company would receive £5,929,811 from the Railway Finance Corporation at 2½% interest. This would be in five annual instalments, and repayment would be spread over 15 years. The shopping list was a long one. Thus came about the Southern Railway's extensions of the third rail as set out in Fig 7.1.

Right:
New Link: Nunhead to Lewisham and Hither Green, 1929.

The first three items in the programme were completed according to plan, but at the following annual meeting in 1938 the chairman said that it had been decided not to proceed with the Hastings and Bexhill scheme. In the Board's view, this was of dubious financial benefit, since the limited size of the tunnels would require heavy expenditure on special rolling stock or, alternatively, enlarging the tunnels. It is of interest to note here that British Railways came to a similar conclusion nearly 20 years later. A rise in the cost of labour and the possibility that traffic would be diverted from the existing electric services via Lewes had also influenced the Board's decision.

However, as a *quid pro quo*, the Gillingham scheme would be extended to cover the Otford to Maidstone East section, and the date of completion brought forward by six months to July 1939.

Nunhead and Selsdon

An important improvement opened on 7 July 1930 was the connection between Nunhead and Lewisham, for which a new flyover was created over the Dover main line. A second link constructed at the same time was that between Lewisham Mid-Kent line platforms and Hither Green. The arrangement is shown in Fig 7.2.

The objective was to free up the busy London Bridge area from freight, as the infrastructure was becoming seriously overcrowded. Freight trains accessed the Southern from the Widened Lines at Blackfriars. Using this newly created route, the freight trains could run via Loughborough Junction, Nunhead and Lewisham to Hither Green. They thus only gained the main line after the Bexleyheath and North Kent line trains had diverged, and train paths were thus available.

Fig 7.1: Routes to be Electrified with Railway Finance Corporation Loan, and Associated Timescales

● Portsmouth No 1: Surbiton to Portsmouth via Guildford, Woking to Alton, Staines to Weybridge	7/37
● Portsmouth No 2: Dorking via Horsham to Arundel Junction, from Three Bridges to Horsham, from West Worthing to Havant, and the Littlehampton and Bognor Regis branches	7/38
● Staines to Reading, Ascot to Aldershot, Aldershot to Guildford	1/39
● Sevenoaks to Hastings and Bexhill West	1/39
● Gravesend and Swanley to Gillingham, and from Strood to Maidstone West	1/40

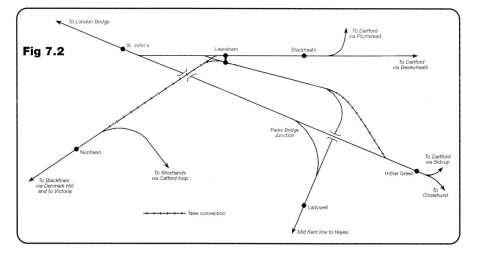

Fig 7.2

The Lewisham-Hither Green loop was electrified on 16 July 1933, and the Nunhead-Lewisham loop on 30 September 1935. Traffic on the Bexleyheath and Sidcup lines had grown so much as to need relief, and five peak hour trains were run by each route, between Dartford and Blackfriars. This also made it possible to offer greatly improved services on the Holborn Viaduct to Mid-Kent and Catford lines without interfering with the main line traffic.

On that same date, the former LBSCR/SER joint line between Woodside and Selsdon, and on to Sanderstead, was also electrified. Steam passenger services over the joint line were suspended on 15 March 1915 and never resumed, although the line remained open for special workings. The former halts, now Bingham Road and Coombe Road, were reopened as stations.

The initial service to Sanderstead was three trains per hour at peaks, mostly from Cannon Street. At other times the service was half-hourly from Charing Cross. A new substation was built at South Croydon. This turned out to be another electric service which did not prosper, and it was withdrawn (although contrary to all expectations, again not finally) on 17 May 1983.

Portsmouth and Alton, No 1

Work on the electrification of the lines from Hampton Court Junction to Woking, Guildford and Havant, Woking to Alton, and Weybridge to Staines commenced in October 1935 and was completed in two stages in 1937. The full electric service was brought into operation on 4 July. At 95 route miles, this was the greatest single electrification ever carried out by the Southern Railway.

Of the engineering works undertaken, by far the greatest was the complete rebuilding of Woking station. This enabled four through platforms to be provided, plus a bay on each of the up and down sides. These platforms are a generous 820ft long. Considerable modifications to stations and track layouts were deemed necessary at Guildford and Haslemere; platforms at these, at Portsmouth & Southsea and Portsmouth Harbour were also extended to the same length. At Havant a new station was started, featuring separate up and down platforms served by loops off the running lines, with an overbridge replacing a level crossing at the western end. As a result, all could now accommodate 790ft 12-car trains of the new rolling stock. A new suburban station at Hersham was brought into use on 28 September 1936.

The new power boxes at Woking and at Havant were part of the resignalling scheme in which many colour lights were installed, although some semaphores remained. At Haslemere, there were up and down platform lines and an up platform loop. The up main and associated crossovers were provided with reversible signalling, so that a slow train proceeding in either direction could be overtaken by a fast. Such arrangements provide much more flexibility to the operator.

A new carriage shed was erected at Wimbledon, the existing sheds and workshops extended, and a mechanical carriage washer provided. Fratton gained a shed and a washing plant, and Farnham a shed.

Power supplies were taken from National Grid substations at Byfleet and at Wymering (near Portsmouth), and distributed to 26 rectifier substations; those as far as Liss were controlled from Woking and the remainder from Havant Control Room. For the suburban area, additional power was obtained by enhancements to the Southern's Durnsford Road installation.

A new electric fleet was obtained for service provision:

4COR, 3101-55

Although constructed only a few years later than the 6PUL/6PAN units for the Brighton electrification, the new trains for the Portsmouth Direct line (as the South Western faction liked to call it, to remind their former adversaries) exhibited some substantial differences. The principal amongst these was the use of gangwayed vehicles, not only within the set but with corridor connections to the adjacent set. Also, the set length was reduced from an unwieldy six vehicles to four.

There were two reasons for this. First, refreshment facilities were only of value if passengers had access. While it is not ideal to have to walk through up to nine vehicles on a moving train to reach a buffet car, this is only possible if the train is gangwayed throughout. The PUL/PAN arrangement meant doubling

Below:
The 4COR units made their debut with the Portsmouth Direct services, and this is unit No 3056 on 6 May 1937. This is in fact a 4RES unit, but marshalled temporarily as a 4COR without the kitchen and dining cars. The location is between Rowlands Castle and Petersfield, the train being on an up working. *Ian Allan Library*

Top:
The Portsmouth Direct electrification included composite trailers in the 4COR sets, and one compartment of each class as shown here, viewed from the corridor side. The first class compartment had the same window pattern and dimensions, but the additional width was used to allow the seat upright to slope back more. The seat itself was of the same dimension in both classes, and the space for legs was also the same. First class passengers were favoured with intermediate armrests. *Author's collection*

Above:
The third class compartment in the 4COR sets saw a more utilitarian approach, seating four instead of three each side. In both cases, the window in the door could be pulled down and then secured in position by pushing the lever to the right-hand side, as shown. Securing such windows so they neither moved nor rattled once positioned was a long-term problem for carriage designers. *Author's collection*

facilities to serve each part, as indeed was done, or one half of the train going without. This meant that either it was expensive for the providers of refreshments or it lost them revenue which they could otherwise hope to gain. As the same problem was to arise again in postwar years with the Hastings diesel units, this consideration may not have been accorded much status.

Of more importance was the reduction in set lengths. Somehow, one feels that six vehicles proceeding eastwards from

Eastbourne to Hastings was never really justified by traffic levels, and four would have been quite adequate then, as it is today. In general terms, the operator must aim to match the accommodation provided with the traffic on offer at that time; if demand levels fall away in the evening, there is little benefit to anybody in operating 12 cars if eight will do. Although the opportunity for serving multiple destinations was a feature more of the Portsmouth No 2 electrification, to be discussed next, a common rolling stock fleet certainly had its attractions.

A disadvantage was that one ends up with more guard's accommodation, van space and driving cabs in 3x4-car units than in 2x6-car units, all at the expense of passenger seats. It followed, though, that if four-car sets were more attractive than six, through corridor connections was essential if any worthwhile restaurant facility were to be offered.

The 29 4COR units for this scheme which resulted had of course to accommodate a driver's cab as well as the gangway connection. This meant that the headcode panel was displaced sideways to the left-hand side of the unit when viewed from the front, taking the place of what would have been a second cab window in a traditional layout. This gave them a curious one-eyed look, from which they quickly acquired the not inappropriate nickname of 'Nelsons'.

Internal layout saw 52-seat driving motor vehicles at each end, with open third class seating, a composite with three third and five first class compartments, and a corridor third with eight compartments and a coupé. Each of the intermediate trailers had a lavatory at each end. They were built at Eastleigh and two 225hp traction motors were carried on the leading bogie of each motor coach. These, and the electro-pneumatic control gear were supplied by English Electric. Each unit had seats for 30 first and 196 third class passengers.

Even so, there was a serious weakness. Each four-car set thus had four traction motors, providing 900hp between them. A 12-car set therefore packed 2,700hp. By comparison, the 6PUL sets each had eight traction motors, thereby offering 1,800hp per set or 3,600hp for the customary 12-car train. The 4COR Portsmouth units and the similar units with which they worked were comparatively underpowered, with little leeway to make up time if delays were incurred.

4RES, 3054-3072

The driving motors of these 19 restaurant car sets were identical, but lavish facilities were provided in the intermediate trailers. The kitchen car, which also had a pantry and was built by BRCW, included 36 dining seats for third class passengers. The adjoining vehicle, a Metro-Cammell product, had 12 first class dining seats and also five first class compartments. Both were provided with a single lavatory. The kitchen equipment was all-electric, the boilers, ovens, etc all using 660V dc from the traction supply, while the grills, hotplates and refrigerator used current from the dynamo mounted on the underframe.

Given that the fast trains covered the 74$\frac{1}{2}$ miles from Waterloo to Portsmouth in 95 minutes, a journey on which snacks and sandwiches are the best that is offered today, one can but wonder at the changes in lifestyles which have taken place over the years. The total seating provision was 42 first class and 140 third class.

Trial running between Surbiton and Woking started in November 1936, and full electric services between Staines and Weybridge, also part of this scheme, began on 3 January 1937. Temporary services using steam timings started the same day between Waterloo and Farnham. These were followed by trial running to Portsmouth in April with full service provision from 4 July 1937.

The basic train service is shown in Fig 7.3:

Peak additions were provided through frequency increases, lifting the fast service up to four an hour. There were also additional services from Waterloo to Chertsey via Weybridge. The normal branch service

Below:
This publicity vehicle was clearly designed to represent the COR/RES/BUF family of rolling stock, with a colour-light signal to show complete modernity. It is seen here at a location thought to be Portsmouth Harbour station around 1937.
C. F. Klapper/Author's collection

Fig. 7.3: Hourly Pattern of Portsmouth and Alton services – 1937 Inaugural Timetable

From Waterloo

xx27	Surbiton, all stations to Portsmouth & Southsea. Divide at Woking, rear part all stations to Alton.
xx50	Guildford (with connections into and out of xx27 from Waterloo), Haslemere, Portsmouth & Southsea, Portsmouth Harbour. Buffet car.
xx57	Surbiton, all stations to Portsmouth & Southsea. Divide at Woking, rear part all stations to Alton.

Left:
In April 1995, Amberley still retained much of its character as a simple wayside station. This is a view looking north. The semaphores were controlled from a box situated on the down side platform, just under the canopy, in typical Brighton style, although it was switched out at weekends. *Author*

consisted of portions detached from Waterloo-Windsor & Eton Riverside trains at Staines, running thence to the north side bay platform at Weybridge. These ran every half-hour, 20 minutes at peaks, nonstop between Waterloo and Richmond.

The then magnitude of summer Saturday holiday traffic is easily overlooked now, but then four fast trains left Waterloo for Portsmouth in every hour from 07.45 to 16.20. Amazingly, all carried restaurant cars, so no wonder such a large fleet was built.

These services were a revolution in traffic facilities west of Woking. Guildford enjoyed a nonstop train from Waterloo every hour in 35 minutes ($52^1/_4$mph), which reached Haslemere in 55 minutes. Aldershot had a regular half-hourly service in 61 minutes, cut to 52 minutes in business hours. Steam haulage had always been constrained by the severe gradients south of Guildford, which included five miles of 1 in 80 from Milford to Haslemere and a fairly sinuous route. The line to Portsmouth was certainly direct compared with the alternatives, but it was not in the top league in terms of its construction. However, it was very much the sort of territory where electric traction, as promoted by the Southern Railway, could offer major advantages.

Portsmouth via Horsham, No 2

This left a wedge of secondary main line between the Brighton and Portsmouth services, for which electrification would clearly offer some benefits. It would also close a coastal gap which, at this stage, had a break of 26 miles between West Worthing and Havant which was steam operated. There were also the awkward branches to both Littlehampton and Bognor Regis, and how to serve all destinations in a reasonably satisfactory manner for all concerned has always been something of a conundrum. This aspect is discussed later.

The decision to electrify this line provoked fears of the live rail among landowners and farmers in West Sussex, to the extent that questions were asked in the House of Commons and a deputation took its apprehensions to the Southern directors. Alternatives suggested included the use of overhead wires at certain points, that the conductor rail should be live only when a train was about to pass, or that it should be boarded in. They received short shrift. In a robust response at the 1937 annual meeting, the Chairman said that none of these

suggestions was practicable. Fatalities to people were few, and were confined to those who got on to the railway for their own purposes. Ten-wire fencing was used on the electrified lines and wire mesh was added where there was a risk that children or animals might get over or through it. The conductor rail ceased where a footpath or cattleway crossed the line; if the former was busy a footbridge was erected, and at the latter wooden cattle grids were provided to prevent cattle leaving the crossing.

Incidental works were numerous and expensive. In the London area, more sidings were electrified at New Cross Gate, and at Streatham Hill carriage sheds were erected to accommodate four 12-car and four eight-car trains. A carriage washer was provided as well as additional berthing sidings. The platforms at Sutton were lengthened to 820ft.

At Dorking the platforms were extended, the down bay became a down loop and the layout altered so that the down line could be used for terminating trains or as an up loop. This was similar to the work at Haslemere. Colour lights were installed from Mickleham, north of Dorking, through to Holmwood, controlled from a new cabin at Dorking. A new station was built at Horsham, consisting of up and down island platforms, with this area also resignalled. Platforms here and also at Pulborough and Arundel were extended to 820ft, and signalling enhanced. At Littlehampton new station buildings were constructed, a bay built and platforms lengthened. A carriage shed was also erected.

The bridge over the River Arun at Ford near Littlehampton included a lifting span to enable vessels to pass upriver to Arundel. The old bridge was worked by hand and took half an hour to lift and then lower. Fortunately, from the railway's point of view, it had not been required to open since 1919. Parliamentary sanction was required to replace the old bridge with a fixed span, and the reconstruction was completed on the weekend of 23–25 April 1938.

At Barnham, Bognor Regis and Chichester the platforms were extended, with new berthing sidings at the first two and a bay at Chichester. The halt platforms at stations between Chichester and Havant were lengthened and booking huts provided, as the halts would be staffed when electric services commenced.

A reversing siding was laid in at West Worthing, to enable trains from Brighton to be terminated clear of the running lines, and on 4 July 1937, a new station was opened at Durrington-on-Sea.

Although some signalling work was carried out, such as the provision of colour lights in mid-section to add to line capacity, much of the area covered by this scheme remained mechanically signalled.

Power supplies were obtained from the National Grid at four different points and

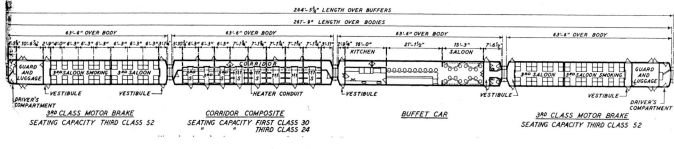

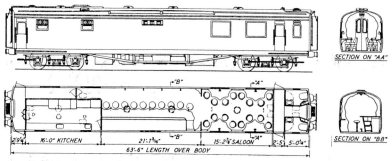

Plan, elevation and section of buffet car for London-Bognor Regis electric services.

distributed to 21 rectifier substations, the whole being overseen by the Havant Control Room. The rolling stock consisted of a further build of 26 4COR units which were matched with a new type, the 4BUF.

4BUF, 3073-85

These 13 sets built at Eastleigh were the same as the 4CORs except for the substitution of a buffet vehicle for the corridor third. The buffet cars contained a food preparation and cooking area, and for the public there was a bar with 10 high revolving stools, a saloon with four specially shaped tables, each with four revolving chairs against a concave backing, and two lavatories. There were no windows in the bar section. The wall décor, so we are told, 'featured plaques of food subjects in antique brass'. There were 30 first and 154 third class seats in total.

Full public electric services began on 3 July 1938.

In addition, there was a half-hourly service of stopping trains from Three Bridges to Littlehampton via Horsham, alternate trains reversing there and continuing to Bognor Regis. For local trains south of Dorking, the two trains an hour from Waterloo to Dorking were extended, one to Horsham and the other to Holmwood only. The Horsham train was looped at Dorking to provide connections into and out of the xx18 service from Victoria to the coast. Additionally, one train per hour from London Bridge to Dorking was extended to Horsham.

The new services included several changes from those which had been offered previously. Notably, Portsmouth services from London Bridge were confined to the rush hour only, and Pullman cars were no longer used on routes via Horsham. Buffet cars were substituted, although catering remained in the hands of the Pullman Car Co. Overall, train mileage was

Above:

The 4BUF buffet cars for the Portsmouth No 2 electrification via Horsham were more modest than their restaurant predecessors, as this diagram shows. Small tables with scalloped edges and seating four were provided, as well as a long counter with bar stools. The objective was to avoid blocking the gangway, while at the same time giving people somewhere to eat their purchases. *Author's collection*

all but doubled compared with the previous steam operations.

This comprehensive range of services nevertheless contained elements which would cause some anguish later. Although the service from Victoria (below) is shown as running via Dorking, the departures at 09.18, 12.18 and 15.18 ran main line, calling at East Croydon, Redhill and Three Bridges instead. Over the years, the growth of East Croydon as an employment and shopping centre, the establishment of Gatwick as London's second airport, and the designation of Crawley as a new town all shifted the commercial balance

firmly towards that route. Latterly, even what became the peak-hour-only services from the coast were diverted away from Dorking, to the great discomfort of the residents of that town. Indeed, even the local services south to Horsham were reduced to very low levels, although these have to some extent been restored. The whole was a classic case in which opposing voices all had valid points, while the railway operator had to balance his commercial instincts against some very loosely defined social obligations.

Chessington

Parliamentary sanction for the loop line from Motspur Park to Leatherhead was obtained in 1930, but construction of the first section as far as Chessington was not started until 1936. This was already a rapidly developing residential area.

The new line diverged in a south-westerly direction from the Raynes Park-Epsom line at the newly created Motspur Park Junction, about half a mile beyond the station. The junction was worked electrically from the signalbox, adjacent to the level crossing at the south end of the platform. Except for a shallow cutting at the junction, and at the Chessington end, the line was formed on embankment. This was largely made up of dry filling from demolitions in London, as the local clay was liable to slip in wet weather.

The line rose at 1 in 96 to Malden Manor, fell at 1 in 199 to the crossing of the River Hogsmill, then rose at 1 in 100 and 1 in 160 to Tolworth. Thence a fall at 1 in 100 was followed by a similar rise to Chessington North. There

Fig. 7.4: Hourly Pattern of Portsmouth and Bognor Regis Services – 1938 Inaugural Timetable	
From Victoria	
xx18	Sutton, Dorking, Horsham, Pulborough, Arundel (connection to Littlehampton), Barnham (train divides). Front, to Chichester, Havant, Portsmouth & Southsea, Portsmouth Harbour. Rear, with buffet car, to Bognor Regis. 132min to Portsmouth Harbour, 102min to Bognor Regis.
xx25	Existing West Worthing service extended all stations to Littlehampton.
From Brighton	
xx03	All stations and halts to West Worthing.
xx17	Hove, Shoreham-by-Sea, Worthing Central and slow to Portsmouth Harbour.
xx20	All stations and Aldrington Halt to West Worthing.
xx33	All stations and halts to West Worthing.
xx47	Hove, Shoreham-by-Sea, Worthing Central, Barnham, Chichester (connection with all stations and halts to Portsmouth & Southsea), Fratton, Portsmouth & Southsea, Portsmouth Harbour.
xx50	All stations and Aldrington Halt to Littlehampton and Bognor Regis.

were seven underbridges, some of them of considerable size, and one overbridge. All were constructed of steel girders encased in concrete, as well as the three-span 140ft-long viaduct over the Hogsmill.

The stations at Malden Manor and Tolworth were built in concrete in a modernistic style as favoured by the Southern. The platform roofings were constructed in reinforced concrete integral with the station buildings, in a novel style of German origin known as the Chisarc system. This gave a completely unobstructed platform, free of all columns. Fluorescent lighting was installed from new. A goods yard was provided on the down side at Tolworth, controlled by a 20-lever frame in the signalbox there.

This was the terminus for the time being, and an inaugural trip was arranged for the local dignitaries on 25 May 1938. Public opening was on 29 May, with the extension of the services which by then were conveniently terminating at Motspur Park. Services from Waterloo ran every 20 minutes on weekdays, from 05.36 to 22.56, then at 23.26 and 00.06. Today, the basic Monday to Friday service is half-hourly only, with timings at 06.06 and every 30 minutes through to 08.06, then 08.22 and at 22 and 52 past each hour until 20.52. There is then a 21.52 and a last service at 23.02. Sunday services show a similar retrenchment with a half-hourly service provided only during the summer months.

The extension to Chessington North and Chessington South was similar in construction, but with brick-built main station buildings. The line was opened on 28 May 1939, and train services were provided by the simple expedient of extending those same trains. The goods yard at Chessington South was not available until 1 July.

A small amount of construction was undertaken south of the yard for 200yd or so, as far as the point where the line would have bridged Chalky Lane. No more progress was made in the direction of Leatherhead, and the route was blocked in the 1980s with the construction of the M25 motorway. While the line could have provided a relief to the railway route via Epsom, the London County Council's Green Belt scheme, made statutory in 1938, was enough to dissuade the Southern from pressing on to Leatherhead. There was thus no building of residential properties in the intervening three miles or so to the outskirts of Leatherhead.

Right:
The new stations on the Chessington branch have splendid roofs which, without any intermediate pillars obstructing the platforms, allow passengers to board and alight from trains without getting wet. As built, and the picture shows a new Chessington North in May 1939, glass inserts allowed natural light to reach the platforms, as seen here. Sadly, Railtrack's recent refurbishment has painted all these over, so artificial light is now used throughout the day.
Southern Railway/Author's collection

The line has thus stayed much as it was when constructed. The footbridge joining what was to have been the up platform at Chessington South to the ticket office on the down side station buildings was never built, and the ticket office itself was relocated on the one operational platform in recent years.

Reading and Camberley

This was the smallest of the schemes carried out under the 1935 New Works arrangements, covering 43 route miles. These were the section from Virginia Water to Reading, and the links from Ascot to Ash Vale, including the line from Frimley round to the main line at Sturt Lane Junction and thence to Pirbright Junction where the Alton line diverged, and from Aldershot North Junction to Guildford.

This included a section of single line from Frimley Junction to Ash Vale Junction, controlled by a tablet instrument. Single line sections on electric railways have never been common in Britain, on the reasoning that if the traffic was not sufficient to justify double track, it was unlikely to support the fixed costs of electric traction either. However, this section is no more than 2¼ miles long anyway.

Electricity supplies were obtained from the National Grid at Reading. There were 10 rectifier substations, controlled from Woking. Station platforms were lengthened, but on

this line to 540ft, or sufficient for eight-car trains. At Ascot, the layout was reorganised to enable combined trains to be run from Waterloo and then split for the two groups of destinations. A new signalbox was built, and the whole commissioned on 16 October 1938. Berthing was provided at the Southern's Reading station, then separate premises from those of the Great Western. The present bay platform at the former Reading General was commissioned in 1965, Reading Southern closing on 4 September that year.

A further build of 2BIL units was produced for this electrification with public services beginning on 1 January 1939. The new train service was simple, being every 20 minutes in weekday busy hours and every half-hour at other times. Trains were fast to Staines and divided at Ascot for Reading (75 minutes) or Guildford via Aldershot. There was a negligible peak service of one morning train at 08.00 from Ascot to Woking via the Sturt Lane chord, and a through service back from Waterloo to Ascot via Woking leaving at 17.37, or 13.37 on Saturdays. There was also a contra-peak service to enable trains arriving from Waterloo via Ascot to be sent on to berth at Woking. The modestly used chord was closed on 21 July 1966, and subsequent attempts at revival have come to nothing. Notably, the new services offered Bagshot, Camberley and Frimley through services to London throughout the day, while there was an 85% increase in the number of trains operated.

The railway also handled the Ascot racecourse traffic with electric trains for the first time on 13–16 June 1939.

Gillingham and Maidstone

The Gillingham and Maidstone scheme was the last expansion before the onset of the war, and covered the lines of the South Eastern Railway from Gravesend to Strood and Maidstone West, with the spur from Strood to the Chatham company's main line at Rochester Bridge Junction. It also covered the Chatham's main line from Swanley to Gillingham, and the line from Otford to Maidstone East. This amounted to a total of 53 route miles. In this, it built on the Sevenoaks electrification of 1935.

This scheme was rather different from that of its predecessors, since although steam working was superseded on the secondary lines, only the intermediate work from Swanley to Gillingham was transferred to the electric trains. These had to be timed over a line carrying heavy steam services, particularly during the holiday season, when a number of relief Continental boat trains were routed via Maidstone East. There was also a considerable volume of freight over the Maidstone West line to serve the industries in the Medway Valley.

The major incidental works included the lengthening and electrification of No 1

platform at Holborn Viaduct, electrifying Platforms 6 and 7 at Cannon Street, and adjusting clearances thence to Gravesend to accommodate 9ft-wide coaching stock. Platforms generally were extended, a carriage shed erected at Gillingham and a carriage washer provided. Goods loops were installed at Cuxton and at Snodland, and New Hythe halt was upgraded to station status.

Swanley Junction station was rebuilt on a new site west of the junction at Swanley, a quarter of a mile west on the London side. Opened on 16 April 1939, this station was intended to be suitable for dividing combined trains with separate portions for Maidstone East and Gillingham. Two 820ft-long island platforms were provided, each a massive 28ft wide.

In anticipation of future housing developments, which in the event never took place, a new station was built at Lullingstone between Swanley and Eynsford. The station was eventually demolished, never having been used for revenue-earning traffic.

A down bay was provided at Maidstone East, and also berthing sidings. Much signalling was also upgraded. Swanley Control Room covered the 13 new substations provided as part of the scheme, with services opened for public use on 2 July 1939. Train operation was in the hands of a new type of Southern electric unit.

2HAL, 2601-92

A fleet of 76 of these units was built at Eastleigh for the Maidstone and Gillingham services, and sported several new features. For one thing, the bodies were 9ft wide as opposed to the 8ft 6in maximum previously allowable for trains on these routes.

Changes in the appearance of the new stock started in the cab design. The driving ends were built of welded rolled-steel sections and panel plates. The rest of the body was made up from steel panelling on hardwood frames with timber roof and floor. The passenger compartment windows which were as flush as possible, were rounded to a larger radius, strengthening the side of the coach and also making cleaning easier. The driving motors

contained the guard's area and seven third class compartments; the driving trailers included a lavatory connected by a side corridor to four first class and four third class compartments. Seating capacity was a total of 24 first and 102 third class.

The electrical equipment was by English Electric and included two 275hp motors with electro-pneumatic control gear. But how did they acquire the acronym of 2HAL? As the description above shows, only one vehicle provided lavatory access. So, two-car but only HALf with a Lavatory. It may be added that an alternative explanation is that they were the equivalent of half a 4LAV unit.

The basic service provision, supplemented at peak, was as shown in Fig 7.5.

An interesting use of electric traction was the Chatham-Portsmouth excursions, previously operated by steam via Factory Junction and Clapham Junction. These became electric units, reversing at London Bridge and travelling via Epsom, Effingham Junction and Guildford.

Electrification Policy

The Southern Railway made a decision to dismantle the Brighton overhead electrification and substitute the third rail, as installed by the South Western company. Over the years, the correctness of this action has inevitably been questioned, and indeed it was to arise again in the postwar years in connection with the system to be used for the Bournemouth line. In 1939, Alfred Raworth, chief electrical engineer of the Southern, gave a spirited defence of why the company had proceeded in the way it did, of which the salient points are as follows.

Raworth began with a basic proposition that electricity was the only means of providing a really adequate train service on a heavily loaded system. This was mainly due to it being possible to concentrate upon a train an almost unlimited supply of power, coupled with the ability of the electric traction motor to exert double its normal horsepower for short periods. Greatly increased rates of acceleration consequently became possible, resulting in faster schedules, while the use of

---

Fig. 7.5: Hourly Pattern of Maidstone and Gillingham Services – 1939 Inaugural Timetable

From Victoria
xx18   Bromley South, Swanley (train divides). Front, fast to Otford, then all stations to Maidstone East. Rear, all stations to Gillingham.
                                65min to Maidstone East, 62min to Gillingham.

From Charing Cross
xx42   Waterloo, London Bridge, Woolwich Arsenal, Dartford, Gravesend, Strood (train divides). Front, to Rochester, Chatham, Gillingham. Rear, all stations to Maidstone West.
                                67min to Gillingham, 81min to Maidstone West.

From Cannon Street
xx55   Trains to Gravesend via Sidcup extended to Gillingham, connection at Strood to Maidstone West.

multiple-unit stock eliminated all idle locomotive movements. This in turn doubled the capacity of the terminal stations.

The question of which system to choose was determined finally by selecting that which, in respect of the first cost and operation and maintenance of the rolling stock, distribution and contact system, gave the minimum annual overall outlay. On the basis of experience, there was no reason to doubt that 660V dc was correct for the suburban area. 'So long as the track is adequately fenced, it is doubtful if there are any real objections to the third rail; it is simple to install and maintain, and it is the cheapest form of contact conductor. It also has a lower maintenance cost and a longer life than the overhead wire.'

On the other hand, third rail uses a comparatively low voltage. This necessitates a comparatively large number of substations, all of which have to be staffed at considerable expense. Overhead wires with 1,500V dc thus gained some popularity, though applications in this period extended only to the Altrincham line of the LMSR/LNER. It was however to be applied to the forthcoming Liverpool Street-Shenfield and Manchester-Sheffield/Wath schemes of the LNER. How suitable was third rail for the main line electrification to Brighton?

Raworth was in no doubts. A then existing fleet of 1,650 third rail dc vehicles which would be enabled to work over the network as a whole was a powerful argument in favour of extending the existing system. The problem was the cost of staffing those substations, which had to be sited about 3½ miles apart. Fig 7.6 indicates just how many there were by 1939.

The problem was solved by devising a development of the 660V third rail system, under which the conductor rail was supplied from single-rectifier substations. All of these could be unattended and controlled remotely from central control rooms. Devised and first installed on the Brighton main line, the system had operated reliably and successfully. It worked on the principle that in the event of any substation becoming unavailable for any reason, the load could be carried by the adjacent substations. Not only this, but the conditions would be such that the voltage drop would not be excessive, and any short-circuit would pass sufficient current to ensure automatic isolation.

Other advantages had been that closer spacing meant a more uniform voltage was supplied to the tracks, and that the spare plant capacity provided was always kept in service and thus instantly available.

The power supply for the suburban area came from the Southern's own plant at Durnsford Road, Wimbledon, and from the London Power Company at Deptford. This was fed to a distribution system at Lewisham. From these two supplies, power was transmitted to the 46 rotary converter substations. For the outer area, that is the post-1931 main line schemes, mercury-arc rectifier substations had been used, all of which were unattended. These were supplied by the National Grid at a number of different supply points. This had helped materially in the extension of electrification, albeit at a relatively high cost.

What it had achieved, though, was the ability to install a 'ring main' system instead of the much more expensive radial feeder system. These ring mains were looped into the substations, which made it possible to provide alternative sources of supply while running only a single 33kV cable along the railway. This applied to all the 112 rectifier substations commissioned from 1933 onwards.

All substations were controlled remotely from central rooms located at Three Bridges, Woking, Havant, Swanley and Ore. The object of the supervisory system was to present a clear picture of the conditions prevailing throughout the high-tension and low-tension systems, and to enable all operations for controlling the supply of power to be carried out from that point.

The growth of the Southern Railway's operations are shown in Fig 7.7.

Thus the Southern was now offering well over twice the train mileage – and it might reasonably be concluded over twice the service – as a result of electrification. Also, it worked, and journey times had decreased by about one third when compared with steam.

There were also considerable savings in operational costs, and on a per train mile basis those for electric trains were again a third less than those for steam. The reduction in wage costs was the major factor here. Not only did one man replace two in the cab, but the men who did the lighting up and the subsequent disposal of the locomotive and its fire were also no longer required. Most importantly, though, the electric trains could be turned round so much quicker at the terminals, as well as running faster between them. Each train crew member was that much more productive as a result. Other electric systems might also have succeeded, but the decision to perpetuate the third rail would certainly appear to have been right for the time at which it was made.

This was in no sense a small business. In 1939, the Southern owned 2,586 electric suburban vehicles, the motor vehicles of which were fitted with 275hp motors and capable of a top speed of 60mph. In addition, there were 603 electric main line corridor vehicles, their motor vehicles having 225hp motors and a top speed of 75mph. The numbers of motor and trailer vehicles were broadly equal.

The Southern thus had 3,189 passenger vehicles for use in electric trains by the outbreak of war, compared with a total of 434 vehicles which the company had taken over a mere 16½ years previously, in 1923. Much of this amazing seven-fold growth was, it is true, achieved by the conversion of vehicles constructed for steam haulage, but the scale of the achievement should not be underestimated. Over that same timescale, the number of passenger journeys on the Southern's electric services rose from 236 million in 1923 to 371 million in 1938, during a period which had been marked by substantial economic depression.

Traffic Growth

The public had responded by voting for the Southern in terms of making many more journeys as shown in Fig 7.8 (overleaf).

Over the decade from the mid-1920s to the mid-1930s, the Southern thus found itself

Fig 7.6: Electrification Progress

Year	Scheme	Route Miles	Track Miles	Substations
By 1931	Suburban area completed	300	800	44
1933	Brighton and West Worthing	52	163	18
1934	Swanley and Sevenoaks	23	50	6
1935	Eastbourne and Hastings	60	134	17
1937	Portsmouth and Alton	96	242	26
1938	Portsmouth via Horsham	75	165	20
1939	Reading and Camberley	43	88	10
1939	Gillingham and Maidstone	53	117	17
Totals		702	1,759	158

Fig 7.7: Additional Train Mileage Following Electrification

1932	Steam train mileage, suburban area, replaced	8,152,820
1932	Electric train mileage, suburban area	20,651,000
	Growth in train mileage, suburban area	factor of 2.53
1939	Steam train mileage, complete area, replaced	18,796,806
1939	Electric train mileage, complete area	41,241,682
	Growth in train mileage, complete area	factor of 2.19

Fig 7.8: Passengers Arriving at London Stations, 1925–36

	07.00-10.00	Non Rush Hour
1925	167,260	82,344
1930	196,929 (+17.7%)	97,401 (+18.3%)
1936	226,807 (+35.6%)	127,407 (+54.7%)

Fig 7.10: Passenger Growth at Selected Suburban Stations

Station	Ordinary Tickets Sold, '000s			Season Tickets Issued		
	1925	1935	Growth	1925	1935	Growth
Welling/Bexleyheath/Sidcup	1,097	4,754	x 4.3	8,959	57,600	x 6.4
	1927	1935	Growth	1927	1935	Growth
Belmont, Banstead, Epsom Downs	330	860	x 2.6	2,964	11,484	x 3.9
	1933	1935	Growth	1933	1935	Growth
Stoneleigh	256	717	x 2.8	5,671	19,422	x 3.4
	1928	1935	Growth	1928	1935	Growth
Tooting	65	601	x 9.2	414	4,353	x 10.5

carrying 35% more passengers into London during the defined three-hour morning peak period, but interestingly the off-peak growth is considerably stronger. These figures, and those that follow, are derived from a paper given by the Southern's E. C. Cox to the Institute of Transport in 1937. Cox suggested that this was due to the area within one or two hours of London 'being mainly residential with a high proportion of a better class of residents having leisure and means for journeying to London for shopping and amusement'.

Cox then provided a breakdown of the number of trains conveying these passengers, set out in Fig 7.9.

Fig 7.9: Passenger and Train Arrivals at London Stations, 1936

	Passengers	Trains	Pass/train
busiest hr	115,000	173	665
07.00-10.00	226,807	520	436
00.00-23.59	354,214	2,427	146

The problem of the peak in terms of crowding, or perhaps overcrowding, is well shown, with the number of passengers per train rising by a factor of between four and five during the busiest hour compared with the daily average. It should perhaps be said

that Cox does not state the number of trains arriving in the busiest hour; this has been assumed to be one third of the total in the 7am and 10am period, but in practice it is likely to have been a little higher – perhaps 40%. However, this does not affect the general conclusions. It may also be added that the problem of passengers crowding to the front of trains so that they are first off on reaching Cannon Street, Victoria or wherever, when there is plenty of space in the rear coaches, was as much a feature of rush hour travel then as now. Statistics compiled for

Below:
Ascot sees a six-car formation of three 2BIL units headed by No 2145 arriving with a train from Reading. This view, taken when the service was new in January 1939, shows that the Southern still used semaphore signals where it suited the company, and also the distinctive concrete platform lamps. The flexibility of the track layout may be judged by the ability to depart for either Reading or Aldershot from at least three of the four platforms in this view.
Southern Railway/Ian Allan Library

1938 show a very similar pattern, but with the numbers of both passengers and trains a little higher, particularly in the peaks.

Turning now to the volumes at suburban stations, with a series of examples Cox demonstrated just how substantial that growth had been. Separate figures were produced for ordinary tickets sold and for season ticket holders, and in each case the growth of season ticket holders was greater. This is shown in Fig 7.10.

The time periods differ, but most run from immediately before electric services were introduced until some years afterwards. Stoneleigh is an exception, as it was a new station in 1932 and was never served by steam trains. There, former farmland was being covered quickly with semi-detached housing. On the other hand, the spectacular results at Tooting, then named Tooting Junction, were achieved in an area which had long been built up.

This period ended with the onset of the World War 2.

8. The Southern at War

'Trains could occasionally escape air attack by diving into a tunnel.'

War on the Line, Southern Railway

The preparations which the company was making were described vividly in the October 1939 issue of the *Southern Railway Magazine* (for staff).

On 1 September 1939, two days before the outbreak of war, the Minister of Transport made an Order under the Emergency Powers (Defence) Act 1939 which allowed him to take control of the undertakings owned by the Southern Railway Company and others.

The Southern relocated their headquarters organisation to Deepdene, Dorking. This was a good move, in view of the bombing damage later suffered at Waterloo and London Bridge. Operationally, a blackout was imposed at night, and this was enforced from 2 September. Initially, interior lighting of coaches was dispensed with or greatly diminished, electric train headcodes were dimmed by the use of blue lamps, and similar lighting was fitted at stations. At platform ends, oil lamps of various kinds showed motormen where to pull up their trains; later these lamps were enclosed in improvised casings, showing the figure eight. As a guide to passengers, portions of station roof supports, edgings of platforms, stairways and all projecting points on buildings were painted white, but windows and other places normally reflecting artificial light were totally obscured. Colour-light signals were dimmed by the fitting of long shades over the lenses, as were handlamps. Motormen were issued with steel helmets. Signs indicating shelters for the staff and public were displayed on stations, 'the appearance of which has considerably changed during the past few weeks'.

Later, train lighting was devised which met Government requirements, and loudspeaker equipment was installed at termini and principal stations for train announcements. Illuminated station name signs were also hung from verandahs at right angles to the platform.

Special regulations were drawn up on internal coach lighting, and copies were posted in each compartment. Passengers were instructed:

- To keep all blinds drawn.
- To keep windows shut except where it is necessary to lower them to open doors and alight.
- To make certain the train is in the platform and to alight on the platform side.

Above:
An early 4SUB unit, No 4163, dating back to LSWR steam stock with additional trailers enters Surbiton. It is October 1946, and this view from the Ewell Road bridge, looking west, has changed little. The down fast line, on which the train is travelling, has no platform. The unit is probably about to take the platform loop to the left to enable it to call.
Southern Railway/Author's collection

- When leaving the carriage to make sure that windows are closed, blinds are lowered and that the door is closed quickly.

This, however, applied to main line stock. Suburban trains were much more difficult to regulate, as stops were more frequent and there were more doors to be opened.

Passenger operations were curtailed from 11 September to run at half-hourly intervals during the peaks and hourly at other times. This proved totally inadequate, notably on the Western section between Epsom and Raynes Park in the mornings, with passengers being left behind. Such was the volume of complaint that normal services were restored a week later.

Restaurant car facilities were suspended 'but arrangements were made for "snack boxes" to be available at the more important stations'. Many cheap fares facilities were withdrawn, although time-restricted cheap day tickets were reinstated from 9 October, as were platform tickets and seat (or compartment) reservations.

There was also the evacuation of schoolchildren, mothers and babies from London and places like Chatham. The destinations were billets in the country and by the sea. With electric services, much of this was achieved by running trains more or less as normal, but cancelling them for ordinary passengers. An example given was the 08.30 Holborn Viaduct to Otford, which called at Bellingham to pick up evacuees and then ran fast to Otford. This enabled the train to fulfil the rest of its booked workings.

Fresh emergency passenger services from 1 January 1940 saw the reinstatement of Pullman and pantry cars on a number of Central Section trains, and restaurant cars to the Waterloo-Portsmouth services. They were withdrawn again on 22 May 1942, this time for the duration. Most of the vehicles were removed from the trains and stored.

Further commercial restrictions were imposed by the Minister of War Transport. On 6 October 1941, first class accommodation was withdrawn from inner-suburban services which both began and finished their journeys in what was then termed the London Transport Area. Longer-distance trains were not affected, but the so-called 'inner' services all lost first class accommodation. The outer limits of this restriction included Windsor, Horsham via Dorking, Coulsdon North, Tattenham Corner and Caterham, Sevenoaks via Orpington and Swanley, and also Gravesend. By and large, a similar situation remains in place today, although some, such as the Guildford New Line (via Cobham), saw first class restored for a time. The idea was to make the maximum usage of all the available seating.

The blackout regulations also caused difficulties for freight movements. The volume was much increased, particularly for food supplies. Owing to lighting restrictions, it was that much more difficult to undertake depot work at night, and more had to be done during the day. This led in turn to more freight movements during the daylight hours and, consequently, fewer paths for passenger trains. The consequential effect by late 1940 was that peak period business trains were about 5% down, but off-peak by roughly 50%. Thus, what was normally a four trains per hour service would become two, and three trains per hour would now be one.

Journey times were also increased, due to heavier loads and longer station stops, and a maximum speed set at 60mph. Electric trains to both Eastbourne and Brighton were being allowed about seven minutes extra running time. It was pointed out by the company that special provision had to be made to give connections with military centres and naval ports, and this might mean additional stops. Suburban electric trains were being allowed 30 seconds per stop instead of 20. After dark, although the stopping point for eight-car sets and other standard train formations was usually marked by a lamp on the platform edge, where the stations were in a low category of permitted lighting it was difficult for drivers to judge their distance from that lamp. It was then much better for them to err on the side of caution, release the brakes and then make another brake application, than to over-run the end of the platform end with the possibility of passengers unguardedly stepping out on to the ramp or the track. Even if that did not occur, setting back under inefficient lighting conditions was fraught with difficulty.

Yet another problem was the time taken by station staff and guards making sure that boarding and alighting was complete and that all doors were shut properly before it was safe to start the train. Such delays were cumulative, and trains could easily arrive at their terminus more minutes late than the length of their layover. The subsequent journey would then be started late, and so on. Part of the answer to that was to introduce turnover trains, if they could be made available, thus deliberately introducing a 'spare' element into the operation.

On main line trains, allowance had to be made for handling parcels and mail on dimly lit platforms. Train services were also thinned out after 20.00, as demand was down anyway under blackout conditions. Thus the last weekday Mid-Kent train from Charing Cross was now to leave at 23.44 instead of 00.21.

The Southern stressed that such schemes could never be perfect and that the company's aim was to give the best possible service to the greatest number of passengers. The services would be kept under review, and constructive suggestions for adjustments would be adopted if they could be made within the framework of national requirements.

To add to such problems, track and signalling maintenance was also made harder, as many of the staff had been called up. Again, the use of powerful lighting to undertake work at night was just not feasible. Likewise, more trains during the day on weekdays tended to rule out that time for maintenance also. This led to an ominous warning from the Southern Railway, the effects of which remain with us to this day:

'On Sundays, the engineers will have to be given the greatest freedom possible in order to carry out a large proportion of their essential work, and this inevitably means a certain restriction of Sunday services.'

Thus was born what became the tradition of massively disruptive Sunday engineering work.

Bombing

On 14 October 1940, a high-explosive bomb hit one of the chimneys of Durnsford Road power station and damaged the boiler house so badly that its capacity was reduced by half. Repairs, which included the erection of a new 100ft steel chimney, were not completed until 12 February 1941. The result of this was that as many trains as could be operated had to run at reduced speed until full power was restored.

Early in March 1941, there had been a heavy air raid on the Waterloo area, with showers of incendiary bombs, extinguished by the staff, and several bombs large and small. Sleepers were torn from some of the tracks, and traffic operations had to begin and end at Clapham Junction. Fig 8.1 identifies each of the lines concerned, although it represents the total incidents of the war years.

Diary of the Waterloo Stationmaster

- All roads out of service at 9pm Saturday.
- Examination of arches at 8am on Sunday morning revealed two large craters in arches in Up Main Through and Up Main Relief. Bomb pierced boundary wall and footings on Down Main Local.
- Up and Down Windsor lines opened for traffic at 9.37am Sunday.
- Roads tested and Up and Down Main Locals opened for traffic at 3.15pm Sunday.
- Crane arrived 1.50pm and two sets of way beams put in on Up Main Through; two other sets unloaded and Down Windsor Local opened at 5pm Sunday.
- Normal working of all steam services from 11am Sunday.
- Down main through opened at 9.8am Monday.
- Crane arrived at 8.54am Monday and way beams etc put in Up Main Relief.
- All squared up by 3.15pm and absolutely normal working resumed by 4pm Monday.

In the great raid of 16/17 April 1941, incendiaries started fires on buildings, platforms and rolling stock at Charing Cross. A landmine fell on the older section of the bridge close to the signal cabin, and became welded to the live rail but did not explode. A

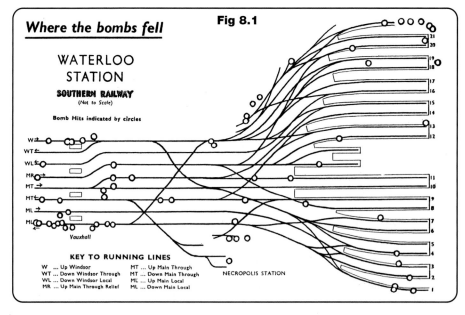

Where the bombs fell Fig 8.1

WATERLOO STATION
SOUTHERN RAILWAY
(Not to Scale)

Bomb Hits indicated by circles

Vauxhall

NECROPOLIS STATION

KEY TO RUNNING LINES

W ... Up Windsor
WT ... Down Windsor Through
WL ... Down Windsor Local
MR ... Up Main Through Relief
MT ... Up Main Through
MT ... Down Main Through
ML ... Up Main Local
ML ... Down Main Local

Above:
**Virginia Water shows its wartime painted
uprights, to guide passengers during the
blackout. This view is taken looking towards
Waterloo, the Chertsey line being on the right and
the other side of the signal cabin. The date is
23 September 1943.**
Southern Railway/Author's collection

fire in the bridge timbers got to within 10ft of
the bomb before it was put out. The bomb
was made harmless and removed.

One of the worst incidents outside
London took place at Portsmouth which, as
a naval base, was the target for many heavy
air attacks. Both stations suffered serious
damage and electric stock was destroyed. In
the raid of 1 January 1941, an electric
train was hit while standing at No 4
platform at Portsmouth Harbour, and a gap
was blown in the viaduct on the landward
side. The damaged vehicles were left where
they were, until lifted out by cranes in
September 1946.

In 1943 the South Coast towns were targets
for 'hit and run' raids by enemy aircraft. In
one of these raids upon Brighton, on 25 May
1943, a 'hopping bomb' passed through a
house and over garden walls to burst against
one of the piers of the 70ft-high London Road
Viaduct on the line to Lewes. This brought
down two of the spans. Temporary repairs
were completed in 15 days and complete
restoration in four months. Extra services
were run from Haywards Heath to Lewes in
the interim.

Shelter from Bombing

There are, at Chislehurst, a number of caves in
the chalk. In the early years of the Blitz in 1940
refugees came nightly. This started as a few, but
numbers grew until the caves were crowded,
their total capacity being around 15,000.

The objective was safety, but there grew up
also a form of nightly community. Large
numbers took an evening train to Chislehurst
as part of the day's routine, the time of their
train varying with the length of the day and
hence that of the blackout. The platform at
New Cross was described as being 'black with
people from end to end, four or five deep', all
waiting to board an arriving train.

Most of the shelterers were regulars, with a
large proportion knowing each other. The
majority travelled by the ordinary services,
but when raids became worse and more
frequent again early in 1944, it was arranged
to run a special train from Cannon Street
when the numbers demanded it. It ran nearly
every night from January to March, a total
anticipated rail usage of 2,000 or more being
needed to justify the additional train.

A great many took season tickets, and
family expenses must have been quite
considerable. The caves may have saved many
lives, and if not that, they saved many
wretched and wakeful nights.

Women on the Railway

In July 1940, an agreement was reached
between the railways and the National Union
of Railwaymen as to the employment of
women in men's places during the war. The
Southern had already been employing women
as carriage cleaners before the war.

With the new accord, the numbers quickly
grew, and by 1942 over 8,000 men had been

released to join the forces – and 8,000 women
had been recruited to replace them. On the
electrified sections, wartime women
employees were to be found most frequently
on station duties or as guards. Brighton
produced the youngest signalwoman, a Miss
Steel aged 22. She worked at the Old
Shoreham Bridge level crossing and also
collected tolls. In her spare time, she was an
Air Raid Precautions (ARP) Warden at
Brighton. By 1944, women nationally
accounted for 16% of the railway labour force.

As to what escaped destruction, it is worth
noting that:

- None of the railway bridges across the
  Thames was damaged seriously.
- The power stations providing the traction
  current were never put out of action
  completely.
- Only one of the eight power signalboxes
  with more than 100 levers, Blackfriars,
  was destroyed, on 19 April 1941.

That said, a great deal of damage was done;
while it is possible to 'patch things up' to

Above:
The prewar railway companies employed few women, but this was to change for the duration of the war. These sketches show Southern Railwaywomen at work, in War on the Line, a 1946 publication by the company. *Author's collection*

enable services to start running again, this does not amount to a full scale permanent repair. That was to become an occupation of the 1950s.

One economy made was to reduce the train heating levels. In peacetime, between October and April, 'full heat' was switched on when the temperature at any one of a number of selected control points fell below 48°F. 'Half heat' was provided on main line trains when the temperature was under 55°F. Wartime conditions reduced the heating season to the five months of November to March, while 'full heat' applied only below 45°F and half heat at a chilly 50°F or less.

The air raids exacted a heavy toll. Fig 8.2 shows the number of red alerts which were received in the 29 Southern Railway warning districts in each year of the war. They are grouped by counties, with Kent suffering the most as might be expected.

Noticeably, Kent and London bore the brunt, while further west the coastal regions were those most heavily affected. Perhaps not surprisingly, this was particularly the case in Portsmouth and Southampton. The pattern of warnings may also be noted; in Kent and the other Home Counties alerts had peaked by 1941, but London suffered a new onslaught as late as 1944. It should perhaps be stressed that these were the number of alerts as opposed to incidents, and that the latter would vary enormously in their intensity and effects.

In the event, the first recorded incident on the Southern Railway was on 19 June 1940. Bombing of the Southern's lines was however heavy, and in the eight months from September 1940, the following incidents were recorded (Fig 8.3):

The V1 'flying bomb' campaign began in the summer of 1944, the first falling in the vicinity of Haywards Heath. These missiles did considerable damage to, for instance, station buildings on the eastern side at Victoria, Wimbledon terminal buildings and the stations at Forest Hill and Charlton. The main girders on a bridge on the Quarry line at Merstham were shifted, and the main lines at Bricklayers Arms junction badly cratered. On 12 July, a bomb fell alongside the plate girder bridge of 110ft span carrying the Catford loop over the South London line at Peckham Rye, causing so much damage that the bridge had to be taken down. The position was complicated by the high-tension cables from Lewisham Distribution Room passing over the bridge; these had to be repaired and placed on a temporary wooden structure before the bridge could be replaced. A temporary bridge of rolled steel joists supported by military-type trestling was erected and normal services resumed on 23 July.

From 2 April 1944, visitors were banned from the whole of the South Coast, in view of the preparations for the invasion of France. Several main line train services were suspended.

The 'flying bombs' were followed by the V2 rockets. One, which dropped on the up side at Hampton Court Junction on 2 November 1944, put the colour-light signalling out of action and did other damage; normal service was resumed on 4 November. On the following morning, the bridge carrying the up main local and South London lines over Southwark Park Road, Bermondsey, was hit and collapsed in the roadway. A similar bridge to the one at Peckham Rye was erected, and normal service resumed on the afternoon of 14 November. Meanwhile, large scale diversions and cancellations were needed.

In October 1944, improved train and station lighting was allowed and by the end of the year most station nameplates had been restored. The 'blackout' ended on 23 April

Fig 8.3: Incidents on the Southern, Inner London, from September 1940 to April 1941

Section	Length	No of Incidents
Charing Cross/Cannon St-New Cross/New Cross Gate	5½ miles	123
Holborn Viaduct-Herne Hill	4½ miles	62
Waterloo-Queen's Road, Battersea	2¼ miles	92

Fig 8.2: Air Raid Warnings, Red, in the Southern Railway Warning Districts

County	1939	1940	1941	1942	1943	1944	1945	Total	%
Kent	5	1,824	2,366	1,128	1,126	610	57	7,116	29.6
London	8	1,805	564	114	469	2,086	104	5,150	21.4
Surrey and Sussex	5	1,372	976	735	907	840	1	4,836	20.1
Berks/Hants/Dorset	1	919	1,064	1,027	664	476	2	4,153	17.3
Rest of Southern Rly	0	822	1,058	467	321	132	0	2,800	11.6
Total	19	6,742	6,028	3,471	3,487	4,144	164	24,055	100.0
%	0.1	28.0	25.1	14.4	14.5	17.2	0.7	100.0	

1945. The last of 3,637 recorded incidents had been on 23 March 1945. The Southern was by far the most affected of the railway companies, with over five times as many incidents per route mile as any of the others. But that, for the Southern, was the price of geography. During the war, 93 electric vehicles were destroyed by enemy action, and a further 1,784 were damaged.

It is difficult to separate the Southern electric services from the matters affecting the system as a whole during the war. The trains run to support the evacuation from Dunkirk were operated undertaken by steam traction, as electrification in Kent was at this time still minimal. In this, electric services had no more than a supportive role.

One benefit which was demonstrated was that electric trains could run during a heavy air raid, if any trains could run at all. In at least one case, electric trains were able to use a bridge which could not withstand the weight of a steam locomotive. For the numerous improvised workings which were necessary from time to time, it was an advantage that electric trains needed no more than a single crossover to reverse.

Disruptions in the War Years

Unconnected with wartime activities was the severe weather experienced at the end of January 1940. Heavy falls of sleet and snow brought down telegraph wires and froze them on the live rail, badly disorganising the services. Outside London, some electric trains had to be piloted by steam locomotives. The situation was made worse by the heaviest fall occurring on a Sunday when only a limited service was running, and trains became frozen in their sidings. Delays caused by bad weather provoked an outburst from the Mayor of Brighton, who accused the Southern of treating Brighton in a most cavalier fashion.

Two short sections of four-aspect colour-light signalling were commissioned. On 21 January 1940 that from North Sheen to St Margarets inaugurated with a new Odeon-style signalbox at Richmond replaced two others. The second was from Clapham Junction to Point Pleasant Junction on 26 May, the box at Wandsworth Town being abolished and a new power frame installed in Clapham Junction E box.

Shoreham Airport Halt was closed on 15 July 1940. Economy measures saw the Crystal Palace High Level branch reduced to a shuttle from Nunhead, while the Wimbledon service via East Putney succumbed on 5 May 1941. It could never beat the main line via Earlsfield for speed, and local traffic south of East Putney was more than adequately catered for by London Transport's District Line. More positively, Hilsea Halt north of Fratton was opened for public use on 2 November 1940, as was Longcross on 3 May 1943. Another wartime opening was Upper Halliford Halt on 1 May 1944, on the Shepperton branch. This consisted of a single platform only, as although the branch was (and is) double track, the up line was being used as a siding. All trains therefore used the down line in both directions. This was controlled by the electric token instruments installed at Kempton Park and used on race days in peacetime. On that same date, Crystal Palace High Level branch was closed for the duration.

The destruction of one third of the City by bombing caused many businesses to move westwards, with the result that much of the peak-hour traffic shifted from the City stations to Charing Cross and Victoria. Evacuation of Government offices and those of other large employers, however, eased the rush hour loads to be carried. Holiday traffic to the South Coast shrank to negligible proportions, and special traffics which had been well catered for in peacetime, such as race traffic, disappeared altogether. On the other hand, travel by members of the armed forces, both on and off duty, was heavy.

In the autumn of 1942, a start was made on altering the suburban sets from three- to four-car units, by adding a vehicle from one of the trailer sets. This was to lead, after the war, to large scale new construction of four-car sets for suburban operation generally.

Aftermath

A fixed rental was paid by the Government to the companies for the greater part of the war, which was considerably less than the monies which the railways would have retained in the same period had they been left under private control.

The 1941 Railway Control Agreement provided for the Southern Railway to receive £6.61 million, as against the £7.1 million

Left:
4SUB units were only able to work in multiple with each other, as they had different control gear to other units. This view was taken on 4 November 1980 at the now-closed Coulsdon North station, where two recently outshopped units, No 4283 (left) and No 4677 (right) were to form the 09.40 departure calling at all stations to Victoria except Battersea Park. *Author*

Above:
November 1945 sees the exterior of Worthing station looking reasonably smart. Services uniforms are noticeable, while a Royal Mail van and taxis wait for the next down train.
Southern Railway/Author's collection

which was the standard revenue which the company would have received under the 1921 Railways Act. Collectively, these rental payments represented only half that which the companies would have earned otherwise. This would have enabled them to provide for the postwar rehabilitation of overworked assets and to pay a dividend which reflected both increased traffic and the effects of inflation. Effectively, they would then have come out of the war that much stronger.

Energetic steps towards clearing up and repairing war damage began as soon as the end of European hostilities was in sight, including the restoration of station terminal roofs where possible. As a result of the German surrender on 8 May 1945, extra trains to the coast started running from 16 June. The public was warned that lack of labour for rolling stock repairs, absence of staff still with the forces, and the large number of special trains still being run for the Government would prevent sufficient long-distance holiday services being provided. Nevertheless, the concourse at Victoria on Saturday, 28 July was accurately described as a 'seething mass'. From 09.18 to 12.00 there were 21 main line electric departures, including no less than 10 to Brighton. This works out as one main line departure every eight minutes for the best part of three hours, and it was reported that all trains were loaded to capacity. How they all got back again is another matter.

The broadcast that the Japanese war was over and that the next two days would be kept as public holidays was made at midnight on Tuesday, 14 August 1945. Unfortunately, few heard it, and most went to work as usual the following day – amid scenes of complete confusion. A similar level of train service to the coast was provided.

A considerable restoration of train services took place from 1 October 1945, and while not amounting to a full return to prewar levels, matters were improved considerably.

Although the war was now over, this by no means solved the many problems confronting the Southern Railway. Staff and material shortages as well as stringent Government controls hampered the heavy task of repairing war damage and restoring prewar services. The new Labour Government of 1945 was committed to the nationalisation of public utilities, and this included transport, coalmines and electricity.

From the traffic point of view, there would be no resumption of the intensive suburban housing development which was such a feature of the period between the two wars, and for many years no major scheme for rebuilding the devastated area of the City would be permitted. History repeated itself; the shortening of the working hours compressed the rush hour traffic into still shorter periods, albeit that the move towards a five-day week slowly eased the midday pressure on Saturdays. For some time to come, travel by members of the services would be heavy, while the public, after six years of blackout and wartime restrictions, was only too ready to resume peacetime travel habits.

Little or no additions had been made to the country's electricity supply system during the war and serious overloading was apt to occur with the return to peacetime conditions. This was especially so in severe weather, which was likely to lead to reduced supplies. The traction side of the electrified lines was not greatly affected, but the working of colour-light signals was often upset by frequency variations and special equipment had to be installed to obviate this.

From 7 January 1946, some eating facilities were restored on trains. The Crystal Palace High Level service was reinstated on 4 March as a shuttle train from Nunhead. Although demand was at an abnormally high level, the company was ill equipped to deal with this. Rolling stock numbers were down by $3\frac{1}{2}$% and the few vehicles which it had been possible to build in 1945 were of a larger capacity suburban design, which it was hoped would go some way towards easing the rush hour problem. Speed restrictions were common and a substantial track mileage was renewed in 1945, the Chairman telling the annual meeting that in 1946 it was hoped to renew a number of bridges and to begin restoring war-damaged stations. Plans had also been prepared for further electrification and for the reconstruction of many stations. The company was in a position to repay the Government loan made in 1935 which had been used for extending the electrified network, although repayment was not due until 1952.

Another sign of peace was that race meetings were resumed in 1946. On Easter Monday, 26 April, about 100,000 people were present at Hurst Park, and a 10-minute service of special trains to Hampton Court was provided from Waterloo. Derby Day at Epsom was Wednesday, 5 June, with services from London leaving as follows over the three hours from 9am to 12 noon:

- Charing Cross to Tattenham Corner
  18 trains
- Cannon Street to Tattenham Corner
  5 trains
- London Bridge to Tattenham Corner
  11 trains
- Victoria to Epsom Downs
  26 trains

These were in addition to the services provided to Epsom, from which a special bus service was provided for the mile or so up the hill to the racecourse.

Erection of a new signal cabin at Blackfriars and the restoration of full colour-light signalling began in January 1946, and the full installation being commissioned on Sunday, 11 August. The four-aspect signals had sidelights and junction indicators, and floodlit ground signals were provided. This enabled the terminal platforms at Blackfriars to be reinstated.

Pullman cars were restored to Central Section trains from 6 May, having been removed on 22 May 1942 together with most other restaurant and buffet facilities. The first stage of restoration of Portsmouth Harbour was completed on 1 June 1946, when two platforms were brought into use, with colour-light signalling and a new signalbox containing a 47-lever frame.

More Electrification?

Following the visit of a delegation to the United States, it was announced in November 1946 that the Board had approved a scheme to convert all lines east of Portsmouth to electric and diesel-electric traction. In many ways, this was what was to happen eventually, although after many years in some cases. What the Southern Railway undoubtedly did was to set out the main elements of what was to become the two phases of the Kent Coast electrification schemes. These matured in 1959 and 1962 respectively.

Fig 8.4 sets out the 1946 scheme, and also the fate of each of the proposals.

The estimated cost of this programme was £15 million. If labour and materials were available, it was hoped to begin work in about

six months and it would be completed by 1955. Sixty substations would be required, with a main control room expected to be at Canterbury. Multiple-unit trains would work about 70% of the mileage on the Eastern Section, while electric locomotives would haul the Continental boat trains and freight services between the principal marshalling yards. Diesel-electric traction would be used on the lines not to be electrified, as well as for local freights and for shunting on the electrified sections.

That however was for the future. What did take place in the short term was the electrification on 16 July 1947 of the (very) short Newhaven Marine branch of a mere 13 chains; this allowed the boat trains for the

service to Dieppe to be hauled electrically to and from Victoria. The usual load was 10 corridor coaches with a buffet car and two utility vans, about 370 tons tare.

Fuel Shortages

From early 1947, the weather was the worst which had been experienced for many years. Heavy snowfalls, severe gales and occasional fogs were accompanied by long spells in which the day temperatures rose little above freezing point and the nights were bitterly cold. At midnight on 29 January, a temperature of -6°F was recorded in Three Bridges Control Room. A short time before, some old trailer coaches had been fitted with equipment for spreading warm oil on the

Below:
One of the new steel 4SUB units completed at Eastleigh in 1941, the 'Sheba' stock. It was photographed on 5 May 1945. An eight-car formation would seat 912, equivalent to 76 compartments each with 12 seats. The Southern was certainly learning how to pack people in.
Southern Railway/Author's collection

Fig 8.4: Southern Railway Electrification Schemes, November 1946

The following sections were to be electrified:	Final Outcome
Gillingham-Faversham-Ramsgate	Kent Coast phase 1, 1959
Faversham-Dover	Kent Coast phase 1, 1959
Sevenoaks-Tonbridge-Ashford-Folkestone-Dover-Deal-Ramsgate	Kent Coast phase 2, 1962
Maidstone East-Ashford	Kent Coast phase 2, 1962
Maidstone West-Paddock Wood	Kent Coast phase 2, 1962
Ashford-Canterbury West-Ramsgate	Kent Coast phase 2, 1962
Tonbridge-West St Leonards	Hastings scheme, 1986
Crowhurst-Bexhill West	Closed, 1964
Christ's Hospital-Steyning-Shoreham by Sea	Closed, 1966
South Croydon-Oxted-East Grinstead	East Grinstead scheme, 1987
East Grinstead-Horsted Keynes	Closed, 1958

conductor rail to counteract freezing. These vehicles were coupled between electric units and sent on a tour of the lines in an area. Apparently they did good work in keeping electric services running.

The fuel position however was much more serious. Blizzards in colliery areas prevented miners from getting to work and disrupted rail transport of coal from the pits. Ships carrying coal to London were kept in port by severe gales. Early in February, the Southern had only a week's supply of coal in hand for all purposes, including electricity generation, and on 10 February the Government stopped the supply of electricity to industry over a wide area. On 5 and 11 February, a large number of suburban trains were withdrawn, with a further batch cut on the 15th. On 4 March a severe gale with rain turned into a blizzard and then froze, causing widespread delays. The 16.25 nonstop from Brighton took over eight hours to reach Victoria, and in some cases motormen in the country areas stopped at stations and waited for the weather to moderate.

A thaw started on 8 March and turned to heavy rain on the 10th. The Sidcup line was flooded at Mottingham and a bad earthslip between Petersfield and Rowlands Castle necessitated single line working. Further heavy rain caused serious chalk falls in the deep cuttings approaching Quarry and Merstham tunnels on the 13th, blocking the Quarry line and leaving only one of the Redhill lines clear. Wholesale diversions and cancellations were necessary, and the 17.45 from London Bridge to Eastbourne was replaced by a steam train via Oxted. All lines were clear by the 17th, but the fallen material was difficult to deal with owing to its liquid and sticky state, and eventually extensive reballasting was necessary. The Staines-Windsor line was flooded and closed for several days. Owing to heavy chalk falls in cuttings between Eynsford and Shoreham (Kent) the line had to be closed, except in rush hours when traffic was worked over a single line. Normal working was more or less resumed by the end of the month, but the restricted train service remained until the fuel position improved.

Twenty-five Years of the Southern

The Southern Railway passed into history at the close of 1947, exactly a quarter of a century after the company had been created under the Grouping. The Transport Act, 1947 provided for a British Transport Commission of five members to control, on behalf of the Government, the main line railways, canals, road haulage and the London Passenger Transport Board's undertaking. For the railways, management was delegated to the Railway Executive. Provision was made in the Act for Users' Consultative Committees and a Transport Tribunal to review rates and charges.

The closing year saw some progress made towards restoration of 1939 standards, but the Chairman told the annual meeting that dwindling supplies, shortage of labour, and rigid controls from the Government were more than enough without the devastating effect of the fuel crisis. War damage was being attended to, and in 1946, 30 acres of glass in station roofs had been replaced and 65 stations renovated. Shortages of steel and other components checked the building of new stock and the repair of existing vehicles, but 127 electric train vehicles had been built. Rolling stock for suburban and holiday services would be short for some time to come. A total of 153 miles of track had been renewed, but lack of sleepers was causing some anxiety.

By October 1946, 84% of the prewar service levels had been restored. However, punctuality was not up to standard owing to arrears of maintenance and signal failures due to power supply shortcomings. Nevertheless, by midsummer, 94% of trains were on time or less than five minutes late. The Board had approved the installation of colour-light signalling from Bricklayers Arms and from Battersea Park to East Croydon and Coulsdon North, to link up with the other Brighton line installations. Four-aspect signals were provided throughout, and this mammoth task was completed in five stages between 1950 and 1955. Most of the signals were of the automatic or semi-automatic varieties, which display a proceed aspect whenever it was safe to do so. The system assumed that all trains would perform the same set of predetermined movements, unless the signalman intervened at a semi-automatic or fully controlled signal to set up another route. Such systems largely run themselves, leaving the signalman to control by exception.

The performance of the last of the services to be electrified before World War 2 was just as encouraging as had been experienced previously. In a British Transport Commission report on electrification in 1951, the following comparisons were offered of passenger numbers before electrification and those in 1947 (see Fig 8.5).

The BTC report added, cautiously, 'the increases in traffic quoted in these examples are not solely attributable to electrification, but are an indication of the general stimulation of traffic which follows conversion to electric traction'. Quite so, but there would have been a few questions asked

if the results had gone the other way.

The Southern never tried to outshine others in the speed stakes; the *Railway Handbook* for 1938–9 lists the fastest scheduled runs in Britain for 1937, being all those above 60mph, and the Southern does not appear at all. (It might be added that the LNER was at the top of the list, at 71.9mph between King's Cross and York.) But this did not make the company's approach unsuccessful. Sir Herbert Walker, the Southern's general manager from 1924 to 1937 died in 1949, and a quote from his obituary in The Times is apposite here:

'He had seen what electrification could do…Eastbourne, Hastings, Worthing, Seaford, Bognor, and finally Portsmouth, were swept into the new timetables, and with every addition traffic and receipts soared, proving anew *that railways could serve the public if they gave what the public wanted* (author's italics). And here lay one of Walker's gifts. He knew what the public wanted…and he had the vision and the will to scrap old ways and ideas to make these things possible…'

Speed is only one attribute of a service; quality embraces also matters such as simplicity in use, reliability, frequency and dependability. Above all, a railway depends upon its staff. In 1937, the Southern's attitude to the public was perhaps embodied in its instructions to its employees. The three key words were: Safety, Courtesy and Care. That for courtesy read as follows:

'Endeavour to make our customers satisfied by doing your utmost to ascertain their wants, by giving them all the help you can in a pleasant manner, and by giving service that will make them wish to use the Railway again. Regard the Railway as a shop, and yourself as its Salesman.'

'The Southern Railway is a fine undertaking – help to make it even better.'

As one of its final acts, the Southern Railway renumbered, consecutively, the platforms at Clapham Junction. There were 17 of them, numbered from the north, and this took effect on 16 November 1947. This was carried out as part of an extensive renovation. At the same time, 160 signboards were replaced by a new pattern in green and white vitreous enamel. Signing can be quite large scale work and correspondingly costly.

Fig 8.5: Passenger Journeys Compared, Before Electrification and in 1947				
Date Electrified	Route	Passenger Journeys (Millions)		Growth
4 July 1937	Portsmouth and Alton, No 1	3.00 (1936/7)	7.25 (1947)	x 2.4
3 July 1938	Portsmouth via Horsham, No 2	3.75 (1937/8)	8.50 (1947)	x 2.3
2 July 1939	Reading and Camberley	1.50 (1938)	4.75 (1947)	x 3.2
2 July 1939	Maidstone and Gillingham	4.75 (1938)	8.75 (1947)	x 1.8

9. Unfinished Business

The formation of the British Transport Commission offered an opportunity to review the electrification systems in use in Britain, and to firm up on a future policy. This was, in part, a rerun of the Railway Electrification Committee (the Pringle Committee) report of 1927; it is discussed here in the light which it sheds on the Southern system as it then existed. The resulting report 'Electrification of Railways' was published by the BTC in 1951.

First, the Southern's third rail scheme dwarfed all the others then in existence in Britain, and a motley collection they were (Fig 9.1).

With the exception of the Manchester-Sheffield/Wath electrification, which was not to be completed for another two years, the emphasis was on the relatively short distance suburban traffics. Electrification elsewhere had made little progress; although the Pringle Committee's preferred 1,500V dc overhead system had been adopted for Altrincham (1931), Shenfield (1949) and Wath, it was only on the Southern that concerted efforts had been made in the intervening years, as we have already seen. What was it like to travel on the Southern?

The Brighton Line in the 1950s

Imagine Angmering, a wayside station on the Coastway line 15 miles 44 chains from Brighton, the best part of half a century ago.

> 'The 1950s were for the Southern mainly a period of rehabilitation and consolidation after the war.'
>
> *H. P. White*

Above:
The Elmers End-Sanderstead shuttle is formed of a two-car BR design 2EPB set No 5770 in July 1978. Viewed from the south end of Sanderstead station, the unit has been given clearance to proceed to the crossover to enable it to return to the up platform on the left. At the time, this was the only electric service at this station. *Author*

It is a cold, clear but dark November evening in 1955, shortly after 6pm. The Southdown No 31 bus, from Portsmouth to Brighton, drops its passengers at the bus stop on the south side of the railway, where the double-decker's route turns right to avoid using the gated level crossing.

Those wanting the London-bound train walk over the crossing to get to the up side, and into the 1848 station via the booking hall. Lighting is adequate but hardly bright. On the platforms, the light bulbs inside their glass globes hang from their concrete posts. Those heading for Victoria walk up the platform, perhaps as far as the concrete footbridge, so as

Fig 9.1: Electrification on British Railways, 1951, Excluding Lines operated by LTE

Scheme	Voltage	System	Route Miles	EMU Vehicles
Southern Region	660V dc	third rail	720	3,289
Manchester-Sheffield/Wath*	1,500V dc	overhead	75	24
Newcastle-South Shields/Tynemouth	630V dc	third rail	42	172
Euston-Watford, North London line	630V dc	fourth rail	38	326
Liverpool-Southport/Ormskirk	630V dc	third rail	37½	182
Liverpool Street-Shenfield	1,500V dc	overhead	23	276
Manchester-Bury-Holcombe Brook	1,200V dc	third rail	14	66
Wirral lines	650V dc	third rail	11	53
Manchester-Altrincham	1,500V dc	overhead	9	76
Lancaster-Morecambe-Heysham	6.6kV ac	overhead	9	5
Mersey Railway	650V dc	fourth rail	5	78
Total, all schemes			983½	4,547
Southern Region percentage			73%	72%
* Under construction				

to be nearer the exit at their destination. While we wait, there is time to marvel at the mountains of boxed flowers and other market garden produce on a fleet of trolleys. These are from the local nurseries, and will shortly start their journey to London's Covent Garden wholesale market by train.

There is a distant crash as the crossing gates are closed against their stops by the signalman and the semaphore clears for a down stopping train. This consists of a pair of well-filled 2BIL units, although the heavily steamed up windows make it difficult to see much of the interior. The sound of doors being slammed confirms that the unseen passengers have alighted, and with the blowing of a guard's whistle the train is shortly on its way to Littlehampton.

The gates open but briefly for road traffic, before being shut again for the up service. Displaying its 16 headcode, 6PUL unit No 3004 arrives with the train for Victoria. By now about 30 people have gathered along the platform, for a service calling at Goring-by-Sea, Durrington-on-Sea (why the difference?), West Worthing, Worthing Central, Hove, Haywards Heath and East Croydon.

A young lad and his mother join the leading driving motor saloon brake third, with its panelled woodwork and dark red upholstery. These trains had the unusual feature of a narrow gangway for public use from side to side of the first vehicle, immediately behind the van accommodation. This had no windows to the outside world other than those in the droplights. A sliding door led to the saloon.

This was an ideal private place to spend the journey; what might now be termed as very modest lighting standards meant that a good view could be had of the passing scene. The calling-on arm at Worthing Central sees the train signalled into the up loop, where the buffers touch with the waiting unit, and some slight heaving to and fro takes place before the driver of what is now a 12-car train does his brake test and is ready to depart.

The best parts of the run come after leaving Hove, slowly rounding the tunnelled Cliftonville Spur to Preston Park and then rapidly picking up speed. The train rattles through Clayton Tunnel and sways over Keymer Junction to the south of Wivelsfield, where the line from Lewes joins, and then it comes to a stand at a brightly lit Haywards Heath.

After that, it is right away for an exhilarating nonstop ride to East Croydon – $27\frac{1}{2}$ miles in 32 minutes, or a breathtaking $51\frac{1}{2}$mph! The lights of the train can be picked out on the ground far below as it crosses the quarter-mile-long Ouse Valley Viaduct, then it is on through Balcombe station before reaching the tunnel of the same name. The four-track section starts soon afterwards, with the slow lines on the west side of the formation and the fast lines to the east. There might be a steam-hauled local for East Grinstead in the down side bay at Three Bridges, but there is no time for more than a glimpse. The dubious riding qualities of these saloons suggest we are travelling faster than we really are.

The train swings to the right to avoid Redhill, and on via the Quarry line. The deep cutting sides make it seem really dark, although this is relieved by the whiteness of the North Downs chalk. At Star Bridge the Quarry line crosses over the slow lines, and the latter become prominent as the train passes through Purley and its junctions for the Caterham and Tattenham Corner branches. South Croydon brings in the line from Oxted, and the train slows for the busy East Croydon stop.

Once through the complex junctions to Selhurst, a succession of local trains may be observed. On the slow lines they might be, but their 4SUB units still show a good turn of

speed in between stops as we overtake them, one by one. One can guess how far in front the next one is by keeping an eye on the colour lights. Our speed is now dropping, as we lumber through Clapham Junction. We pass Battersea Power Station before reaching Grosvenor Bridge over the Thames and the final descent of the bank into Victoria, where we come to a punctual stand in Platform 15. The overall journey time has been 1 hour 38 minutes for the 66 miles, at an average of 40mph, including the stops as described.

Suburban Woes, the 4DD, 4001-2

Those, however, were the express operations. What was happening in the suburban area? Rebuilding of the war-damaged Elephant & Castle station started in 1948, while late evening and Sunday services began more nearly to resemble their 1939 counterparts. But it was becoming more difficult to accommodate the traffic which was now on offer. Or, perhaps, demanding to be carried. For some time, complaints had been made of overcrowding on rush hour services from Charing Cross, and a press photograph was published which purported to show 26 people standing in a guard's compartment. Although the introduction of six-per-side compartment vehicles was easing the situation, complaints persisted and the matter was raised in the House of Commons. Speaking at Lewisham in April 1948, the Minister's Parliamentary Secretary hinted that double-deck trains might be the answer for South East London, and the Southern Region were pursuing this.

Two four-car double-deck units designed by O. V. S. Bulleid emerged from Lancing late in 1949, although two lots of modifications meant that full service running did not start until 6 January 1950. These were not double-deck in the true sense, but with an arrangement of compartments at high and low level, the high level ones being reached from stairs in the centre of the low level ones. Seating in the standard length eight-car train was 1,016, to which could be added 88 tip-up seats, making 1,060 in total. This compared with 772 or thereabouts in the 4SUB units then coming off the production line. On the face of it, a large increase in the seating capacity was a very worthwhile benefit; was this to be the style of the future?

The answer turned out to be no. For a start, restricted clearances required the windows on the upper floors to be fixed, and although pressure ventilation was fitted, the results were said to be unbearably stuffy. Secondly, the trains themselves were higher than standard sets, and this restricted their use to between Charing Cross or Cannon

Street and Gravesend. While clearances could be increased on other routes to cope, this can be a costly exercise, as those installing 25kV electrification elsewhere have found.

Far more important, though, was that the new trains failed to do the job for which they were designed. To carry an extra 43% of passengers is fine, but there was no corresponding increase in the number of doors. The net result was that standard station stop times were massively exceeded, and this slowed the succeeding services. Each train may carry more, but if the result is that you can run only a reduced frequency service, the net gain may be quite small. Given also the other difficulties mentioned, the conclusion that no more such trains would be built would have come as little surprise when it was announced in December 1950. The original pair of units remained in service, however,

until they were withdrawn on 1 October 1971.

If increasing the capacity of a train by adding high level compartments did not work, the main alternative approach was to lengthen trains. The South Eastern, in common with the rest of the suburban areas, was able to take a maximum of eight cars. The greatest train length possible is determined fairly obviously by the length of platforms, but also by the length of loop lines serving

them, the ability of stations and passageways to cope, the placing of signals and their spacing, and depot stabling, inspection and repair facilities. If nothing else, two additional cars on each eight-car train raised the stabling requirement by a straight 25%. It should also be recognised that it is virtually unworkable to reassemble trains into 10 cars only as they leave depots, so some increase in siding lengths was also required.

And so it was concluded, and a four-stage plan for running 10-car trains on the Eastern Section was produced. The trains were to consist of two four-car units coupled to a two-car unit, providing a total of 958 seats in an overall length of about 649ft. The scope of work was not unlike that of the original electrification of the 1920s; sample works undertaken were:

- Extending platform lengths and altering the track approaches at Charing Cross.
- Removing the Platform 5 up loop at London Bridge to allow Platform 4 to be lengthened.
- Retaining walls erected at St Johns and at Blackheath.

- Rebuilding the war-damaged station at Charlton.
- Overbridge rebuilt at Bexleyheath.
- New Eltham platform extension required removal of the signal cabin so colour-light signals could be installed and sidings controlled from a ground frame released electrically from Sidcup.
- Five new berthing sidings laid in at Slade Green depot, inspection shed extended 82ft and new track connections made.
- Four up side berthing sidings extended at Dartford, No 1 signal cabin at Dartford abolished and signal control transferred to No 2 box; all lines track circuited.

The 10-car scheme was brought into use in stages between 1954 and 1957.

Also required was additional power supply capacity for longer and more frequent trains. The power stations at both Deptford and Durnsford Road were in need of replacement, while the rotary converter substations, which needed an attendant on site, were nearing the end of their economic life. The Railway Executive approved a scheme to replace the existing power supply equipment with 50Hz equipment, with remotely controlled rectifier substations.

The Durnsford Road establishment would not be replaced and the whole of the current required would be taken from the British Electricity Authority, whose Deptford

generating station had been re-equipped for that purpose. Feeder cables from the latter would be taken to 66kV-33kV outdoor transformers at Nunhead, Lewisham, Brockley and South Bermondsey. Feeders from other BEA generating stations, at 33kV, would be taken to supply points at Northfleet, Wimbledon, Leatherhead and Croydon. From these points a cable network would serve the railway substations. These cables would be laid in concrete ducts, buried in the ground or taken across bridges in asbestos concrete tubing. Of the 71 substations, 45 would be new, 24 located in existing buildings and two in arches. The new substations consisted of a brick building containing from one to five 2,500kW mercury-arc rectifiers and the necessary switchgear, with an outdoor transformer. Their equipment provided for the live rail voltage to be raised to 750V if necessary in the future. The three control rooms at Raynes Park, Lewisham and Selhurst came into operation between 1954 and 1955.

Despite the growth which this suggests, it was not uniform across the Southern's territory. Two service reductions early in the life of the nationalised railway both paved the way to future closures. Thus, on Sundays from 3 October 1948, the Crystal Palace High Level branch was closed, while on 26 September 1949, the weekday off-peak trains from Cannon Street to Sanderstead were withdrawn. Four trains an hour ran from Charing Cross to Hayes, with alternate trains having connections at Elmers End, to Addiscombe and Sanderstead.

Rolling Stock Design

What of the passenger accommodation? The Southern had long followed the approach of maximum seating and maximum accessibility for its suburban passengers, which resulted in the production of straight through compartments with a slam door each side. If that was one's aim, so be it, but there were alternative approaches.

The use of some form of internal gangway between compartments makes it possible for passengers to distribute themselves more equally within the vehicle, and to some extent the possibilities are enhanced by gangways between vehicles. Both however have their drawbacks; 10 compartments at six-per-side gives 120 seats; use a semi-saloon and the seats go down to 102. More conventional gangwayed vehicles cut the accommodation even further, but other considerations are seat spacing and seat pitch. The former revolve around the argument as to whether a three+gangway+two (3+2) layout is acceptable, or whether one can afford the relative luxury of 2+2. Seat pitch refers to the knee room; crudely, the tighter you make it, the more seats you can cram in.

Another point concerns passengers who have to stand, or choose to do so. The latter include those travelling short distances, for instance between Charing Cross and Waterloo East only, for access to trains from Waterloo main line station. Standing is not very comfortable in open saloons, but it is downright uncomfortable for everybody – seated or standing – in straight through compartments. Pity, too, shorter people or children, who when standing are unable to reach a luggage rack and thus have absolutely nothing solid within reach on which they can steady themselves.

While gangways have an operational advantage in that they permit ticket issue and inspection while the train is on the move, they also allow passengers access to toilets and to buffet cars, if provided. In terms of more recent developments, they also permit refreshment trolleys to perambulate the length of a train if doorway dimensions and other obstructions allow. However, such niceties are of minimal value in the short-distance suburban market. It is though a consideration that the capital cost of providing full gangways, their maintenance, and the seating forgone, need to have some positive aim in mind before they can or perhaps

should be justified. The longer the passenger journeys undertaken, the more likely it is that such benefits can be demonstrated.

There is also another approach, and that is the use of powered external sliding doors. While other British systems pursued these, notably on the Wirral services in Merseyside and then on the 1949 Shenfield electrification, they were totally ignored by the Southern. Again, space taken up by doors cannot be used for seats. While the more doors that are provided makes access and egress faster, the number of seats diminishes as a result. Power doors only became part of the Southern repertoire with the delivery of the Class 508 units, but this was not until the 1980s.

The Southern Region's rolling stock procurement policy of the period resulted in three types of electric and, later, diesel-electric units:

- A high-density suburban layout with open saloons and some compartments, no gangways between vehicles and no toilets.
- An outer-suburban layout basically similar but with some first class compartments with side corridor access and toilet facilities, but no gangways between vehicles.
- An express passenger layout with open saloons and compartments with side corridor access, toilet facilities and in some cases buffet and bar facilities; fully gangwayed throughout, including the driving ends.

Below:
The repair shop at Chart Leacon, Ashford, sees the body of a driving motor of 4EPB No 5320 being lifted on to its bogies on 5 September 1961. On the right is 4CEP unit No 7140. Photographically, all-green livery is little more appealing than all-over blue. *Author's collection*

Above:
A pair of 4EPB units led by No 5041 arrive at Grove Park with an up service from Orpington to Charing Cross on 30 April 1984. These trains were improved considerably by the application of blue and grey instead of all-blue livery. *Author*

Right:
Until its abolition, the signalbox at Epsom was one of the more curious railway sights to be seen in the Home Counties. A Waterloo-Horsham service leaves Epsom in January 1978, with SR-design 4EPB set No 5122. *Author*

The future rolling stock basis was the Mk 1 locomotive-hauled coach design of 1951. Its features included the all-steel body and roof panel, a similar curved side panel to that already in use on the Southern to make the maximum use of the width available, a separate steel underframe and, for express stock, buckeye couplers and Pullman-type gangway connections. All bodyside access doors opened outwards and were identical at a standard 1ft 11½in width. Southern versions were built on the longer 63ft 5in underframes, although a derivative of the Southern design, as used by the London Midland Region on the Broad Street-Richmond services, was built on the shorter 56ft 11in version, due to tighter clearances. Initially, bogies were to a single bolster leaf-spring design, but this proved thoroughly disappointing since they were rough riding at speed once they began to wear. Modification eventually made the ride passable, but these bogies mostly had to be endured by passengers travelling on the suburban stock until the end of its days. The express stock was favoured with the cast-steel frame coil-spring Commonwealth bogie, which performed well but was a ton or so heavier and more costly to construct.

The whole episode, which was mirrored in the locomotive-hauled stock, resulted in serious research into the whole field of bogie dynamics and the emergence of new British Railways designs. These took the form of the B4/B5 bogies, which were coil-spring fabricated designs. The variations were accounted for by the load which they were expected to carry, and the limitations imposed by the third rail on the Southern in terms of clearances. These bogies weighed in at a little over 5 tons each, compared with 6.75 tons for the Commonwealth design. They were applied to all subsequent deliveries until the 1980s.

Vehicles are classified in terms of their original number series and descriptions.

4EPB, 5001-260

In 1951, the first of a new series of four-car suburban units was built at Eastleigh, although they conformed to Southern Railway design standards. Dimensions and seating were standard, and the whole weighed in at 136 tons. English Electric equipment included 2x250hp EE507 traction motors and electro-pneumatic control gear in each end vehicle. Current for lighting and control purposes was taken from a 70V motor-generator and battery mounted below the motor coaches. Electro-pneumatic brakes (EPB) were fitted in addition to the Westinghouse air brakes, and the motorman's controls and instruments grouped into a desk. Roller blind indicators were installed, replacing the metal stencils which were put in place manually. Buckeye couplings were provided, and the control cables and brake hoses placed so that coupling and uncoupling could be done without going between the cars at ground level. Duplicate connections were placed on each side of the unit so that the ability to do this did not depend upon the side of the train on which the platform was situated. A rubbing plate at buffer beam level allowed them to run with Pullman gangwayed stock, but of course there was no connection for passenger use. These were 75mph units with a balancing speed of 63mph; they had an acceleration rate of 1 mile/h/sec up to 27mph.

They were used primarily on the Eastern Section as part of the 10-car project, but also on the Central Section. Later classified Class 415/1, they were refurbished at the end of the 1970s and became Class 415/4. One substantial change was the conversion of the (one) compartment vehicle into a semi-open saloon layout.

2EPB, 5701-79

The first of the two-coach motor sets, No 5701, nominally anyway for use in 10-car trains, appeared from Eastleigh in 1953. These were in most respects similar to their 4EPB counterparts, and the driving motors were effectively identical. However, the driving trailers comprised a half-open saloon and half compartment layout. Overall, this produced the same proportion of accommodation of each type as in their 4EPB counterparts!

Where these units differed was in their being based on British Railways designs, although the distinctions were minimal. Thus there was now no small window (quarter-light) above the droplights in the doors, and gutters and rainstrips were more prominent. They were in fact a modified version of the BR loco-hauled suburban Mk 1 coach, albeit with ends based on main line stock. These were created by the simple expedient of having holes cut into them for a couple of cab windows.

The first of these sets was sent to the South London line to replace the side-gangway sets which had been working there since ac days in 1909. The last of these was withdrawn in September 1954, when the 2EPBs assumed full control. They were also used on the Wimbledon-West Croydon route, and the shuttle services from Elmers End to Addiscombe and Sanderstead. These units became TOPS Class 416/2, and refurbished versions Class 416/4.

The large numbers of suburban units constructed for the Southern over the years contain many minor variations. This is due, in part, to the policy of rebuilding earlier stock, but also to the vast numbers needed to run an operation of this size. Electric trains are long lasting, since there is no vibrating diesel engine. Provided body corrosion and similar problems can be kept at bay, their life can in theory be extended time and again. How acceptable elderly designs are to passengers who have a choice of their means and frequency of travel is another matter. Expectations are one thing, but the reality is

that few of the Southern's commuters had — or have — any real choice in the matter.

The remainder of the Mk 1 versions of suburban stock are therefore discussed here. In later years, there were a number of re-formations, not the least as a result of the disbandment. This enabled 'new' four-car units to be created, for instance. New ideas also surrounded the diesel-electric units, and are mentioned in that context. The last of these electric vehicles to remain in front line revenue-earning service, until 2001, were the 10 driving motor brake second opens, used on 'Gatwick Express' trains. These started life in 1959 as the powered part of 2HAP units and had their passenger accommodation stripped out for use as luggage accommodation, but also so they could fulfil a role as a powered leading vehicle on the 'Gatwick Express' push-pull operation. For this, they were reclassified Class 489, BR luggage van. This freed up the same number of driving trailer composites. A few remain in non-passenger-carrying roles such as on Sandite duties for Railtrack.

4EPB, 5301-70

This further build did not appear until 1960, but it incorporated the redesign first seen with the 2EPB vehicles already described. Compartment accommodation was retained in half of each of the two intermediate trailers. Somehow the Southern had the

persistent ability to appear to be behind the rest of the world. Another anachronism was the continued installation of unshaded tungsten light bulbs; fluorescent strip lights were still many years away.

On a brighter note, it was on one of these units that the B5(S) bogies were first trialled, with very satisfactory results. Classified under TOPS as Class 415/3, and then as updated and renumbered from 1982 as Class 415/6, these units were fitted with electro-pneumatic camshaft control, but were able to work in multiple with earlier stock. An economy measure saw the motor-generators being confined to one of the driving motor vehicles only. These trains were to be found principally on the South Eastern, although later batches were used on South Western services.

2HAP, 5601-36

These were rebuilds on the 2NOL underframes for outer-suburban and semi-fast duties; as a result they had express gear ratios which gave them a top speed of 90mph. They were built in 1957/58 and were a 'modern' version of the prewar 2HAL units with EP brakes. The units as built were formed of a driving motor brake second saloon and a driving trailer composite. The latter had an internal side corridor. There were three first class compartments at the lavatory end and five second class. This gave 126 second class and 18 first class seats in total.

They were constructed to an outer-suburban specification for the Kent Coast electrification, but their subsequent transfer to South Western services saw them downgraded to second class only and the lavatory locked out of use. Later still, in 1970, they became part of the Coastway operation centring on Brighton. Lo and behold, first class was restored and the lavatories unlocked. It was but a short respite, and these Class 418/1 units were downgraded again in 1976 for use on Central Division London suburban services before withdrawal.

2NOP, 5651-84

These were Southern Railway design units, although they were late on the scene. Built at Eastleigh from 1959, they were the final manifestation of old underframes, again from the withdrawn 2NOL units of 1935/36. The 'P' addition refers to the EP brake, but they later became 2EPBs.

As such, they were similar to the original 4EPB vehicles, with both the end cars fitted with the semi-saloon arrangement. 'Semi' in the title reflects the fact that there was a central partition dividing the whole into two open saloons of approximately equal size. These units were built for the Windsor lines of the Western Section.

Following a 1979 refurbishment in which Class 416/1 became Class 416/3, they were renumbered to the 63xx series and found

alternative work on the Central Section. The two saloons on the driving trailer second were connected, and this gave them some scope to be used on the North London line services. Window bars were fitted to units Nos 6313-6328 and they became the providers of the newly electrified extension through to North Woolwich. They remained on the Southern as an operating base and for maintenance purposes.

They were replaced on the North London by Class 313 units, and subsequently large sections of the third rail were removed eastwards from Acton Central and replaced by 25kV ac overhead. On this the dual-voltage Class 313s have no problem, but it does create the curious result of a section of third rail network, on what was once the Eastern Region, being totally disconnected from other third rail operations.

2EPB, 5781-95

This small group of 15 units was built for use on South Tyneside in 1954/5, where their stay was cut short by the decision to de-electrify that service. They were built at Eastleigh as a

Below:
The South Tyneside 2EPB sets, for that is what they were in reality, spent by far the largest part of their lives south of the Thames. Unit No 5785 heads a Hounslow Loop service from Waterloo via Brentford as it passes the ornate Barnes station on 1 March 1980. Small features distinguished these EPB units from others, one such being the small, two-character headcode panel. *Author*

slight variation on the 2EPB sets described earlier, the principal change being the reduction in seating bays by one to enable greater van space to be provided. Destination blinds were fitted and a series of marker lights, which were quickly removed and replaced with headcode blinds when transfer to the Southern became the only sensible option. These Class 416/2 EMUs were used on less busy routes on the South Western and Central Divisions.

2HAP, 6001-173

These units had similar accommodation to the 5601-36 style 2HAP units, but were built new to British Railways designs. They were introduced on South Eastern services in Kent from 1957, but there was a subtle difference in the design of the driving trailer composite. The three first class compartments remained much as before, but the short corridor led to a much smaller lavatory in the centre of the vehicle, to which they had exclusive access. Second class passengers had a saloon rather than compartments and their own lavatory in the 'other half' of that part of the centre of the vehicle. As with the former NOL-based 2HAPs, there were no lavatories at all if you were in the other vehicle.

The result of this redesign was that the number of first class seats increased by one, but the number of second class seats was exactly the same. Why, one wonders, did anyone bother? The later batches in this

group, from No 6147 onwards, were given Commonwealth bogies from new.

These units too were later declassified to second class only into the 59xx number series and then reclassified before final withdrawal. They were contained within TOPS Class 414 with various suffixes.

The 1955 Modernisation Plan

The 1955 plan rehearsed the case for electrification as it then stood, and it must be borne in mind that steam traction, then, was far from dead. New steam locomotives were to be built for a further five years, and the first of the Southern's rebuilt Bulleid Pacifics would not appear for another year.

Steam, said the Plan, had the virtues of low first cost, simplicity, robustness and long life. Against it was the shortage of suitable coal, dirtiness, air pollution and the lack of acceleration. It was also a prodigious user of labour for what were, essentially, unattractive jobs.

Electricity was seen as the ideal, provided the traffic was sufficiently heavy to cover the higher fixed costs. It was also reliable and clean, with good acceleration. The disadvantage was the associated engineering work on the infrastructure, which was complex, took up considerable planning time, and some service disruption during its execution. That the work was rather less complex with the dc third rail, particularly in the matter of clearances, was not stated.

A 'further consideration', said the Plan, was that 'in some cases in the past, the riding qualities of electric multiple-unit stock have not equalled those of modern vehicles hauled by a separate locomotive'. Despite the pious hope then expressed for an improvement, this problem was not to be solved for some time.

Diesel traction was seen as the halfway house, with some of the same advantages but to a lesser extent, but also with the ability to be introduced quickly with little civil or signalling work. Diesel traction could also be redeployed elsewhere. What, then, was proposed for the Southern? The Plan was quite specific, and is quoted verbatim:

'On the Southern Region, the greatest early advantage will be secured by employing diesel locomotives to replace steam services between Waterloo and Exeter, and Waterloo, Southampton, Bournemouth and Weymouth.'

Extensions of Southern Region Electrification

'It has always been the intention that, as soon as circumstances permit, all the main routes of the Southern Region east of a line drawn from Reading to Portsmouth should be electrified. This will extend to the coast the electrified zone which now terminates at Gillingham, Maidstone and Sevenoaks, and carry the electric train services to Ramsgate, Dover, Folkestone and (via Ashford) to Hastings. In conjunction with the diesel services to be

introduced, this will effect the elimination of steam traction from all the lines of the Southern Region in the area mentioned.

'This programme will entail electrifying about 250 route miles of line at a cost of approximately £25 million for the fixed equipment.'

Elsewhere, there would be the use of diesel multiple-units for secondary and cross-country routes, and branch lines. And so, more or less, it came to pass. Electrification of the Kent Coast assumed priority; the plans for this scheme had long been drawn up, and implementation was thus relatively straightforward. The British Transport Commission approved the complete scheme in February 1956.

On 3 June 1956, third class travel was finally abolished in Britain as part of a European initiative, and it became second class.

Gatwick, London's Second Airport

The name Gatwick is today associated firmly with the airport of the same name, but it was not always so. The map of the former LBSCR system which is still displayed at Victoria (if you look carefully enough) shows in large type Horley and Three Bridges, but a smaller and thus relatively insignificant station in between for the Sussex village of Gatwick.

There were once two stations. Gatwick Racecourse station, at 26m 47ch from London Bridge, was opened in 1891. It was joined by Tinsley Green (27m 34ch) on 30 September 1935. Both were subsequently renamed, Tinsley Green becoming Gatwick Airport on 1 June 1936. However, it was the original 1891 station which was chosen for development, and this was completely reconstructed. Today, it is a six-platformed station on a four-track main line. It was renamed Gatwick Airport on the completion of the initial work on 28 May 1958. The former Tinsley Green station was closed and demolished.

The station was built as an integral part of the new airport terminal, and its opening actually preceded the first commercial flights by a couple of weeks. The one and only railway ticket office is within the air terminal building. As *Trains Illustrated* commented, a little sniffily, local passengers who had to make the detour 'would at least have the consolation of access to the airport restaurant and buffet'.

Of the original Gatwick Racecourse station, only the signalbox remained. The rest was all 'handsomely contemporary and lavishly lit by fluorescent tubes displaying the station's name'. The latter was then a new idea, to replace the small metal notices attached to each lighting column. It had the advantage of being thoroughly visible at night from the inside of a train.

Initially, the main train service consisted of a half-hourly Victoria-Bognor Regis service, from which the rear two-car unit was detached at Gatwick Airport. This then allowed air passengers to take their time in alighting from the train, while the rest continued south. The unit remained in the platform (Platform 2) so that arriving air passengers for London could join it. When the next up train from Bognor arrived, the whole was coupled up and set off for Victoria.

Journey time was around 40 minutes, calling at East Croydon and usually (but not always) stopping at Redhill. A weakness was the time spent by the detached unit at Gatwick, typically between 16 and 25 minutes, during which it was acting merely as an expensive waiting room. While the service arrangement had the advantage for airline passengers of having their part of the train always at the buffer stops end at Victoria, it also meant that the unit could be sited just about as far from the station entrance/exit as one could get at Gatwick. This, of course, depended on the length of the train to which it was attached.

The Southern has always been keen to exploit the possibilities for joining and splitting trains en route, and the signalling at

Gatwick Airport incorporated calling-on signals and reversible working on three platforms to facilitate such manoeuvres.

The only other trains to call at the new station were the all-stations stopping services between Brighton and, alternately, Victoria and London Bridge. It might be added that in 1958 Gatwick itself was aimed at catering only for Channel Islands traffic and later, perhaps, for some cross-Channel services.

The explosive growth of air travel soon caused the rail service to be revised, and an early response by the Southern Region was to introduce stops at Gatwick by other services. Twenty years hence in 1979, Gatwick Airport could boast ten trains an hour in each direction, with only a single Brighton fast service passing through nonstop. Nevertheless, the long-established 'expresses' from Victoria at 25 minutes past the hour (Littlehampton), 30 minutes past (Portsmouth via Horsham), 40 minutes past (Brighton), and 55 minutes past (Eastbourne/Ore), all stopped at Gatwick to pick up only in the down direction, and set down only in the up.

This was symptomatic of a much wider problem. The aim was to keep relatively short-distance passengers (Gatwick is only just over half the distance between London and Brighton) off the principal trains serving the coast. Otherwise, passengers for Worthing, Chichester and Lewes could have difficulty in finding seats and it was they who, in practical terms, paid the railway substantially more for their journeys. To some extent, it was possible to enforce this separation by the use of different platforms and in taking care of how trains were announced. However, regular travellers soon get wise to such edicts and how to circumvent them.

More difficult still is the nature of airline passengers, particularly those arriving in

Britain. After a long-haul flight, with at least their fair share of luggage, passengers tend to flop down on the nearest seat, spread their luggage liberally around them – and go to sleep. They are then less than pleased to be woken by an angry commuter joining at an intermediate station, who sees no reason why he should stand when there should be seats available, 'but they are all taken up with your junk…' Strong words were at least a possibility.

Joining and alighting times for airline passengers are also likely to be higher, which has its effects on line capacity. Departure times for trains which did pick up at Gatwick Airport were littered with codes to the effect 'Arr. 3 (or more) minutes earlier'. Again, regular domestic travellers found journey times getting longer for what they might have considered no good reason.

The VEG Era and 'Gatwick Express'

The Southern Region met this challenge in two ways. The first attempt, in 1978, was to provide more luggage accommodation in a limited number of the by now ubiquitous 4VEP units (yet to be described). This was done by substituting luggage racks for a few seats in the standard class accommodation, and the 12 units concerned were branded 'Rapid City Link – Gatwick-London' to distinguish them. Otherwise, they were in standard blue/grey livery. Numbered 7901-12, they were given the classification 4VEG, the G being for Gatwick. While this might have lessened any direct cause for fisticuffs, it addressed only part of the problem. The trains were converted back to normal VEP seating arrangements in 1983.

The second assault was the inauguration of the 'Gatwick Express' service, on 14 May 1984. The trains were formed from the Southern's own over-large fleet of Class 73 electro-diesel locomotives, surplus air-conditioned, locomotive-hauled sets of Mk 2f coaching stock displaced by the delivery of new HSTs elsewhere, and driver motor brake vehicles from 2HAP electric units. This was an economical move of which Sir Herbert Walker would have been justly proud! In this form, they lasted for 17 years until 2001, when they were replaced by the new build of Class 460 electric units for the Gatwick Express Train Operating Company.

The whole concept was made possible by the major reorganisation of the track and signalling in the junctions north of Croydon, which provided additional line capacity, plus resignalling. The aim was to complete the separation of airport and non-airport passengers, and to offer the former a much higher quality of service than could be provided in the 3+2 seating arrangement of a 4VEP.

The original 'Gatwick Express' fleet consisted of the following:

- 14 dedicated Class 73/2s with vacuum brake isolated and passed for 90mph running. The diesel engine was available, but not normally used.
- 77 coaches formed permanently into 10 two-car sets (one vehicle in each being first class) and 19 three-car sets of standard class vehicles. Respectively, these were Class 488/2 and 488/3. Conversion included a new seating layout by removing one complete bay and one lavatory in the standard class, to provide extra luggage space. In the first class, one seat and table were removed to create a wheelchair space, with again the removal of a lavatory to give more room for luggage. Electro-pneumatic brakes and also a handbrake were fitted, while the buffing gear within sets was removed.
- 10 Class 489 GLVs, converted from Class 414/3 2HAP passenger-carrying vehicles built from 1958. The conversion saw all seats removed and windows in the saloon

panelled over to provide van space. Three pairs of double doors were fitted, as in a locomotive-hauled gangwayed brake (BG) vehicle. The guard was given access to the rest of the train through the fitting of a gangway connection. These vehicles retained their third rail pick-up shoes and traction motors. The latter supplemented those in the locomotives, but the arrangement also ensured that the train did not become stranded by 'gapping', with none of the shoes anywhere on the train in contact with the conductor rail – and thus the traction current.

These trains always operated in push-pull mode, with the locomotive at the south end of the train. The luggage van was thus always nearest the barrier at Victoria. The formation was one each of Class 488/2 and 488/3 in winter, making five passenger vehicles, with an additional Class 488/3 set in the summer months offering eight vehicles. The trains were maintained at Stewarts Lane. All were painted in the then new InterCity livery of pale cream bodywork with a red stripe below window level, and a dark grey window band. The service was later to become part of the InterCity Anglia/Gatwick profit centre, which paved the way for 'Gatwick Express' to be created as a separate Train Operating Company under the much later franchising regime.

Initially, the service was operated at regular 15-minute intervals in each direction, starting at 05.30 from Victoria and 06.20 from Gatwick. Last trains were at 23.00 and 00.05 respectively. The journey time was standardised at 30 minutes nonstop. The diagramming built in 20 minutes turnround at Gatwick and 25 minutes at Victoria to cope with luggage, making a complete cycle of 1³/₄ hours. The service thus required seven trains to operate it, and there would always be at least one train stationary at each terminal. Customers might thus always expect to be able to board immediately.

Kent Coast Phase 1

In terms of new electrification, this covered in effect all lines east of Gillingham:

- The route along the Kent Coast to Margate, and to Ramsgate for access to the depot.
- The route from Faversham to Canterbury East and Dover.
- The branch from Sittingbourne to Sheerness-on-Sea.

This made a total of 78 route miles. The Chatham main line was thought to be a very suitable electrification candidate, as much of it was steeply graded at 1 in 100 or so with

Southern Electrics for the Kent Coast

Start June 15!

The Southern proudly introduce a regular interval service of new trains on the busiest railway line in the world. Every hour of the day expresses will run between London and the coast, shrinking journey time to Whitstable to only 75 minutes, Margate just 100 minutes, Ramsgate 114 minutes and Dover via Canterbury to a little under two hours. With these expresses, semi-fast trains from Charing Cross to Ramsgate and Dover and from Victoria to Sheerness-on-Sea will maintain a half-hourly service. And for the first time there will be a direct service between Sheerness-on-Sea and Dover.

Morning and evening business trains will operate a fast and intensive service.

Extra trains at summer week-ends will enable Londoners to travel quickly and in comfort to the coast and enjoy a few hours by the sea. Special fast holiday trains will run non-stop during the height of the season to the larger resorts.

Buffet cars will run in many of the expresses and some of the business trains.

This new electric service is the first stage of the Southern's Modernisation plan, designed to serve the needs of today and tomorrow.

BRITISH RAILWAYS MODERNISATION

Left:
An advertisement for Phase 1 of the Kent Coast Southern Electrics, which were introduced on 15 June 1959. *Author's collection*

several service slacks. It also carried a heavy summer Saturday traffic to the coast.

A great deal of work was needed on the existing electrified railway to increase capacity. Starting at Victoria, the platforms on the Chatham side, except Nos 3 and 4, were lengthened to take 14-car trains. This required the bridge carrying Eccleston Road across the station to be rebuilt as a single girder span. By thus eliminating the supporting piers, the whole of the track layout could be moved further out, and this work required complete closure for a series of eight weekends.

At Stewarts Lane an electric loco shed was built, with workshop accommodation. The existing carriage shed was extended to contain 14 roads and eight berthing sidings were provided outside it.

The first major engineering work was necessary between Shortlands and Bickley Junction. At Shortlands Junction, the double-track exit from Victoria via Herne Hill converged with the double track carrying a suburban service to and from Holborn Viaduct, and trains taking the alternative route out of Victoria via the Catford Loop. From Shortlands through Bromley South to Bickley there were four tracks which were previously paired by direction, so that the paths of down trains from Herne Hill and up trains to the Catford Loop or Holborn conflicted at Shortlands Junction. Moreover, as it crossed the layout there, up local traffic to Holborn Viaduct blocked the path of up fast trains via Herne Hill to Victoria. The entire layout from Shortlands to Bickley Junction was reorganised, pairing up and down lines throughout with the fast lines on the south side. In addition, curvature was eased to allow speed restrictions to be raised by 20mph.

The curvature was also tackled at Bromley South to raise speeds from 30mph to 60mph on the outer platform faces. The platforms were lengthened to take 12-car trains and the buildings modernised. Additional crossovers were laid in before reaching Bickley Junction to allow more scope for sorting the conflicting streams of traffic, some of which was towards Tonbridge and Folkestone as opposed to Gillingham and Ramsgate.

The Chislehurst curves were completely reorganised. Four tracking on the Kent Coast line previously terminated at Bickley Junction, but was extended through St Mary Cray to Swanley, with up and down lines paired. Eleven bridges and a viaduct in the five-mile stretch between Bickley Junction and Swanley had to be rebuilt to provide sufficient width for the two additional tracks, and old bridges were demolished. The alterations of the layout on this route demanded modifications of its connections with the four-track Charing Cross-Folkestone main line, and offered an opportunity to relocate the sharply curved spurs, over which seven speed restrictions had been necessary in the past. Boat trains could now take the connections from west to south at 50mph instead of 30mph. St Mary Cray station was completely rebuilt.

At Chatham, the main station platforms were extended to take 12 cars, and as a result, the up and down slow lines and the up sidings were taken out. It was to offset the loss of these that new up and down loops were provided between Rainham (exclusive) and Newington (inclusive). Thus, trains requiring to stop at Newington have to be routed via the 2¼-mile loop. In all, 35 stations had to be rebuilt to some degree to accommodate longer trains; several new footbridges were installed and all level crossings fitted with cattle grids.

The Sheerness-on-Sea branch had not figured in previous electrification proposals. This was then a single-track branch from Middle Junction, Sittingbourne, then

Fig 9.3

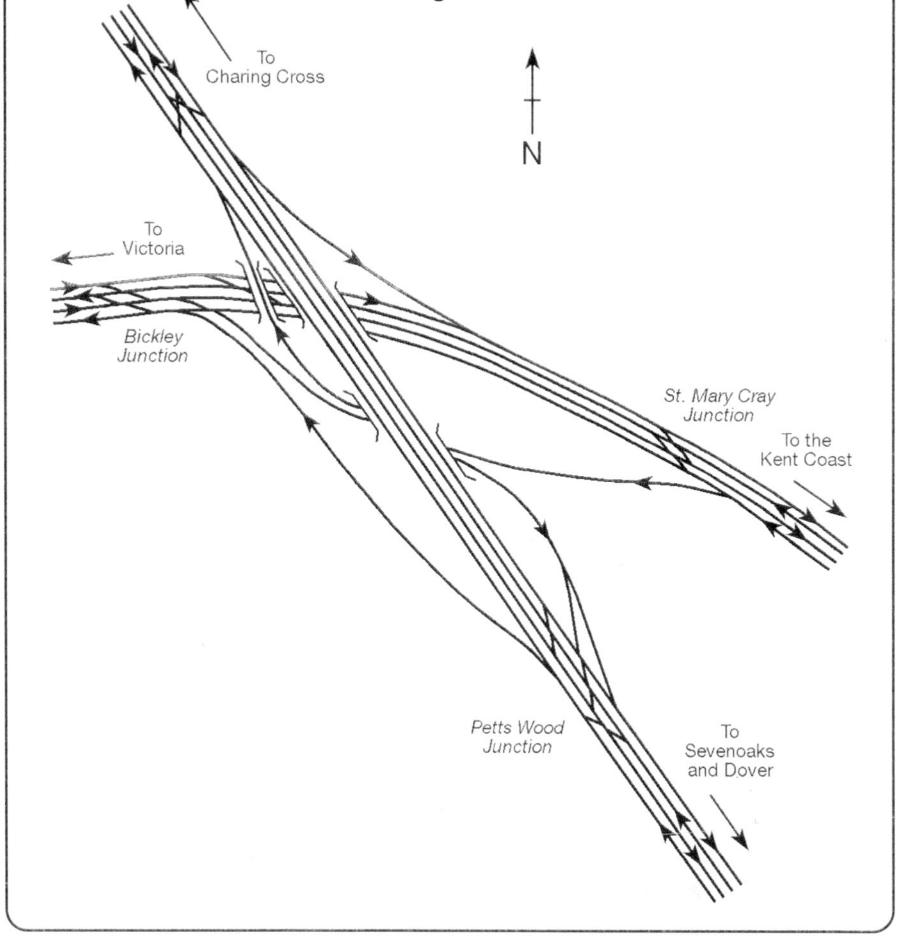

To Charing Cross

N

To Victoria

Bickley Junction

St. Mary Cray Junction

To the Kent Coast

Petts Wood Junction

To Sevenoaks and Dover

Left:

Track layout changes, Shortlands Junction to Bickley Junction, 1959.

Top:

Track layout changes, the Chislehurst curves as reconstructed, 1959.

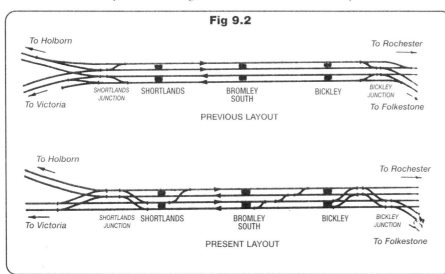

Fig 9.2

To Holborn

To Rochester

SHORTLANDS JUNCTION   SHORTLANDS   BROMLEY SOUTH   BICKLEY   BICKLEY JUNCTION

To Victoria

To Folkestone

PREVIOUS LAYOUT

To Holborn

To Rochester

SHORTLANDS JUNCTION   SHORTLANDS   BROMLEY SOUTH   BICKLEY   BICKLEY JUNCTION

To Victoria

To Folkestone

PRESENT LAYOUT

controlled by electric train tablet, with two passing loops. This was doubled for three miles to a point south of Swale Halt, which was essential to allow the planned three-trains-per-hour service to operate without obstructing freight traffic.

The line then crossed the River Swale by means of a road and rail bridge, which was funded by the Ministry of Transport, British Railways, Kent County Council and Bowaters paper mills and which replaced the previous structure. The new bridge included a span of 120ft, electrically raised between two concrete towers 130ft high, to give a waterway 90ft wide, with three approach spans of 80ft on each side. The branch was diverted to cross the new King's Ferry Bridge and a concrete platform was erected for Swale Halt. Trains began to use the new bridge on 10 August 1960.

Colour-light signalling and track circuiting were installed throughout, providing for a 2½-minute headway between stopping trains and expanded to three minutes between expresses. The scheme included the completion of eight new signalboxes at Shepherd's Lane (controlling three junctions in the Brixton area), Beckenham Junction, Shortlands (also controlling Bromley South), Chislehurst Junction (controlling the Bickley Junction-St Mary Cray and Elmstead Woods-Petts Wood sections, with the Bickley and Chislehurst loops), Farningham Road, Rochester, Rainham (controlling the loops to Newington), Sittingbourne and Faversham. At Rainham the level crossing gates were worked hydraulically by oil under pressure, and at Sittingbourne a separate panel controlled the whole of the Sheerness branch. This programme allowed the abolition of 31 boxes on the main line, although another 23 were still in use.

Current was taken from the National Grid at five points and distributed to 23 rectifier substations for conversion to 750V dc. There were 21 track paralleling huts and the control room was situated near Canterbury West station.

Public services began on Monday, 15 June 1959, and the hourly service pattern is shown in Fig 9.4.

Fast services and any boat trains to Dover Marine were in the hands of the 4CEP/4BEP units, others from combinations of HAL and EPB stock. The only regular passenger service which was not a multiple-unit was now the 'Night Ferry', on which the new E5000-type electric locomotives were used; the 'Golden Arrow' remained steam-hauled via Tonbridge for the time being.

Kent Coast Phase 2

This brought electrification to the South Eastern main lines south of Sevenoaks, where they were left by the Southern. The lines concerned were:

- Sevenoaks to Tonbridge and thence to Ashford, via Dover and the coast to Deal and Ramsgate.
- The branch from Paddock Wood to meet electric services at Maidstone West.
- An extension of the Maidstone East electrification to Ashford and thence via Canterbury West to Minster.
- The Folkestone Harbour branch.

Omitted because of dubious economic prospects was the Ashford-Hastings branch, but the programme agreed still amounted to 132 route miles added to the electric network.

Ashford station is a five-way railway junction, and the station was provided with two additional platform loops by the conversion of the bay platforms at the Dover end, quadruple tracks for half a mile on the London side of the station and a long passing loop on the up side at the Dover end of the station. The platforms were lengthened and a footbridge incorporating the ticket office was erected at the London end, together with new platform buildings and fluorescent lighting. Both up and down marshalling yards were electrified with overhead conductors.

From Cheriton box there were two down and one up line to Folkestone West (then Shorncliffe). A widening to four lines right through to Folkestone Central was undertaken, to make room for the increased service without hindering Continental boat trains and relief services, particularly in view

of the possible irregularity of inward services because of delayed boat arrivals. While platforms were lengthened at Folkestone West, Central underwent a complete reconstruction. Situated on a high embankment, it emerged with two island platforms connected by subway to a new low level ticket office. It was flanked by a new approach road.

Electrification of the steeply graded and mile-long Folkestone Harbour branch eliminated the need for banking engines on up trains. The average gradient is 1 in 36 and SER 'R1' class 0-6-0Ts monopolised the job for many years. One locomotive was allowed to take 127 tons, two locomotives 254 tons, three locomotives 400 tons, and four locomotives 450 tons. When two or more were used, at least one had to assist at the back of the train. Such were the economics of steam traction! All trains need to reverse at the sidings at the top of the incline.

On the Maidstone East line, passing loops were laid east of Otford (up side), west of Borough Green & Wrotham (down side), and at Lenham (up and down sides) to permit passenger trains, particularly boat trains, to overtake others. At Maidstone East, the existing middle road became a short reversible loop. Generally, platforms were lengthened and reconstructed as required.

A new depot for Continental fruit and vegetable traffic from the Dover-Dunkerque train ferry was opened at Hither Green on 10 October 1960, with capacity for unloading 50-60 Continental wagons. Overhead wires were provided on the reception lines, while berthing sidings, inspection sheds and carriage washers were provided for the electric stock, notably at Ramsgate and Grove Park. At Ashford, extensive repair shops for both diesel and diesel-electric stock were built at Chart Leacon.

Power supplies came from the National Grid at Tunbridge Wells, Folkestone Junction and Canterbury West and were supplied to 32 substations which were normally about 3½ miles apart. The substation at Marden was built on a concrete platform in an attempt to avoid it being flooded. The control room was situated at Paddock Wood.

Fig 9.4: Hourly Pattern of Phase 1 Kent Coast Services via Gillingham – 1959 Inaugural Timetable		
From Victoria		
xx10	Bromley South, Swanley (train divides). Front, all stations to Sheerness not via Sittingbourne. Rear, stations to Maidstone East.	90min to Sittingbourne.
xx40	Bromley South, Chatham, Gillingham (train divides). Front, with buffet car, to Whitstable, Herne Bay and all stations to Margate and Ramsgate. Rear to Sittingbourne, Faversham and all stations to Dover Priory except Selling and Bekesbourne.	100min to Margate, 114min to Ramsgate, 114min to Dover Priory.
From Charing Cross		
xx40	Waterloo, London Bridge, Woolwich Arsenal, Dartford, Gravesend, Strood and all stations to Ramsgate.	147min to Ramsgate.
From Sheerness-on-Sea		
xx16	All stations to Sittingbourne.	18min to Sittingbourne.
xx36	All stations to Dover Priory via Sittingbourne and Faversham. 88min to Dover Priory, including 11min stand at Faversham for connections.	

From Charing Cross

xx00   Waterloo, Ashford (train divides). Front, to Folkestone Central, Dover Priory and all stations to Ramsgate, buffet car. Rear, to Canterbury West, Ramsgate.   Ashford 60min, Ramsgate 105min, Dover Priory 94min

xx10   Waterloo, Orpington, Sevenoaks, Hildenborough, Tonbridge (part detached for all stations to Ashford), Paddock Wood (connection for Maidstone West), Ashford (connections for Margate via Canterbury West and for Hastings), then all stations to Folkestone Central, Dover Priory and Margate via Minster.   Dover Priory 112min

From Victoria

xx14   Bromley South, Swanley, and all stations to Ashford via Maidstone East.   Ashford 100min

xx49   Bromley South, St Mary Cray, Borough Green, Maidstone East, Bearsted, Lenham and all stations to Margate via Ashford, Canterbury West and Minster.   Ashford 89min

Colour-light signalling was installed generally, with new cabins at Hither Green, Orpington, Sevenoaks, Tonbridge (also controlling Paddock Wood and the up loop at Headcorn), Ashford (including the Headcorn down loop) and Folkestone Junction (including lines from Cheriton and the Harbour branch). Provision was made for a headway of 2½ minutes for stopping and 2min for fast trains from Hither Green to Sevenoaks and 3 minutes for fast trains beyond. To achieve this, it was necessary to provide signals inside the tunnels at Chislehurst (650yd, down lines only), Polhill (about 1½ miles) and Sevenoaks (nearly two miles). There were 32 cabins abolished.

Temporary electric workings began to steam timings from as early as January 1961 in some cases, but the full electric timetable

had to wait until 18 June 1962. The 'Golden Arrow' all-Pullman boat train was hauled by electrics from 12 June. The new service is set out in Fig 9.5.

For both the Phase 1 and Phase 2 services together, the train mileage under electric traction rose by 73% compared with that being provided by steam immediately previously.

4CEP, 7101-211

Two new types of four-car, all-steel corridor 'express units', gangwayed throughout, were built at Eastleigh in 1956. These were what became the CEP units, and the BEP variant, which had a buffet vehicle in place of the trailer second. A total of six units were constructed initially, consisting of 4x4CEP and 2x4BEP. Despite what many may have thought, they were not destined

automatically for the Kent Coast scheme. The 6PUL/5BEL combinations were showing their age through some very rough riding, and in each case it was found that the equalising beam type of bogie fitted had deteriorated to the extent that replacement was necessary. It was felt timely to design and build some new express units for service evaluation; at the least, the Central Division was short of power and could use some extra resources.

Below:
The rebuilding of the CEP units took place at Swindon Works, where two driving motors from units Nos 7156 and 7211 were seen in May 1979. The extent of the task is apparent from the large chunks of bodywork missing, including the guard's area behind the cab, which became a passenger seating bay. *Author*

No 7153 at Eastleigh in 1975. Tungsten lighting gave way to strips, public address was fitted, the interiors completely gutted and rebuilt, and Commonwealth bogies became standard, courtesy of other withdrawn rolling stock. The rebuilding was judged successful, and the whole fleet underwent treatment at Swindon Works from 1979 to 1984. In the production version, the sliding quarter-light windows became the hopper type. They emerged as TOPS Class 411.

As rebuilt, the revised formation and seating became:

• Driving motor second saloon	-	64S	-
• Trailer brake composite corridor	24F	6S	2T
• Trailer second saloon	-	64S	2T
• Driving motor brake second saloon	-	64S	-
Total seats	24F	198S	4T

This was achieved by removing the brake (and guard's) accommodation from the two end

Below:
Commonwealth bogies have a distinctive outline, and they were the saviour of the riding qualities of BR's EMU fleet. One is seen here at Slade Green on 27 March 1992 beneath Class 411/5 unit No 1550. *Author*

Above:
Canterbury East has a signalbox raised high above platform level; this is done usually to provide better visibility where there are obstructions. A single 4CEP unit, No 7187, arrives from Dover Priory with a train for Victoria on 15 August 1981. *Author*

The experimental 4CEP (corridor, electro-pneumatic) units were built on standard underframes and with 24 first and 200 second class seats. As built, the formation, seating and toilet (T) provision were as follows:

• Motor brake second saloon	-	56S	-
• Trailer composite corridor	24F	24S	2T
• Trailer second corridor	-	64S	2T
• Driving motor brake second saloon	-	56S	-
Total seats	24F	200S	4T

The units went into production for Kent Coast services in 1958 and continued so until 1963. There were a number of modifications to the original vehicles, including later types of electrical equipment, roller bearings, Formica panelling to replace wood finishes, and double glazing of the windows. This last proved to be something of an own goal, since the means of sealing such units had not been perfected. This led to water being trapped between the panes, and accelerating backwards and forwards in time with the movement of the train. It was from such misfortunes that mischievous inquiries were made as to whether the Southern had

considered filling the gap with extra narrow goldfish? No, the Southern hadn't, and single pane windows were substituted.

The problem of ride quality reached its most critical with these trains. Excluding the motor bogies in which the damping was adjusted, later batches from CEP unit No 7155 and BEP unit No 7013 onwards were fitted with Commonwealth bogies from new.

With many years of life still in front of them, the CEP/BEP units were considered in need of an update, but another reason was their blue asbestos insulation content. Experimental work was carried out on unit

vehicles and converting the space which was freed up in each to another seating bay, and creating a replacement in the composite vehicle. Here, two second class bays were removed and turned into brake accommodation. This left one former second class compartment, which thoughtfully had its existing seats removed and replaced by two sets of three and a rather useless rack at floor level. Seemingly for no good reason, what was eight seats became six. The trailer second was gutted, and its eight compartments were replaced by an open saloon with the same total seating capacity.

The CEP units have soldiered on, some with their trailer seconds removed and making them 3CEPs.

4BEP, 7001-22

These vehicles were similar to the 4CEP units apart from the trailer seconds being replaced with a buffet car. By today's standards, the provision of a fleet of 22 sets with buffet car seems remarkably generous, and so it has proved. Some sets had their buffet cars replaced with former locomotive-hauled second class saloons suitably adapted to their new role, thus becoming 4CEPs. The seven 4BEPs which survived and became Class 412 remained in service, but the buffet facilities later became disused.

MLV, S68001-10

From 1959 to 1961, 10 motor luggage vans (MLVs) were built at Eastleigh for use on Continental boat trains. While being capable of propelling themselves on the third rail, they were also able to work over non-electrified lines on the quayside. For this, current was supplied from a 230 amp/h battery, charged from a 200V motor-generator set. Control gear and lighting current were furnished by a 70V generator driven by the same motor. These vans, later Class 419, could haul 100 tons in the guise of locomotives, and had been known to work parcels trains elsewhere on the Southern.

These useful vehicles weighed a hefty 47 tons, and included two motormen's positions, guard's, long and short luggage compartments

Above:
Dover Western Docks station sees motor luggage van No 68001 with a 4CEP unit behind it forming a boat train departure to Victoria via Meopham on 24 August 1979; on the right is 4CEP No 7124 with a stopping service over the same route. *Author*

and a vestibule. The smaller compartment was intended for bonded consignments and the three double doors on each side were wide enough to admit pallet trucks. Their equipment included two English Electric 250hp motors, EP and vacuum brakes and buckeye couplers. As single vehicles, they carried no set number.

TLV, S68201-6

Six brake gangwayed vehicles (BGs) were adapted for multiple-unit working as trailer luggage vans (TLVs) in 1968 to be used in conjunction with the MLVs, but of course these did not have their own driver control positions. They were, however, suitable for inserting between the MLV and the train of CEP stock to which it was coupled, to provide extra carrying capacity. The TLVs were withdrawn in 1975, but the MLVs lasted until the effective end of boat train operations, following the opening of the Channel Tunnel.

Electric Locomotives

The middle of a war seemed an unlikely time to launch the first of what turned out to be a small fleet of new locomotives, but this was the culmination of work started before the outbreak of hostilities.

Up until then, the extensive electrified network of the Southern Railway, amounting to about 40% of the company's track mileage, had been used solely by multiple-unit passenger trains. The very few electric locomotives in the company's possession were used purely for service purposes, in a power house or at car sheds. To obtain the fullest use from the electric traction equipment, it was thought necessary eventually to introduce locomotives for freight, parcels and milk traffic, and also for haulage of trains such as the Newhaven boat expresses which varied in make-up from day to day. Consequently, in 1936, plans were made, and construction at Ashford was well advanced by the outbreak of war in 1939. The locomotive was completed in summer 1941 and had been making test runs on the Brighton main line.

Designed by Bulleid (mechanical parts) and Raworth (electrical), the locomotive No CC1 was capable of accelerating a 1,000-ton freight to 24mph in 100 seconds, while passenger trains could be operated at up to 78mph. The box-like body was carried on a pair of six-wheeled bogies. Each axle was driven by a specially designed 250hp traction motor. The controller was provided with deadman's equipment and had 26 notches for speed control. This could be run through twice, the second time on field weakening positions. There were thus 52 effective notches, which made for extremely smooth acceleration.

An outstanding problem on the Southern Railway with third rail current collection was that of successfully operating loose-coupled

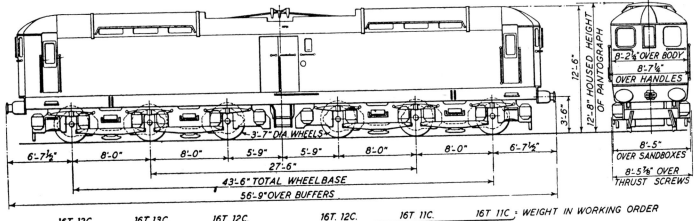

The all-purpose electric locomotive made its debut on the Southern in 1941. No CC1 is seen here with something like a 12-coach train at an unknown location on 19 November 1941. A steam heating boiler was fitted, which accounts for the leakage between the second and third vehicles. *Southern Railway/Author's collection*

Above:

Dimensioned drawing of the Southern's No CC1 locomotive. *Author's collection*

freight trains through conductor rail gaps. On multiple-unit trains gaps are bridged by the jumper cable running from end to end of the sets so that collector shoes somewhere remain in contact and prevent 'gapping'. The electric locomotive, however, with a length over buffers of only 56ft 9in had its extreme collector shoes only 35ft apart.

This was overcome by the use of a 'booster' unit which was a flywheel-driven generator, enabling some power to continue to be supplied to the traction motors while the locomotive traversed gaps of up to 250yd. There were two boosters per locomotive,

each supplying the three traction motors on each bogie, which were linked in series.

To enable the locomotive to work freight into sidings, where a conductor rail is wholly undesirable, a pantograph was fitted into a roof well. Later, some sidings would be wired, tramway style. A steam heating boiler was installed for use with passenger trains in winter.

A second locomotive, No CC2, was delivered in 1943, and this was fitted with jumper cables for multiple-unit working. A third appeared in 1948 as No 20003 under British Railways. This was a more powerful machine and had an adapted 4SUB front end to give a different appearance.

The initial livery for No CC1 was workshop grey with three parallel white lines and black bogies. After the war this became malachite green lined out in yellow, and under BR, black and with aluminium for lining, roof and bogies. A darker shade of malachite followed, with a thin red and grey lining band halfway up the sides, but this was dropped later. The final version was rail blue with yellow ends.

The principal use of these locomotives was on the Central Section, where they worked through freight trains from Norwood Yard and New Cross Gate as far east as Polegate and west to Portsmouth & Southsea. Their load-hauling capabilities gave them a considerable advantage over steam for these tasks. They also monopolised the Victoria-Newhaven boat trains. Among their other duties was the annual haulage of the Royal Train carrying HM the Queen to Tattenham Corner for the Derby meeting in May or June, for which the chosen locomotive would be specially prepared. All were withdrawn by 1969.

If the original electric locomotives might have been thought of as large and ponderous machines, the build for the Kent Coast electrification was much smaller and also lighter. The products of Doncaster Works, they were intended to be much more powerful to enable them to maintain close headways in between multiple-unit services and to deal satisfactorily with stretches of the Chatham line to the Medway towns which has gradients of 1 in 100. Haulage of 900-ton

Fig 9.6: SR-based dc Electric Locomotives

Year Introduced	SR No	BR Nos	hp	TOPS Class	Type	Builder	Length	Weight	Withdrawn
1941	CC1	20001	1,470	70	Co-Co	SR Ashford	56ft 9in	99 tons	1969
1943	CC2	20002	1,470	70	Co-Co	SR Ashford	56ft 9in	99 tons	1969
1948	-	20003	1,650	70	Co-Co	SR Ashford	58ft 3in	105 tons	1968
1958	-	E5000 -E5023*	2,552	71	Bo-Bo	BR Doncaster	50ft 7in	77 tons	1977

*No E5000 was later renumbered E5024

freights was also in the specification, as well as Continental passenger traffic. The 'Night Ferry' could load to 700 tons, and they also hauled the all-Pullman 'Golden Arrow'. Large trains of train ferry wagons were also in their job specification and they were capable of a 90mph maximum.

The number of booster units was reduced to one, and provision for steam heating of coaching stock was eliminated. Roller bearings were fitted, while each of the four axles had a 638hp traction motor. Electrically driven camshaft control, giving 33 notches, was operated from a master controller. All locomotives were fitted with a central pantograph in a depression in the roof. An initial order of 13 locomotives was followed up with a further 11 in 1960.

When new, these locomotives sported a fine malachite green livery, with grey window surrounds and a thin red line, edged with white, along the bodysides between the cabs. The profile was that of Mk 1 coaching stock. The slightly sloping cab front could give a mildly curious effect at times. Later, the green became darker, small yellow panels were added and the lining disappeared. This was succeeded by rail blue and all-yellow ends.

Availability at 90% was achieved, but this in itself emphasised that the total fleet was rather larger than was really required in the turbulent times for the railway during the 1960s. Ten were stored for eventual conversion to electro-diesels intended for the Bournemouth electrification. The rest soldiered on for another decade, but all were withdrawn en masse in November 1977. One locomotive, No E5001, has been preserved by the National Railway Museum.

Electro-diesels

The wiring of yards and sidings could only be partial, and even if it was not, there would always be occasions when traction current was switched off from the third rail. This might be for engineering works, in which case a locomotive with dual power sources could prove itself very useful. Locomotives might also be required to visit non-electrified parts of the system. The next development therefore was to introduce the electro-diesel concept, which it was hoped would combine the best of both worlds.

Below:
The 'Golden Arrow' was for many years one of the Southern's prestige Pullman trains. It is seen here leaving Victoria behind new-looking No E5015 on its run to Dover Marine. The headboard fits neatly on the brackets provided for it, and the locomotive carries the two arrow symbols on its sides as well as the British and French flags below the cab windows.
Ian Allan Library

Fig 9.7: SR Electro-diesel Locomotives

Year Introduced	BR Nos	hp Electric/Diesel	TOPS Class	Type	Builder	Length	Weight	Withdrawn
1962	E6001-6	1,600/600	73/0	Bo-Bo	BR Eastleigh	53ft 8in	75 tons	
1965	E6007-49	1,600/600	73/1	Bo-Bo	EE Vulcan Foundry	53ft 8in	76 tons	
1967	E6101-10	2,500/650	74	Bo-Bo	BR Crewe	50ft 7in	85 tons	1977

Left:
The Class 71 locomotives were first stored and then withdrawn. At Ashford, on 28 May 1977, from left to right, are Nos 71003, 71010 and 71011. All three were cut up at Doncaster in 1979/80. Even in their rebuilt form as Class 74, these locomotives lasted no longer, and none was in service after the end of 1977. *Wyn Hobson*

Below left:
The electro-diesels have played a valuable part in the Southern's fleet. A Class 73 takes five empty mineral wagons and a brake van through the basic facilities of Fishersgate on 16 September 1977 as it heads for Hove. *Author*

The Southern Region had long thought along these lines, and in 1959 they obtained approval from the British Transport Commission. Six prototypes (Type JA) were constructed at Eastleigh Works for a mixed traffic locomotive, seen as the equivalent of a Class 5 steam locomotive (eg the BR Standard 73000 series 4-6-0s). The first, No E6001, began trials of its 600hp English Electric 4SRKT diesel-generator set between Eastleigh and Basingstoke; after that, it moved to Stewarts Lane to test its 1,600hp straight electric plant. The four English Electric axle-mounted traction motors are common to both means of power supply.

They appeared in 1962, the epitome of the box-on-wheels approach. This was perhaps excusable, in that use on the Hastings line was one of the requirements, and this was still in the days of the very constrained loading gauge. The squareness of these machines and their slab sides is a direct result.

The locomotives could be controlled from a remote driver's cab whether in diesel or electric mode, and the diesel engine could be started from a remote driving position. The changeover from electric to diesel or vice versa could be made at any time, and did not involve stopping the train.

The prototypes performed well. One problem which had not been foreseen was the effect on the track of a 75-ton weight concentrated on a comparatively short 40ft 9in total wheelbase and this led to some speed restrictions on older bridges. Generally, the locomotives were very successful, and this led to an order for 43 more, with minor variations, from English Electric's plant at Newton-le-Willows (Type JB).

These are versatile locomotives, particularly in their ability to couple in multiple with electric stock. They are also extremely reliable, to the extent that they became the Southern's favoured motive power for Royal occasions. Soon after their introduction, it was found that one mixed train formation of particular operating convenience was a 4CEP multiple-unit followed by an electro-diesel, itself hauling a train of vans and all controlled by one driver, in the CEP. These were the newspaper trains then running from Victoria and Holborn Viaduct. The use of diesel power was sufficient to get these trains over any breaks in the current supply where permanent way work was in progress. This and other experiments convinced the Southern of the utility of such locomotives, given also that their capital cost (in 1963) was claimed to be over one third less than the Sulzer Class 33 diesel-electrics which the Southern had also just purchased.

A later variation was the creation of Class 73/2, a dedicated sub-class for the 'Gatwick

Below:
The London, Chatham & Dover Railway's branch to Crystal Palace had about as much luck as the Great Northern Railway's branch to Alexandra Palace. The LCDR station was a barn of a place. It is seen here on 13 July 1954, and was closed a couple of months later. The building had a structural weakness and was demolished. *H. C. Casserley/Author's collection*

Express' operations for which 14 Class 73/1 locomotives were modified in that the vacuum brake was isolated and their maximum speed increased from 75mph to 90mph. This duty used fully their push-pull capability, with a train of air-conditioned coaching stock, which became sub-sets of Class 488/2 (two-car sets) or 488/3 (three-car sets), the ensemble being completed with a Class 489 driving motor luggage van – half a former 2HAP unit, as described above. These trains were replaced progressively during 2001 with a fleet of eight new Class 460 'Gatwick Express' stock trains.

The future of the Bournemouth line was debated strongly in terms of the options available. These were:

- dc electrification to Weymouth.
- dc electrification to Bournemouth and diesel operation from there.
- ac electrification.
- Diesel operation throughout.

The use of more powerful electro-diesels was seen as one way of retaining a through service to the extremities, these latter to include Weymouth Quay boat trains where third rail operation along the quayside was clearly a non-starter, and also to Southampton Docks.

Here entered the 10 Kent electric locomotives, which were dispatched to Crewe to have the pantographs removed and a 650hp Paxman diesel engine fitted. They emerged as what became TOPS Class 74, but for the time being they were numbered in the E6101-10 series and classified Type HB. They were required to be able to work in multiple with the Class 33 diesel-electrics and the Class 73 electro-diesels, as well as with multiple-units, and to operate in push-pull mode when controlled remotely. Like their earlier Class 73 counterparts, the pick-up shoegear retracted when not in use to avoid fouling and lineside equipment.

Reliability and availability figures in the early days were described as 'almost disastrous' at around 1,500 miles per casualty. Although this was improved, it never reached acceptable levels. This non-standard class was withdrawn after less than 10 years' service, when it was found that their duties could be performed quite adequately by the existing fleets of Class 33 diesel-electrics and Class 73 electro-diesels.

Elsewhere on the Southern Region, the Bournemouth line never received its proposed diesel traction, except as occasional visitors and the use of a Class 47 from time to time on services such as the 'Bournemouth Belle'. The ubiquitous Class 33s were also to be seen on the route, as were the Class 73 electro-diesels, but eventually the move was direct to electrification of part of the line as described later.

10. Diesel to Hastings, Electric to Bournemouth

'Hitherto, we have been led to understand that push and pull working in this country was restricted by ancient statute.'

Trains Illustrated, *December 1961*

With the Kent Coast scheme in the course of completion, there were still a number of gaps in the electrified network. For these, a fleet of diesel-electric multiple-units was constructed. These were for separate groups of services, and several variations arose. Broadly, the groups were:

- The Hastings line.
- The Berkshire and Hampshire lines.
- The Oxted/East Sussex lines.

However, before considering the units themselves, it is perhaps worth while to examine why the Southern Region, alone, decided on diesel-electric rather than diesel-mechanical (or even diesel-hydraulic) transmission.

As has been shown, electrification on the Southern has a long and essentially distinguished history. To build upon success by using the same traction motors but driven by a diesel engine instead of the third rail seems a worthwhile development. Thus it came to pass. The benefit to the Southern was that much of the electrical equipment was standard, and that Southern staff had many years' experience in its design, maintenance and operation.

Having said that, there were some substantial disadvantages to the path chosen. For a start, the diesel-mechanical route of the Modernisation Plan builds employed an underfloor diesel engine, which by its location took up no space which could be used for earning revenue. The English Electric 4SRKT 500hp diesel engine used by the Southern took up valuable body space and, moreover, it was very much heavier. Against a weight of around 36 tons for the all-up weight of a diesel-mechanical power car, the diesel-electric power cars came in at a hefty 56 tons. This was thanks to the weight and bulk of the diesel-generator set, but it also limited the number of seats. Thus a Hampshire Class 205 power car had 52 seats, compared with 65 seats in a Derby Class 116 of the same length.

Some of this can be put down to interior layout design, but the generator set in the Southern units had the additional problem in that it made it impossible to provide through gangway connections. When it came to the Hastings main line, running as 12-car trains and thus two six-car units, one only of which was equipped with a buffet car, the problems were obvious. Passengers had to have the necessary knowledge to make sure they

travelled in the right part of the train if they wanted to make use of the facility.

There was also the question of noise levels, but this is a more subjective subject. The 'thump, thump, thump' associated with the Southern units was arguably at least no more irritating than the quite different pitch of the mechanical units, and the diesel-electrics did not induce a feeling in the traveller that the whole vehicle was about to shake itself to pieces. In all cases, the diesel engine was mounted at the cab-end of the power car, but the two EE507 traction motors on the inner bogie. This had the effect of distributing the vehicle weight as equally as possible.

Perhaps, though, the major indictment of the Southern's choice was that the capital costs for the diesel-electrics exceeded those of their mechanical cousins by a factor in excess of two. High costs were the last thing that was wanted for trains intended for use on secondary services and branches.

The Hastings Units

First to appear were the Hastings units, from 1957. There were three variations. All six-car trains, the first vehicles were already under construction at Eastleigh on short 58ft underframes (6S). These were to be used as hauled coaching stock. Incorporation of diesel engines in each of two end cars was a late alteration! They were followed by a generally similar design but built on standard 63ft 5in underframes (6L). The third type again had the longer underframes, but a trailer buffet was substituted for one trailer second (6B).

All had the unenviable distinction of being built to Hastings loading gauge, which was considerably narrower than that applying normally. This was due originally to the contractors building the line not lining the tunnels sufficiently, and correcting their error by placing additional layers of bricks on the inside of that which had already been constructed. While this made the tunnels safe, it left the line with a permanent handicap by limiting the types of stock which could use it – and special stock it had to be.

The Hastings units were built to a maximum width of 8ft 2½in, which made

them very cramped indeed for width. As built, all second class accommodation was in saloons, the first class in compartments. Doors were provided on the basis of three per vehicle side or two on the power cars. A curious exception was the compartment trailer firsts, which had a separate door to each of the eight compartments (long vehicles) and four doors on the corridor side. Each six-car unit had a power car at each end, providing a total of 1,000hp.

The Hampshire and very similar Berkshire units were built originally with two cars only (2H), but traffic growth saw an additional intermediate (and very slightly shorter) trailer constructed or, in four cases, commandeered rather later from elsewhere. They thus became classified as 3H. There were some modest differences in the seating capacity between individual members of this class, caused by the provision of more, or less, van space, or by altering the balance between first and second class accommodation. All seating bays had external doors on both sides, and the general construction was that of the electric 2HAP units as built for the Kent Coast electrification. As Fig 10.1 shows, these units had the advantage of being standard width.

These units exemplified the curious attitude of the Southern towards the provision of lavatories. No gangways were provided between vehicles, so each was self-contained in terms of facilities. In the driving motor brake second, there was an open second class saloon, but no toilet. In the centre trailer seconds, there were two separate saloons, but again no toilets. The needy had to travel in the driving trailer composite. In this, the second class saloon had access to one toilet, the first class compartments (sometimes with, sometimes without a second class one) had access to a different toilet. There was no connection between the two, so it was hard luck if the one to which the passenger had access was out of order.

Last to appear, and considerably later, were the three-car units for the Oxted line. This was a possible candidate for electrification, but that decision was deferred for some years,

and then only implemented partially. Again, width restrictions were deemed relevant, but the Oxted units were a little wider that the Hastings stock. A limitation here was Grove Tunnel which connected Tunbridge Wells West and Tunbridge Wells Central, now closed.

Externally, these 3D units had a slightly more rounded look and, by common consent, were the most attractive of the rather ugly diesel-electric bunch of units. This time, a single toilet was offered in the trailer composite in the centre of the train, available equally to both first and second class passengers. The writer well remembers travelling back with a colleague from Oxted to East Croydon late one evening after a few beers; by the time we reached Riddlesdown the situation was becoming desperate. The guard kindly allowed us time to change to the essential vehicle before he gave the driver the starting signal!

Above:

A train of 6L vehicles formed of Class 202 unit No 1014 approaches Crowhurst on a down Charing Cross to Hastings service on 16 October 1978. The tracks are separating to serve the side platforms; the centre through roads had long since disappeared. The curious appearance of these trains is evident in this view; the fourth vehicle contains the (only) first class accommodation, and the unusual window pattern is the result of providing as many as four sets of doors on this side of the vehicle. *Author*

In the Hampshire units, the 500hp engine was considered inadequate for the job when these were upgraded to three cars. This was achieved by the fitting of a larger Napier turbocharger to provide 600hp and a consequential improvement in performance. The Oxted units had these from new.

As a group, the total number of diesel-electric vehicles was reduced by the Hither Green accident of 1967, and the buffet cars were all withdrawn by 1980. There were obvious capacity shortcomings in the short Hastings units, and some of these were disbanded. Several re-formations of this stock were undertaken over their lives, notably to create what were known as the 'Tadpole' units.

There was an urgent need in 1964 to provide trains for the Reading-Redhill-Tonbridge line, which survived with steam traction and no replacements in sight. The decision was made to disband some of the 6S short Hastings units and use one driving motor brake second and one trailer second together with a surplus 2EPB driving trailer second from an electric unit. This created a three-car unit of mixed vehicle widths. Two at 8ft 2$\frac{1}{2}$in wide and 58ft long were married to one at 9ft 3in wide and 63ft 11$\frac{1}{2}$in long. It made an odd combination, and the name 'Tadpole', once conjured up, stuck fast.

Fig 10.1: Diesel-electric Units, as Built

TOPS Class	SR Code	Year Intro'd	No Series	Description	Body Length	Body Width	Seats 1st	Seats 2nd
201	6S	1957	1001-7	Hastings six-car short	58ft 0in	8ft 2$\frac{1}{2}$in	42	200
202	6L	1957	1011-19	Hastings six-car long	64ft 6in	8ft 2$\frac{1}{2}$in	48	240
203	6B	1958	1031-7	Hastings six-car buffet	64ft 6in	8ft 2$\frac{1}{2}$in	48	201
205	3H	1957-9	1101-33	Hampshire three-car*	64ft 0in	9ft 3in	13	206
207	3D	1962	1301-19	Oxted three-car	64ft 0in	8ft 6in	24	160

* Built as two-car units, additional centre car added from 1959 onwards.

Six such units were created to undertake this duty. As the EPB trailer had no gangway connection, it was used normally for van space only. This was a line on which tickets were issued on the train, and the ex-Hastings vehicles were quite suitable. Nevertheless, the units as thus restricted could accommodate only 74 seated passengers, or about the same as a self-respecting double-deck bus. Given the growth of Gatwick, they proved inadequate for their task, and the operation of this route was transferred to the Western Region's Reading-based operation. The 3R 'Tadpoles' were disbanded from 1979 onwards.

At this stage, four of the Hampshire units were still running as two-cars or 2H units. The opportunity was taken to use the now third-hand EPB driving trailers to strengthen them to three cars. The driving cab of the EPB vehicle was taken out of use and disabled, and the car was then used as the centre unit of the 3T or Class 204 set. They thus became minor variants of the Hampshire units and were used as such. Like their Class 205 close cousins, though, the lack of through gangways made

Left:
'Tadpole' 3R unit No 1206 of Class 206 leaves Ore for Ashford on 17 August 1981, with the empty car sheds on the right of the picture. This is the furthest extent of the third rail system, for the time being anyway. *Author*

Above:
The earlier versions of the Hampshire units were built as two-car sets, but traffic growth demanded a third coach. This was provided for most, but not all, of them. When the Class 206 'Tadpoles' were disbanded, the spare EPB driving trailer was pressed into service to form the middle car of this small class which was known as 3T Class 204. Unit No 1404 passes Millbrook as it approaches Southampton with a Salisbury-Portsmouth service on 14 June 1981. *Author*

them basically unsuitable for use on a rural network where many stations were unstaffed. If the railway wants to employ conductor guards to collect fares and issue tickets, the design of the trains must make it reasonably possible to do so.

Later, there were other changes in the make-up of the diesel-electric sets, but this was more to do with keeping the best vehicles in an ageing fleet operational.

A trial refurbishment of 3H unit Class 205 No 1111 was undertaken at Eastleigh in 1979/80, in which gangways were provided within the vehicle and it became second class only. Fluorescent lighting was also fitted; this was quite a novelty as the Southern had traditionally always used ordinary light bulbs. This unit, one of the first to receive British Rail blue and grey livery as opposed to all-blue became, and remained, the sole example of Class 205/1 until its withdrawal.

One factor in the refurbishment was the need to strip any asbestos out of diesel units by the end of 1987, and this was enough to press the case for a number of electrification schemes that much harder. Increasing age

TOPS Class	SR Code	Year Intro'd	No Series	Description	Body Length	Body Width	Seats 1st	Seats 2nd
204	3T	1979	1401-4	Hants/Wilts/Berks three-car*	64ft 0in	9ft 3in	13	168
206	3R	1964	1201-6	Reading-Redhill three-car*	58ft 0in	8ft 21/2in	-	74

* One vehicle was 63ft 111/2in x 9ft 3in, ex-Class 416/2

makes it more and more difficult to justify such work, as opposed to scrapping them, and most dated from the 1950s.

Yet, there were, and are, still some duties for which there are no other units available. These concern the two remaining branches in the heart of Southern electric territory which still have no third rail: the lines between Ashford International and Hastings, and between Oxted and Uckfield. In the case of the latter, trains run beyond the 'branch' to offer a peak service to and from Victoria and London Bridge (one each) on Mondays to Fridays, plus positioning movements.

These are operated by the refurbished remnants of the Hampshire Class 205 and Oxted Class 207 units. Three of the ex-Oxted sets are now gangwayed within the set, the centre vehicle having been replaced by a Class 411 trailer taken from a 4CEP Kent Coast unit. They are classified Class 207/1 and have become standard class only. However, they may run as two cars without the intermediate trailer in the winter months.

There is also a preserved Class 201/202 combination of four vehicles, plus a Class 411 trailer. This unit is based at St Leonards, but those still in service with Connex SouthCentral are maintained at Selhurst.

Assessment of the DEMUs

How well have the Southern's diesel-electrics performed? The answer seems to be that they have worked well, although they have been noted for their rough riding. The destructive and highly regrettable Hither Green derailment of 5 November 1967, in which 49 passengers were killed and 78 injured, was caused by a broken rail. However, it was widely believed by the users of the service to be the result of an extreme case of poor ride quality in a Hastings unit. The concern was such that a special test run was made on the East Coast main line between King's Cross and Grantham, and on several Southern Region main lines at the behest of the Railway Inspectorate. At that time, the ECML was acknowledged to be one of the best aligned

and maintained lines in the country. The cause of the accident was however more prosaic. That it was a pair of Hastings diesel-electric sets which came to grief was little more than coincidental. Of considerable concern though

Below:
There was a time when Uckfield was just a passing station on the line to Lewes, but the section south from Uckfield was closed on 4 May 1969. This left the station inconveniently sited on the south side of the B2102 road, with nothing beyond it other than the platforms. As seen here, Class 207 3D unit No 1308 awaits departure. There is now a single platform on the north side of the crossing, but it is a good three miles before double track is regained at Greenhurst Junction. There are long-standing aspirations to once more project this line to Lewes and indeed electrify it. *Author*

Below right:
Dover is an unusual place to find a member of the diesel-electric fleet, but No 207103 and Class 423 No 3424 were covering for engineering work. The ability to find a diesel-powered unit when electricity might have to be switched off can be useful. The date is 6 March 1993. *Author*

was the Inspecting Officer, Col McMullen's conclusion that 'the general condition of the track on the Southern Region lines, although by no means unsafe, was notably inferior to that on the Eastern Region lines'.

Operationally, the diesel-electric fleet seems to have done what was asked of it, after some early troubles. All classes had a speed ceiling of 75mph, but they seem to have mixed in satisfactorily with the electric multiple-units on common sections of line. This included, in particular, north of Tonbridge, but also north of South Croydon.

The interior design did however leave much to be desired, as has already been discussed. Writing in 1986, the design specialist Brian Haresnape had some scathing comments to make: 'As pieces of machinery they have been very successful, but as a mode of conveyance they have kept the passenger firmly in the final days of steam-oriented thinking in terms of aesthetics and amenity design.' *Trains Illustrated* was even harsher in its view of the first Hastings main line units: 'The slab sides have obviously been dictated by the restricted clearances . . . but to combine them with the standard front end of a modern SR suburban electric unit and produce a drabber box on wheels than anything yet turned out by BR, cannot have been equally inescapable.'

The external colour scheme was initially completely unrelieved Southern green apart from a small BR lion-and-wheel totem on the power cars. This progressed through rail blue and small yellow panels, to overall yellow panel ends, and blue and grey livery under BR ownership. The double arrow sign was carried below the driving cab window. In the earlier liveries, an orange vee on the brake ends of the Hampshire units and others was designed to ensure that the station staff could locate that end quickly. This became an inverted black triangle when the small yellow panels were introduced. Connex colours of yellow and off-white have been applied to the units still remaining in service.

The next developments will be a matter for the incoming franchisee of the South Central services, GOVIA, and electrification is the most likely option. There are opportunities within this for revising services along the South Coast; there would after all then be no need to terminate at either Hastings or Ashford, and the possibility arises of (say) a Portsmouth to Margate service – albeit that it would need three reversals en route at Brighton, Eastbourne and Ashford. Prospects for the Uckfield branch are perhaps more related to the possible restoration of the link to Lewes which would create an alternative route to Brighton from the main line via Haywards Heath, although only south of Croydon. Nevertheless, north of Croydon there are separate lines to Victoria and to London Bridge, plus Thameslink.

Finally, there are the lines on which the DEMUs operated. Fig 10.3 (overleaf) does not claim to cover all such services, but it does perhaps indicate the range of duties undertaken. Perhaps even more to the point, it indicates what has been the fate of the lines concerned, and why their activities reduced over the years. With the authorisation of the Hastings, East Grinstead and Solent electrification schemes, their spheres of operation were reducing and withdrawals followed quickly. Even the Clapham Junction-Kensington Olympia service, on which they were used for a time, was electrified.

Substantial improvements were made both to journey times and to train frequencies, compared with the steam services which they replaced. With the winter timetables of 1957, the running times between Portsmouth and Southampton came down from 70 minutes to 55 minutes, while the time for the service between Winchester and Southampton Terminus was reduced from 35 minutes to 24 minutes. Train mileage in the Hampshire area was more than doubled compared with steam, in this first flush of enthusiasm.

On some lines, the use of diesel-electric units was temporary or intermittent. This included the Lymington branch, where the DEMUS were a short-term fill-in during the transition from steam to electrification. Other Southern branches such as the line to Bexhill West and that from Romsey to Andover did

Fig 10.3: Selection of Lines on Which the Southern DEMUs Were Used

Brockenhurst-Lymington Pier	Electrified, 8 May 1967
(London)-Tonbridge-Tunbridge Wells-Hastings	Electrified, 6 May 1986
(London)-East Croydon-Oxted-East Grinstead	Electrified, 26 September 1987
Eastleigh-Fareham	Electrified, 9 May 1990
Portsmouth Harbour-Fareham-Southampton	Electrified, 9 May 1990
Clapham Junction-Kensington Olympia	Electrified, 26 July 1993
Redhill-Tonbridge	Electrified, 6 March 1994
Reading-Guildford-Redhill	Services now provided by Thames Trains
Reading-Basingstoke	Services now provided by Thames Trains
Basingstoke-Salisbury (local services)	Services now provided by SWT Class 159s
Southampton-Salisbury	Services now provided by Wales & West
(London)-(East Croydon)-Oxted-Uckfield	DEMUs still in use, 2001
Ashford International-Hastings	DEMUs still in use, 2001
Crowhurst-Bexhill West	Closed, 15 June 1964
Romsey-Andover	Closed, 7 September 1964
Totton-Fawley	Closed, 14 February 1966
Christ's Hospital-Shoreham	Closed, 7 March 1966
Southampton Terminus and approaches	Closed, 5 September 1966
Three Bridges-East Grinstead-Tunbridge Wells	Closed, 2 January 1967
(Ashford)-Appledore-New Romney	Closed, 6 March 1967
Polegate-Hailsham	Closed, 9 September 1968
Uckfield-Lewes	Closed, 4 May 1969
Romsey-Eastleigh	Closed, 5 May 1969
Wareham-Swanage	Closed, 3 January 1972
Alton-Winchester	Closed, 4 February 1973
Tunbridge Wells Central-Eridge	Closed, 6 July 1985

not have long before closure, even if the units did find work on them for a time. Other lines closed before they became available at all, although some may have seen occasional workings.

Also, it should not be assumed that operations on these routes were necessarily self-contained. Thus there might be through services between Salisbury and Reading via Basingstoke or, more adventurously, between Reading and Portsmouth via Winchester and Fareham. Other booked workings might take them out of their usual sphere of operation, such as a Saturdays-only Brighton-Exeter service in the first half of the 1970s.

Brighton Re-equipping

All good things come to an end, and by the early 1960s the original trains used for the Brighton and Eastbourne electrification schemes were nearing 30 years of service and around three million miles of travel per unit. Re-forming of units took place to meet new requirements. It turned out that these would centre on the refreshment facilities to be provided, and retaining the best of the old units. Given that so many of the suburban units in particular comprised stock of various ages, this gave plenty of opportunities. Pullman cars were taken out of 6PUL Brighton sets and used to replace restaurant cars in some of the 4RES Portsmouth sets, which then became 4PUL. While that might have been seen as even less availability for Pullman car custom, these sets had through corridor connections and were thus able to serve the whole 12-car train.

In other 4RES sets, a second class trailer from a 6PAN set replaced the restaurant car. In yet other re-formations, 10 six-car sets were made up from spares in 6PUL and 6PAN units to provide what was known as 6CORs – units with no refreshment facilities at all.

4CIG, 7301-438

None of this was of more than temporary duration, as the need was for new trains. These emerged from the BR Workshops at York from 1964, carriage building at Eastleigh having ceased the previous year. The new deliveries consisted, initially, of 54 four-car sets, of which 18 included a buffet car. They were given the codes 4CIG (Corridor, Brighton – IG being the LBSCR telegraphic code for that location) and 4BIG, denoting buffet. Their arrival heralded the end of Pullman cars on the Brighton line fast trains, and these ceased with effect from the 18 April 1966 timetable. The 'Brighton Belle' itself, though, was to soldier on for a few more years.

Fig 10.4 shows how the accommodation provided by the CIG units compared with those they replaced when in a 12-car formation. For a train of very similar overall length, the CIG/BIG/CIG formation has notably more seats, and also shows a move towards more second and less first class accommodation. There is also much less space dedicated to eating facilities, and that provided was classified as second class. Curiously, second class passengers were nominally better off in the PUL/PAN days when the unit had a Pullman car. However, the total weight of the new trains compared with the old came down from 510 tons to 456 tons, a considerable saving. Put that together with considerably more powerful traction motors, and it became clear that the future lay in performance of a different order.

The new units had clearly seen some Design Panel attention, as the rounded ends and recessed boxes containing the jumper cables and brake hoses on the fronts of the units were less severe than their 4CIG predecessors. Like them, they were gangwayed throughout.

The lessons regarding quality of ride had by now been learned, and the B5(S) version of the new BR bogie was fitted to all trailer cars. This was a modified version to deal with the heavy overloads of passengers to which

Fig 10.4: Make up of 6PUL+6PAN Formation Compared with 4CIG+4BIG+4CIG

	Seats	PUL/PAN		Seats	CIG/BIG/CIG
Driving motor brake second		52S	Driving trailer composite	24F	28S
Trailer corridor second		68S	Trailer second		72S
Trailer corridor composite	30F	24S	Motor brake second		56S
Trailer Pullman composite	12F	16S	Driving trailer composite	18F	36S
Trailer corridor composite	30F	24S	Driving trailer composite	24F	28S
Driving motor brake second		52S	Trailer buffet second		40S
Driving motor brake second		52S	Motor brake second		58S
Trailer corridor second		68S	Driving trailer composite	18F	36S
Trailer corridor first	42F		Driving trailer composite	24F	28S
Trailer pantry first	30F		Trailer second		72S
Trailer corridor second		68S	Motor brake second		56S
Driving motor brake second		52S	Driving trailer composite	18F	36S
Total, 6PUL+6PAN	144F	476S	Total, 4CIG+4BIG+4CIG	126F	546S
Weight of 12-car train		510 tons	Weight of 12-car train		456 tons
Traction motor rating		1,800hp	Traction motor rating		3,000hp

The 4CIG units were the last 'proper' main line EMUs to be built new to Mk 1 designs; the Bournemouth trains were not conventional EMUs and were mostly conversions. Class 421/1 No 7309 arrives at Lewes from Brighton with a Coastway service, meeting No 7388 in the reverse direction. *Author*

Southern trains are subjected from time to time, which meant that the coil springs on the bogie bolster had two rubber springs to assist with overloads. Also, it was modified so it could be used at the cab ends of the driving trailers. Here, it carried the beamless shoe collection gear, which was specially designed to fit this bogie.

Internally, the new units had the first class compartments at (both) the extreme ends, but with one compartment only downgraded to second. At the time, it was said that this could be upgraded later if necessary, although the tendency has been entirely in the other direction.

The desire to provide a mixture of first class compartments and a second class open

saloon in the end vehicles led to an uncomfortable arrangement of what seems to have been termed a half compartment in the centre of the car. Passengers with their backs to the cab sit on a bench seat for four with doors on both sides, and either face down the centre gangway or admire a blank partition. That said, the interiors generally are to a very acceptable standard, and the seats properly sprung. The windows are also well positioned for looking out. In short, it has the hallmarks of the best of the Mk 1 designs. Nearly 40 years later, the CIG units still compare well with many later offerings.

When new, tungsten lighting was fitted, although subsequent upgrading has seen this replaced by fluorescent strips. A more

Below:
This drawing shows the general arrangement and seating of the 4CIG units, and the half compartment created at the ends of the full compartment accommodation in the driving trailer composites. That feature apart, the internal arrangements are generally very pleasing.
English Electric/Author's collection

substantial rebuild was that undertaken for the units used on the Coastway services. These were reduced to three cars by removing the trailer second and converting all compartments to become part of the open saloons and standard class only. However, the side corridor remains, and the passenger is confronted with a series of four-a-side seats which lead to a fixed window and no door (in three out of the four former compartments). The overall effect is reminiscent of the upper deck of the double-decker low bridge buses of the 1950s which had a very low offside gangway and similar bench seats to reduce the vehicle height as far as possible.

Over the years, this became an extensive build of 138 four-car units, the later batches not being turned out until the early 1970s. The later versions dispensed with the asbestos insulation (subsequently removed from earlier vehicles); the power cars were given the new B6 motor bogie and there are other minor differences. In TOPS terms, all are variations of Class 421.

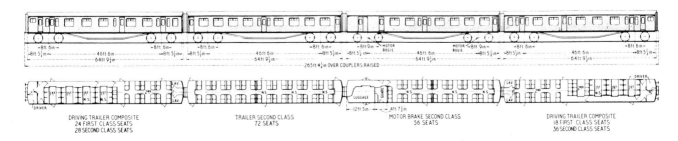

DRIVING TRAILER COMPOSITE
24 FIRST CLASS SEATS
28 SECOND CLASS SEATS

TRAILER SECOND CLASS
72 SEATS

MOTOR BRAKE SECOND CLASS
56 SEATS

DRIVING TRAILER COMPOSITE
18 FIRST CLASS SEATS
36 SECOND CLASS SEATS

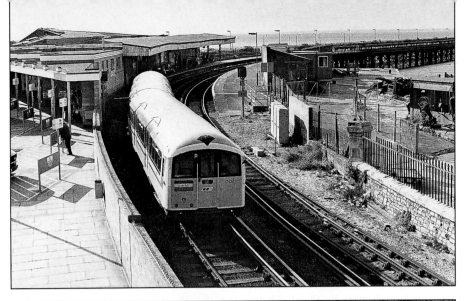

4BIG, 7031-58

These units are similar, with a buffet taking up almost half the vehicle which would otherwise be a trailer second in the CIG series. These are of TOPS Class 420.

Isle of Wight

That the British Railways Board planned to close all the remaining railways on the Isle of Wight is a matter of fact, but the Ministerial decision of 1965 to reprieve the Ryde to Shanklin line caused some considerable head scratching. By common consent, the existing steam locomotives and rolling stock were past redemption; the main problem was the substandard clearances. The most difficult of all was Ryde Tunnel, and the 12ft 3⁹/₁₆in loading gauge height restriction is about 10in less than that on the mainland. The choice of available rolling stock was thus limited, and although 10 of the BR Standard Class 2 2-6-2 tank locomotives (Nos 84010/3/4/5/6/7/9/25/6/8) were transferred (on paper) to Eastleigh in November 1965 for possible height reduction work, it would not have solved the coaching stock problem. The locomotives were withdrawn for scrap.

The capital budget was fixed at a modest £0.5 million, so purpose-designed stock was not possible. Dieselisation would have needed the establishment of a maintenance depot to look after very few trains (the line is only 8m 31ch long), and there was the physical impossibility of incorporating a diesel engine within the restrictive contours of the coaches, Hastings style. It might have proved possible to use diesel shunters regeared for higher speeds, but this would have meant running round trains at terminals and higher operating costs.

Being the Southern, third rail electrification, albeit at the reduced voltage of 630V dc was chosen as the simplest option. It just so happened that London Transport was in the process of replacing the Central and Piccadilly Line rolling stock, and the pre-1938 or Standard stock trains were being withdrawn. While these units had had their day for intensive Underground usage, the Southern decided to purchase a quantity of them. Even before the Minister's decision was announced, it was thought that the Ryde Pier Tramway would need to be kept in being even if the railway proper was allowed to close.

After some considerable rehabilitation work, the trains were formed into 4VEC (two driving motors and two trailers) and 3TIS (driving motor, trailer, driving trailer) units. Formations were initially either seven cars, making the Roman Vectis name for the Island, or a four-car unit on its own. There were six units of each type, plus a spare driving motor.

Electrical and mechanical overhauls were carried out by London Transport at its Acton Works. The trains were then hauled to Wimbledon and worked under their own power to Stewarts Lane depot, Battersea, for repainting and internal alterations. Exteriors were painted in the new Rail Blue livery, with large yellow ends. Internally, ceilings and window frames were white, other parts mushroom. Shelves for passengers' luggage replaced one bank of longitudinal seats adjacent to each set of double doors. Electro-pneumatic brakes were fitted and the air-

worked doors retained, operated by the guard from one of the vestibules. There was accommodation for other luggage or parcels etc, which was loaded on to road vehicles on the mainland, ferried to the island, and delivered by road. Passengers were advised that trains could carry only hand luggage and that advantage should be taken of the now long-defunct 'Luggage in Advance' system for heavy articles.

Power for the traction supply was taken from the Southern Electricity Board's 35kV ac supply to substations at Ryde St Johns Road, Rowborough (north of Brading) and Sandown. There, the supply was taken into a transformer and a silicon diode rectifier and was output at 650V dc. Ryde Works was converted for its new role as an electric train depot.

The track layout was much reduced and has since been simplified further; the original 1967 layout is shown in Fig 10.5 (overleaf). Compared with steam days, all run-round facilities and locomotive spurs became surplus other than for some works trains, and the rest were removed. The four platforms at Ryde Pier Head were similarly reduced to one single sided and one double sided. The latter was worked on the principle that passenger flows were separated so that they alighted from one side and boarded on the other. Platforms at Ryde Esplanade were lowered to suit the former tube stock, but at the other stations the track was raised.

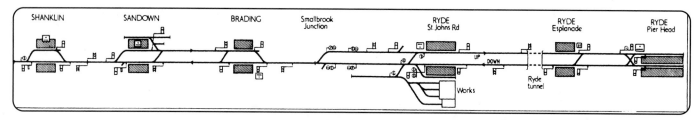

Above:
Isle of Wight electrification, 1967.

Right:
At St Denys, the line from Portsmouth joins the South Western main line. Class 205 3H unit No 1110 is leaving with a local service to Southampton in September 1975. This fill-in electrification was completed in 1990. *Author*

Signalling was simplified, with boxes retained at Ryde Pier, Ryde St Johns Road, Brading, Sandown and Shanklin. Normal block working was used on most of the double line, with track-circuit block between St Johns and Smallbrook Junction. The single-line sections became the first installations of tokenless block on the Southern.

The initial train service was generous compared with what was to be offered some years hence, and is shown in Fig 10.6. The timings are given for a specific hour; during the summer, train frequencies on Mondays to Fridays reduced to two trains per hour and on Sundays there was only one train per hour by mid-afternoon. The services shown are the maximum that was offered, and these were timed with particular regard to connections with ferry sailings. The normal running time was 22 minutes throughout, compared with 28 minutes down and 26 minutes up with steam traction.

During the summer service, all trains consisted of a seven-car VECTIS set with 238 seats, and all sets were in use. The winter service was worked by two four-car trains on weekdays and one on Sundays. The three-car sets were not used on their own as they had current collector shoes at one end only. They would thus have been vulnerable to 'gapping'. All sets carried a red tail disc in place of a tail lamp. Electric services commenced on 20 March 1967, after a total shutdown from 31 December 1966 to carry out the necessary work.

Rationalisation

On a positive note, the Isle of Wight has seen two stations opened since electrification: at Lake for the local housing and at Smallbrook Junction. This increased the total from six to eight, and where else has the number of stations risen by one third? Smallbrook Junction was a special case; there is no public access from any road or path, but there is cross-platform connection to the Isle of Wight Steam Railway which operates between there and Wootton. Consequently, Island Line trains stop there only when the steam railway is running.

Less satisfactorily, Shanklin loop has been removed, and while Sandown still has a loop, the track to Brading and indeed to Smallbrook is now single throughout. The crossover at Pier Head has also gone.

The ex-LT Standard stock came to the end of its life and was replaced by Underground 1938 stock in 1990. The number of vehicles shrunk to eight sets each of two cars only, making 16 cars in all, although a spare two-car set was acquired for possible rehabilitation and use. That did not come to pass, and subsequent withdrawals and flood damage in Autumn 2000 reduced the total stock available to four operable sets, with others stored unserviceable. A two-car set of Class 483 stock, as it became, seats 84.

Services are now noticeably thinner, too, and these are constrained by the long single-track sections. At the time of writing there are two trains per hour daily, but unevenly spaced at 20- and 40-minute intervals. The

Fig 10.6: Departures of trains 11.00-11.59 from Ryde Pier Head – Initial 1967 Service			
Summer Mondays to Fridays		**Winter Mondays to Fridays**	
11.18	All stations to Sandown	11.18	All stations to Shanklin
11.25	All stations to Shanklin		
11.48	All stations to Shanklin		
Summer Saturdays		**Winter Saturdays**	
11.09	All stations to Shanklin	11.18	All stations to Shanklin
11.21	All stations to Shanklin		
11.33	All stations to Shanklin		
11.45	All stations to Shanklin		
11.57	All stations to Shanklin		
Summer Sundays		**Winter Sundays**	
11.18	All stations to Sandown	11.23	All stations to Shanklin
11.25	All stations to Shanklin		
11.48	All stations to Shanklin		

service reduces to hourly in the evenings, and all day on Sundays in the depths of winter.

An uneven headway such as this is not generally helpful, especially in connection with ferries which run at a basic half-hourly interval between Portsmouth Harbour and Ryde Pier Head. However, the sad fact is that the track simplification makes the operation of a 30-minute frequency on the Island Line impossible. A 20-minute service might be offered, but this does not get over the ferry problem.

New Timetable, 10 July 1967

In a major mid-1960s exercise, the Southern decided to ascertain in some detail exactly what passenger requirements were as the basis for a new timetable. The aim was to obtain the most out of the existing facilities of traction, signalling, rolling stock and power supplies. Essentially, peak services would be increased to the maximum amount possible, provided the demand was there.

The numbers of passengers arriving at the London termini during the heaviest peak hour in October 1966 were as shown in Fig 10.7.

The total of 180,000 passengers on the Southern was carried on 228 trains, equivalent to 789 persons per train. However, demand was not uniform, with the most difficult situation occurring on the South Eastern lines out of Charing Cross/Cannon Street where nearly one in five passengers were having to stand. Conversely, some of the

Fig 10.7: Passengers Arriving and Seats Provided in Heaviest Hour, 08.15-09.15, October 1966			
	Passengers	Seats	Ratio Pass/seats
Charing Cross) Cannon Street) Waterloo East)	58,496	47,346	1.24
Victoria SE	9,520	8,136	1.17
Holborn Viaduct) Blackfriars)	16,761	15,280	1.10
Victoria (Central)	26,183	25,263	1.04
London Bridge (Central)	27,079	32,215	0.84
Waterloo Main	41,819	43,508	0.96
Total, Southern termini	179,858	171,748	1.05

Central Division services were relatively overprovided, while Waterloo might be described as 'comfortable'.

However, such figures do not distinguish between individual trains, or even groups of trains. Were the problems more to do with long-distance commuting, or on the inner suburban services? Were the trains over-full at the front and half-empty at the back? And whatever the answers, how far, or for how long, were passengers having to stand? There is a world of difference between standing from New Cross or Clapham Junction into London, and being wedged in the corridor all the way from Tonbridge or Haywards Heath.

It is also not irrelevant that the latter unfortunates pay considerably more in fares for the privilege. There is more revenue, though not necessarily more profit, in carrying people longer rather than shorter distances, and railway business managers need to recognise this.

Physical counts were supported by on-train and off-train passenger surveys and an examination of future planned developments

Below:
A REP+TC+TC combination headed by Class 430 4REP No 3013 passes Adelaide Crossing north of Southampton with a Weymouth to Waterloo express on 11 June 1981. *Author*

such as new housing or industrial parks. The capacity of the network was examined and a series of minor works put in hand. These included items such as new crossovers to turn back trains at Sidcup and Kent House, as well as the signalling alterations and additional berthing sidings. All running times were revised for modern stock, with 90mph authorised for the four main lines from London to Ramsgate via Chatham, to Folkestone via Tonbridge, to Brighton, and to Bournemouth. This applied to electric stock with Commonwealth, B4, B5 and Mk 6 bogies. The resulting acceleration was worth two minutes for Charing Cross to Folkestone, five minutes for Victoria to Brighton and 11 minutes for Waterloo to Southampton.

The results of all this activity identified another 42 possible train paths in the busiest hour. The new timetable from 10 July 1967 used 33 of these, so 261 trains were being run where 228 sufficed previously. The number of seats was increased by 25,556, or 14%, which was a substantial benefit.

As an example of how this was achieved, one way of getting more trains through the London Bridge area was to run them nonstop through the station. Once a train leaving London is full (however one determines what 'full' is), it might as well run nonstop initially anyway. To compensate for the loss of stops at London Bridge, the train plan reduced the need for interchange there. This was done by providing the Dartford Loop and the Bexleyheath lines flights of trains on a regular pattern: first a Charing Cross, then a Cannon Street, then a Holborn Viaduct, then another Charing Cross. The whole pattern was repeated every 20 minutes. Where interchange between Charing Cross and Cannon Street trains was necessary, the idea was that it would be done at Sidcup or Eltham Well Hall, into semi-fast trains which skipped the last few stations before London.

However, while to suggest that it all ended in tears is an exaggeration, the results were less than satisfactory in an operational sense. The Southern had a choice between more trains and a decrease in punctuality when incidents occurred, or no more trains and a slightly higher standard of punctuality. The management deliberately chose the first option.

Making the maximum use of the capacity available is a laudable objective, and one that was to be heard much later in the 'flog those assets' approach. One matter thought to have caused problems was allowing insufficient time for trains to clear junctions. Longer trains will occupy track circuits for just that greater length of time, especially at junctions, and this can cumulatively become critical in capacity terms.

Planners must be careful not to go too far as this leaves little (and as it transpired, too little) margin for error. Timekeeping problems that occur when the system is at full

Fig 10.8: Deployment of SR Rolling Stock and Locomotives as at 10 July 1967

Type of Traction	Programmed Workings by SR Division			Total Traffic	Special Traffic	Maintenance	Total
	SE	Cen	SW				
Suburban EMUs	246	168	138	552	-	90	642
Main line EMUs	256	237	227	720	-	127	847
DEMUs	19	27	20	66	-	12	78
20001 class	2*	-	-	2	-	1	3
Class 71	12*	-	-	12	-	2	14
Class 73	21*	-	18	39	1	9	49
Class 74	-	-	3	3	2	5	10§
Class 33	23*	-	34	57	13	14	84
Diesel shunters	41	27	50	118	3	21	142

Notes: Special traffic allocation for all multiple-units is not distinguished separately from maintenance spares; for suburban EMUs this figure also includes three Regional spares and for main line EMUs 10 Regional spares.
  * Shared by SE and Central Divisions.
  § Pending delivery, work to be covered on temporary basis by Class 47 locomotives borrowed from WR.

Fig 10.9: SR Daily Passenger Train Mileage as at 10 July 1967

Division	Mons-Fris	Saturdays	Sundays
South Eastern	53,578	44,907	32,641
Central	53,961	42,508	31,492
South Western	57,011	50,686	35,849
Total	164,550	138,101	99,982
% by day of week	100%	84%	61%

stretch are very difficult to rectify, in the sense of getting the service back on time, with trains and train crew all in the right place. There needs to be *some* judicial slack in the train plan *somewhere*.

The Southern came in for much criticism from the press and from union sources. Lack of staff consultation but also inadequacies in the planning and pre-briefing also seem to have been issues, while a coincidental escalation of technical defects in points and signal failures hardly helped. The exercise did demonstrate, though, how close the Southern was to providing as much capacity as was feasible without more fundamental infrastructure work.

Rolling Stock Situation

The introduction of the 10 July 1967 timetable coincided with the Bournemouth electrification, considered separately. This date also saw the virtual elimination of locomotive-hauled rolling stock from the Southern, and totally for steam traction. The only remaining use of locomotive-hauled coaching stock from that time was the Weymouth, Southampton and Newhaven boat trains, the 'Golden Arrow' and the 'Night Ferry', all since defunct, Oxted line business trains which are now either electric (to East Grinstead) or use the remaining DEMUs to run to Uckfield, the West of England services which subsequently were turned over to Class 159 diesel units, and Brighton-Plymouth

services, also DMUs for services proceeding west of Southampton.

Fig 10.8 shows the total rolling stock resources available to the Southern Region with the Bournemouth line stock delivered, and split between the Divisions.

In interpreting such figures, it should be borne in mind that the number of units does not specify whether they are of two cars, four cars or six cars, and that the number making up a train will vary according to circumstances. In terms of passenger train mileage, this was remarkably consistent across the Divisions, as Fig 10.9 shows.

This also shows the effects of different service patterns on each day of the week, with Sundays being accorded appreciably less traffic than Saturdays. This was of course the summer timetable, and the remains of the summer Saturday holiday peak will have contributed to these figures. There is no distinction in these mileages between electric and diesel-operated services, but as Fig 10.8 shows, the EMU fleets formed by far the largest part of the rolling stock.

Borough Market Bottleneck

The further growth of peak hour travel was taking place on a system which had not expanded to match. Furthermore, if the Kent Coast electrification was successful in stimulating traffic, the results would inevitably impinge on the area of the London termini, and no more so than in the difficult approaches through London Bridge and thence to Blackfriars or, more particularly, Cannon Street and Charing Cross.

The earlier practice of running some trains via Cannon Street to Charing Cross has already been discussed. However, the relative growth of the West End for commuter traffic and the stagnation if not decline in the City were creating new demands which were not being met. The key problem was in the four tracks approaching Borough Market Junction from the east, where in simple terms trains approaching London were on the south side of the formation and trains leaving London were on the north side. This created an immediate conflict, quite apart from any headway considerations relating to service frequency. All trains going *towards* Cannon Street on the four-track line needed to cross all trains *from* Charing Cross on the two-track line at Borough Market Junction, and this was a very real constraint upon the quantity of service offered.

This is not a minor difficulty, since around 1,000 trains pass through Borough Market a day, and 100 of them in the peak hour. Some progress was made in the 1967 revisions by timing trains so that moves took place in parallel, such as trains to and from Charing Cross both being timed to reach the junction together, and likewise the Cannon Street services. This was taken further, so that flights of trains might make moves on one pair of routes, then a series of trains on the other. However, success in such areas depends upon very precise timekeeping by everybody, including passengers, for it is also essential that the booked platform times are not exceeded. While parallel running in such a manner can undoubtedly help, it is really no more than a palliative.

Nevertheless, Borough Market Junction was only a symptom of what was wrong. The Southern Railway resignalled the area in the 1920s, but it did not tackle the problem of the conflicting junctions between there and New Cross on the South Eastern lines. The complications arose because of the large number of branches converging on to a four-track main line in the Lewisham/St Johns area, and the addition of the Greenwich line at North Kent East Junction. By this point, the four tracks had become six, all in up and down pairs. Eastwards towards London

Above:
London Bridge is at one end of an exceedingly busy stretch of railway. This picture of May 1990 with Class 411/5 No 1540 shows just how many tracks there are to be reckoned with, running side by side. *Author*

Bridge, the tracks were rearranged in two stages, using flat crossings, to produce a six-platform layout at London Bridge station using three islands.

This layout meant that almost every up train crossed the path of a down train at another point as well as Borough Market, and sometimes more than once. Thus an up train from Greenwich to Cannon Street crossed down lines on four separate occasions.

The solution – or as near perfect a solution as was attainable – was seen as resolving the conflicting moves further out. This was to be associated with a complete rearrangement of tracks, so that all trains proceeding to and from Cannon Street occupied the three tracks on the north side of the formation, and those for Charing Cross the three on the south side. There would also be some provision for reversible working. If this could be achieved, Borough Market Junction would be effectively eliminated.

Of course, one major problem was the amount of passenger interchange at London Bridge, which included those going to and from the Brighton platforms. This letter to *Modern Transport* from a Vivian Carter summed up the situation admirably:

'Passengers dismount from their usual Cannon Street train and wait in crowds on the platform at London Bridge to see on the

indicator whither they are to rush to pick up the next Charing Cross train. If this train should be on another platform, a stampede up the staircase and over the bridge takes place. As often as not, a similar stampede on the part of people waiting for a Cannon Street train takes place from the other side, and the two crowds meet on the bridge and staircase and engage in an unseemly struggle.'

That letter was dated 24 January 1920, and half a century later nothing much had really changed. So, sensing the need for action, the Southern built a nice, new, 30ft-wide enclosed footbridge with enough space to cater for about 2,000 passengers at a time. Unlike its predecessors, the new bridge included the Brighton platforms. Its provision was coupled with the realisation that there was going to be more need for passengers to change trains if conflicting train movements really were to be minimised.

Below:
Track layout changes, Charing Cross to New Cross, in association with London Bridge resignalling.

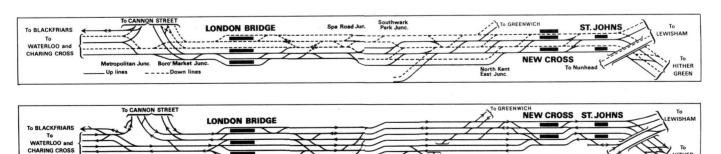

103

A major feature of the scheme in sorting trains between Charing Cross and Cannon Street was the provision of an effective flying junction at St Johns. Thus all up trains calling at Lewisham could either continue as previously on a route which led easily to Cannon Street, or be routed via the line to Nunhead and cross the South Eastern main lines by the existing flyover. A new (reversible) link was constructed down to the fast lines, which the viaduct crossed. This resulted in the trains from Lewisham being positioned ideally for the lines to Charing Cross.

Other new 40mph flat junctions at Parks Bridge were installed to allow trains from Sidcup or those already on the main line at Hither Green to be sorted into Cannon Street or Charing Cross destinations before being joined by the trains from Lewisham. This routeing facility was already available for trains on the Mid-Kent line via Ladywell.

Such work can only be carried out in conjunction with a complete resignalling, and the new London Bridge box was commissioned in stages during 1975 and 1976. It supervised 47 track miles on both the South Eastern side as far as Woolwich Arsenal, Bromley North and Hayes, and on the South Central to Crystal Palace and Denmark Hill. While the South Central panel offered two operating positions, that for the South Eastern was divided into seven sub-panels. These were of the conventional entrance-exit type, with double push buttons serving both these functions as required.

One new feature was a flashing white light when the entrance button was pressed, displayed on the track diagram on the section concerned, and remaining flashing until the route had been established and proved. This was designed to draw attention to a route which was not set successfully, as opposed merely to a gap in the series of white lights appearing on the diagram. Another new feature was a means whereby a train could itself reset a route after it had passed without any outside intervention.

Automatic turnback working was established at the terminals of Hayes and at Bromley North. With this, the route is cleared into the specified platform. After the train has arrived, the outward route is established without any further action from the signalman, and when the train has departed the route is reset for the next incoming train.

Most running line points were fitted with electric point heaters, with timers to cut them out after a given period of time. Hot axle box detectors were provided at Elmstead Woods on the up lines and at Brockley Lane on the down route at Nunhead.

Signalling power supplies were taken in duplicate from the CEGB via the traction supply substations, with a second emergency supply direct from the local public electricity company near the signalbox. If one supply fails, changeover to the alternative is automatic. The Southern's philosophy here was that if electricity was not available for signalling, it would not be available to run the trains either.

The Bournemouth Electrification

The fulfilment of the Kent Coast electrification plans of the Southern Railway, at the beginning of the 1960s, was the last of the major works to be undertaken which had been delayed by World War 2. It was, however, still what might be termed an interim result. The choice in the area east of a line drawn roughly from Reading to Portsmouth was further electrification, dieselisation or closure. As will be shown, the situation reached by the late 20th century was a mixture of all three, the operation of diesel trains being made possible by the Modernisation Plan.

Only careful examination of a 4CEP unit running between Victoria and Faversham on 28 September 1960 would have shown that it was making runs of special interest. One motor coach of the unit, No 7114, had had its traction motors removed, and the other was fitted experimentally with two BR Mk 4 motor bogies. The unit was thus converted into a push-pull train.

The next day, further trials were conducted, this time in company with two 2HAP units coupled on one side of it, and two motor luggage vans on the other. The traction equipment of the 2HAPs was cut out and with these two units leading and the power provided by the rear motor car of No 7114 and the two MLVs, the formation was run from Victoria via Swanley, Faversham and Canterbury to Dover Priory, returning via Ashford, Sevenoaks and Bromley South. There were thus seven idle vehicles being propelled by the three powered cars at the rear. Speeds in excess of 80mph were obtained between Ashford and Paddock Wood, the old racing stretch of the South Eastern main line, with no stability problems being experienced.

The trials were conducted to assess the suitability of four-motor power cars on high-speed push-pull workings, with a view to the possible operation of the Waterloo-Bournemouth services by these methods. These trials preceded many others, with electro-diesels and 12-car trains at up to 100mph and Class 33 Sulzers propelling unpowered six-car sets. Much later, trains propelled by locomotives became commonplace. Electric multiple-units are rather different, although a four-car unit with a power car in one of the central vehicles might be said to be propelling either one or two other vehicles, dependent upon direction of travel.

By push-pull methods, turnround times at the ultimate termini need to be no longer than those of ordinary multiple-units, albeit that the division of the train and transferring haulage to a diesel locomotive wherever the interface occurs will occupy both time and space. Also saved are the run-round facilities to release the locomotive on the incoming train for its next duty.

The Modernisation Plan envisaged 25kV ac electrification between Waterloo and Weymouth and to Salisbury, and from Waterloo to Byfleet via Richmond, Feltham and Chertsey. This was discarded eventually, partly due to the complexities of dual systems over the congested network between Clapham Junction and Waterloo, and the lack of interavailability of rolling stock.

The 90-route-mile and 750V dc scheme which was built was authorised in September 1964. This also included extensive civil work and colour-light signal installation on a large scale. Bournemouth would be the break point for passenger trains, but electrification was to continue the $2\frac{1}{2}$ miles to Branksome station for depot access.

This was a cut-price scheme, where the specification was kept to the minimum achievable. Thus any redundant freight facilities were to be removed, together with associated points and crossings, while the multiple-units to be ordered were to include 123 refurbished locomotive-hauled vehicles, in true Southern fashion! The rehabilitation of the viaduct leading directly into the Bournemouth West depot was discarded in favour of a time-consuming reversal at Branksome on each and every occasion access to the new depot on the line to the former Bournemouth West station was wanted. Diesel traction was to be used west of Bournemouth, but, importantly, through services were to be maintained. One enhancement which did creep in was the new unstaffed station for Southampton Airport; by 1991 this was attracting 1,000 boarding passengers daily. It has since been upgraded and fully staffed.

The civil engineering work included re-laying the through lines to Worting Junction, where the line to Bournemouth leaves the West of England main line west of Basingstoke, and beyond with continuous welded rail (cwr). Rail was transported to site in 600yd lengths for further welding there. At the same time, deep ballasting was carried out to permit 90mph running. Track layout revisions were undertaken at Basingstoke where four berthing sidings were laid in.

Station platforms were lengthened as necessary. Southampton acquired new buildings on the up side, which necessitated the demolition of the clock tower. At Eastleigh, the existing shed for DEMUs was more than doubled in size, while carriage servicing facilities were also provided.

The Lymington branch was reduced to long siding status, but this was not to prevent the operation of as many as three through trains from Waterloo on summer Saturdays. (There were another three to Swanage.)

At Bournemouth Central, the down and up middle lines through the station were taken out and replaced by two berthing sidings at the Poole end, one suitable for a locomotive and 12 cars and the other for a locomotive and eight cars. This was to enable a train which finished its down journey at Bournemouth to be serviced quickly before it was required for an up service. The up platform was lengthened to 800ft to take a 12-car train, a footbridge replaced the previous subway and extensive improvements were made to the station offices. Both down and up platforms were signalled for two-way working. A bay for four-cars was retained at the London end on the up side. In more recent times, a large bus/rail interchange has been constructed on the down side.

Colour-light signalling was eventually to be installed throughout from Hampton Court Junction to Branksome, but some pockets of semaphores remained initially. Provision was made for headways of three minutes on fast trains and three to five minutes for stopping services. The new signalling installation from Brookwood to Basingstoke replaced one of the oldest lengths of automatic signalling in the country, consisting of semaphore signals operated by compressed air and controlled by track-circuit. Dating back as far as 1902, many retained their LSWR lower quadrant arms to the end.

High-tension current was supplied by the CEGB from the National Grid at Basingstoke, Southampton and Bournemouth, and further distributed to 19 substations with intervening track paralleling huts. These substations were of a new type, using air-cooled silicon diode rectifiers. With their associated transformers and switchgear, these were housed in prefabricated aluminium alloy huts. While some were operated from the existing Woking Control Room, the rest came under a new control room at Eastleigh. In a rare fit of environmental sensitivity, the substations in the New Forest were painted green rather than standard grey.

Conductor rails weighing 106lb/yd were laid, but in Southampton Tunnel and on the

Lymington branch the weight was increased to 150lb/yd. The live rails on the local lines from Pirbright Junction to the former Sturt Lane Junction were still in place, the little used connection to the Ascot-Ash Vale line having been removed in July 1966.

4REP, 3001-15

These were the four-car tractor units. This enabled them to work with up to two unpowered four-car 4TC trailer units to form 12-car trains which they propelled from Waterloo to Bournemouth and hauled back again. They were formed of two newly built driving motor open seconds, with two motor bogies and with two EE546 348hp traction motors each. Intermediate cars consisted of a trailer buffet car and a trailer brake first. Both of these were converted from locomotive-hauled stock. The total seating capacity was 24 first and 153 second class.

There were 11 units built originally, supplemented later by a further four. The specifications differed from the original sets inasmuch as RB (restaurant buffet) trailers substituted for the RUs (restaurant unclassed) vehicles of the first build. They became TOPS Class 432.

Below:
The full 258yd length of a 12-car train formed in this case of a 4REP (leading) and two 4TC units is brought out in this New Forest view near Beaulieu Road in May 1977, yet, a Eurostar is over half as long again. Trains of such length have implications for the station infrastructure and the ability to handle so many passengers simultaneously, quite apart from matters such as signal spacing. *Author*

Above:
The 17.00 Waterloo-Salisbury was at one time formed of a Class 33, a 4TC set and 2x4VEP sets. The locomotive and the TC set would detach at Basingstoke and continue under diesel power only, while the 2x4VEP formation would continue to Eastleigh and terminate there. Such a move made full use of the ability of the whole to couple in multiple. On 27 July 1983, No 33103 and 4TC No 418 arrive at London Waterloo with the locomotive propelling, to couple to the VEP units already in the platform. *Author*

4TC, 401-34

The trailer units were all conversions from locomotive-hauled vehicles and were provided with new B5 bogies. The make-up was driving trailer second, 64 seats converted from a TSO; a trailer first corridor, converted from an FK; a trailer brake second corridor, converted from a BSK; and a further driving trailer second. In the TSOs, the lavatories became the driving cabs, which solved the problem of how to retain 64 seats in the vehicle but caused others. Originally, 28 Class 491 4TC units were built together with three as 3TC units which were identical but omitted the trailer first. The 3TCs were later converted to four-car units and supplemented with a further 3x4TC. The seating of the 4TC units comprised 42 first class and 169 2nd class.

Class 33 Diesel-electrics

These were an essential part of the scheme. Of the Southern's fleet of 98, 19 were modified for push-pull operation with multiple-unit stock and fitted with buckeye couplers. They could double-head if necessary with Class 73s, and became sub-class 33/1.

4VEP, 7701-894

The original build of Class 423 4VEP units was intended for outer suburban and stopping trains to Bournemouth. As such, they had suburban type 3+2 seating and in open saloons for second class, and slam doors to each and every seating bay. There were four first class compartments with a side corridor in each driving trailer composite.

The powered vehicle was the non-driving motor open brake second, and there was also a trailer second. This followed the 4CIG units towards ac practice where the traction is concentrated in a single intermediate vehicle rather than powering both end cars.

Total seating as built was 48 first and 232 second. Subsequent alterations to this large class of units, which were used all over the old Southern Region, saw declassification of one, later two, first class compartments and the conversion of part of the van accommodation to seat 18 additional passengers. A table showing the effect of these capacity changes appears, with the discussion on the Class 442 units, in Chapter 12. The VEPs were originally fitted with curtains, all later removed, while the sliding ventilators were fixed in the closed position. Nineteen units have had their first class accommodation permanently downclassed for operation on the Connex South London Metro service and have become 4VOP units.

Operations

The method of working was as follows. A train leaving Waterloo would have, at the rear, a high-powered 4REP unit complete with buffet car. This would be propelling either one or two 4TC units. The train would be driven from the cab at the front of the first TC unit in the normal way; to the uninitiated, the whole looked much like any other multiple-unit formation.

On arrival at Bournemouth, a Class 33 diesel would back down on to the front of the train, and one (or occasionally both) of the TC units would be uncoupled and attached to the diesel.

This would then haul the TC to Weymouth. Meanwhile, the TC+REP unit would repair to the sidings in between the tracks to be serviced and to await the next up working.

After arriving at Weymouth, the return train would be propelled by the Class 33 from the rear, the driver now occupying the TC cab. Before its arrival at Bournemouth, a REP+TC unit would leave the berthing sidings and proceed to the far end of the up platform, ready for the TC+Class 33 formation to be attached to its rear. The diesel would then be detached and what was now an all-electric train would depart for Waterloo. The basic service pattern was as shown in Fig 10.11.

The Southern was put in considerable difficulties by the late delivery of some of the rolling stock for the Bournemouth line, to the extent that many thought that some steam locomotives might be retained for a little longer. This did not happen, although in the event it might have been a sensible move. As it was, the start of the timetable was put back a month, and the electric services commenced on 10 July 1967. There were a number of problems:

- The 4REP traction motors and shoe beam pick-up gear were giving a good deal of trouble.
- While the last 4REP unit had been delivered to the Southern, it had still to be fitted out with its traction equipment.
- The delivery programme for the 4VEP units from York Works was running behind time, with two or three yet to come.
- None of the fleet of 10 new electro-diesels in the E6101 number series had been delivered, and they were not in the event available for traffic purposes for the best part of another year.

Improvised arrangements to provide alternatives saw Class 33 diesel-electrics and Class 73 electro-diesels married up with 4TC units for use on the main line through to London. They could be either hauled or propelled. These trains however would have had no buffet facilities, so some loco-hauled buffet cars were fitted temporarily with air brakes and electrical connections, and incorporated in the formations. Even suburban units of the 2EPB and 4EPB types were to be found in these trains. A not untypical formation was recorded on 18 November

1967 for the 10.30 Waterloo-Bournemouth. This consisted, from the country end, of 4TC unit+3TC unit+RB S1758, all propelled by electro-diesel No E6013.

Perhaps the most macabre result was the creation of the curious 8VAB unit in 1968, when one feels matters must have becoming desperate! One particular problem was the 15.30 fast service from Waterloo, which was additional to the basic service pattern and included a portion for, in those days, the Swanage branch. This was made up from Rail Blue vehicles taken from 4VEP units Nos 7741 and 7742, plus an additional motor brake second and a blue/grey RB restaurant buffet from the hauled fleet. It worked as an indivisible unit, No 8001, TOPS code Class 480, the formation and seating accommodation provided being as shown in Fig 10.12. On the right is a comparison with the 4REP+4TC formation which it replaced.

As can be seen, the 8VAB accommodation had more seats, due largely to the 3+2 rather than 2+2 seating in the second class. The VAB did, however, provide an extra motor car, giving three instead of two for an 8-car formation. Thus, it was reckoned, it could propel a single 4TC unit to and from Bournemouth, for which it would provide the same traction power as a 'normal' 12-car formation of 3x4VEP. This gave the bonus that the 4TC unit which it was likely to propel could then be taken over by a Class 33 in the normal way for the journey on to Swanage. But there is always a snag, and in this case it was a lack of means of heating the TC unit. In the depths of winter, Swanage passengers would have been really cold by the time the

Class 33 was hooked on at Bournemouth.

More seriously, the overall shortage of units was addressed, and more 4REP and 4TC units were built in 1974 as already discussed. This activity allowed the 8VAB unit to be disbanded at the end of the same year.

The 'Brighton Belle'

For what turned out to be little more than a curtain call, the three 5BEL Pullman sets were renovated at Eastleigh in 1968/9 and painted in blue and grey livery. The Pullman Car Co had now been acquired by British Railways, and the Pullman umber and cream did not reflect the corporate image. The cars had the double arrow symbols at each end, with the words Brighton Belle on the waist panels, and yellow ends and the first class cars lost their names. Upholstery was charcoal and grey check in first class, and blue and green check with navy blue arm- and headrests in second class. Mustard colour carpets and orange window curtains were fitted.

The timings proved not to be completely sacrosanct, as from September 1963 the number of return trips had been increased from three to four. 13.25 for the first 'Belle' from Brighton always seemed unconscionably late, and the introduction of a 09.26 up departure was still well after the dawn chorus. A late down run was also begun, leaving Victoria at 23.00 and calling at Haywards Heath. This also involved the trains being stabled at Brighton rather than at the London end of the line. Further changes came in 1967. The 'Belle' was limited to 75mph, whereas the new CIG stock had a 90mph capability. Thus the old trains had to fit in as

Fig 10.12: 8VAB Unit from 7x4VEP Vehicles and Buffet Car, Compared with 4REP+4TC

	Seats	8VAB		Seats	4REP +4TC
Driving trailer composite	24F	38S	Driving motor saloon second		64S
Non-driving motor brake second		58S	Trailer brake first	24F	
Trailer buffet		19S	Trailer buffet		19S
Non-driving motor brake second		58S	Driving motor saloon second		64S
Driving trailer composite	24F	38S	Driving trailer saloon second		64S
Driving trailer composite	24F	38S	Trailer brake second		32S
Non-driving motor brake second		58S	Trailer first	42S	
Driving trailer composite	24F	38S	Driving trailer saloon second		64S
Total, 8VAB	96F	345S	Total, 4REP+4TC	66F	307S

Fig. 10.11: Hourly Pattern of Waterloo to Bournemouth Services – 1967 Inaugural Timetable

xx13	Surbiton, Woking (detach portion for Portsmouth & Southsea), and all stations to Basingstoke	62min
xx30	Even hours only. Southampton, Bournemouth, Poole, Wareham (connection for Swanage), Wool, Dorchester, Weymouth. Buffet car to Bournemouth	100min to Bournemouth, 141min to Weymouth
xx43	Surbiton, Woking, Brookwood (detach portion for Alton), Farnborough and all stations except Southampton Airport to Bournemouth	174min
xx47	Woking, Basingstoke, Winchester, Eastleigh, Southampton Airport, Southampton, Brockenhurst (connection for Lymington Pier), New Milton, Christchurch, Bournemouth. Even hour departures from Waterloo (only) continue all stations to Weymouth	127min to Bournemouth

The fast services at xx30 overtook the xx43 stopping service (previous hour) at Southampton, providing connections into and out of the latter.

best they could, and some timings were reduced to 55 minutes. 'Brighton in the hour' might have impressed the previous generation, but it represents only a tiny fraction above a pedestrian 50mph average.

In March 1971, it was announced that the all-Pullman service, the 'Brighton Belle', would be replaced by ordinary electric stock from 1 May 1972 due to increasing age and decrepitude, although the press release expressed it more prosaically. This was after nearly 40 years of service, albeit that the stock was stored during part of World War 2.

On the last day, Sunday, 30 April 1972, special arrangements were made. Besides the normal services, a 'cheese and wine' special was laid on from Brighton at 18.50 at a fare of £7.50, and a 'champagne special' from Victoria at 22.30. This was due at Brighton at 23.52 and the fare of £10 included a cold meal and champagne. A relief train left Victoria at 22.02 for Brighton, returning at

00.30 with calls at Redhill and East Croydon, arriving Victoria at 01.30. Ordinary platform ticket sales were suspended and 500 souvenir platform permits were issued at Victoria, and 250 at Brighton, priced at 50p each.

On 9 May, the organisers of the Brighton festival hired the 'Belle' for a special trip to Brighton and back, and this time a £10 fare covered the journey, dinner at the Royal Pavilion and champagne. The cars were sold, including six to a firm of brewers and four for use as restaurants.

Modern Railways regretted its passing. In an editorial, the magazine fantasized about a set of redundant East Coast Pullmans converted for push-pull operation with one of the Southern's electro-diesels at one end. This could shuttle between Victoria and Brighton 'not three or four times a day, but to a day-long intensive diagram, which would release a standard CIG/BIG set for duty elsewhere'.

Instead of bringing all services down to a basic level, it could have provided the one service in the country where the ordinary passenger who was not an expense account business executive could have travelled on a train with that extra special luxury.

Little did *Modern Railways* know how 'Gatwick Express' would take up that operational concept in another decade's time. The use of the Class 73s even came as close to this as painting No 73101 in real Pullman livery for the Brighton line's 150th anniversary celebrations in 1992, which it retained until 2001.

11. The Other Railways

There are a number of railways which do not quite fit the traditional Southern Electric image, but which are certainly entitled to be included in a wide-ranging book of this nature.

'A margin was built into the estimates for the costs of construction in order to lessen the risk of eventual overspending.'

British Railways Board, Report on Cross-Channel Rail Tunnel, 1979

Southern Heights Light Railway

Every now and again in railway history, there arises a curious undertaking which subsequently slowly sinks out of sight, with no physical work ever undertaken. Such was the Southern Heights Light Railway, which in the mid-1920s it was proposed to construct from Sanderstead on the Croydon and Oxted joint line of the Brighton and South Eastern Railways, to Orpington on the South Eastern main line.

This railway would have occupied an area bounded by Croydon, Bromley, Tonbridge and Oxted, into which only the Hayes branch presently enters. The terrain on the edge of the North Downs was decidedly difficult, and it would have been necessary to have crossed many deep gullies in the chalk. This 15$^{1}/_{2}$-mile line was intended to be routed via Chelsham, Tatsfield, Westerham Hill, Downe and Green Street Green. The route was chosen for the promoters by that mildly eccentric collector of obscure minor railways, Col H. F. Stephens.

Prospects augured well, since the Southern Railway agreed to work the line for 75% of the gross receipts and to guarantee interest at 5% on the £330,000 debenture stock. The ordinary capital was to have been £500,000 and the company was to have paid the Southern Railway £140,000 in cash or shares to meet the cost of the single track which it was at first proposed to lay. The proposals were strongly attacked by the town planners, but even so the undertaking obtained its Light Railway Order in 1926.

However, nine years later in 1937 little more had been heard of the company, and it was made known that no attempt would be made to exercise its powers.

East Devon Electrification

Worting Junction is where the Southampton line leaves the West of England main line, a couple of miles or so west of Basingstoke. This had long been the haunt of locomotive-hauled trains, including such well-known named services as the 'Devon Belle' and the 'Atlantic Coast Express'. These were in the days when the Southern route was not just to Exeter, but very much a through line to a number of destinations in North Devon.

A boundary reorganisation from 1 January 1963 saw the West of England main line west of Salisbury ceded by British Railways Southern Region to the Western Region, and there is at least circumstantial evidence that Paddington never gave the ex-Southern line its due. The services began to be whittled away, a process which was hastened by the removal, one by one, of the Southern branches west of Exeter. Today, the Barnstaple branch, itself truncated from its former Ilfracombe terminus, remains. There are other services to Okehampton, sponsored by Devon County Council while, east of Exeter, the branch to Exmouth alone retains a passenger service. The question of what to do with the Southern main line has always been complicated by a track layout which results in the route arriving at Exeter St David's facing towards London rather than pointing further west. It should be added, though, that the Barnstaple line is a continuation in the same direction from Waterloo.

Sections of the Waterloo to Exeter main line were singled west of Wilton in 1967. A long passing loop was retained between Templecombe (but not including the station platform) and Yeovil Junction, while station loops exist at Gillingham (Dorset), Chard Junction (no station) and Honiton. Double track is regained at Pinhoe. Many intermediate stations were closed, and this included those whose main purpose in life was as a junction station for the coastal branches. This draconian step was later reversed, to the extent that Feniton (formerly Sidmouth Junction) was reopened in 1971, and both Templecombe and Pinhoe in 1983. In each case, there was a judicious local authority grant towards the costs.

Eventually, the decision was taken not to electrify the 122 miles from Worting Junction to Exeter; instead a variant of the Class 158 DMU fleet of Regional Railways was ordered. The 22-strong fleet of Class 159s were all three-car units, which took over from the

Right:
The damp morning of 15 April 2000 sees Seaton Tramway car No 16 at the Harbour Road terminus, ready to make the trip to Colyton. This car was built in 1921 as a 3ft 6in-gauge Bournemouth open-top car No 106, and was rebuilt at Seaton between 1974 and 1991. *Author*

Western Region-based Class 50 and early Mk 2 non-air-conditioned stock in 1994. Up to three units may be found working together.

However, electrification did reach East Devon in an unusual manner, which justifies its inclusion. Among the branches which closed in the Beeching years was that from Seaton Junction to Seaton, a line which had two intermediate stations at Colyton and Colyford. It followed the western bank of the River Axe with splendid views of the estuary and the wading birds, terminating at an inconveniently sited Seaton station, well to the east of the town centre.

In the summer of 1956, the Seaton branch boasted 14 down and 12 up trains on Mondays to Fridays, and 17 down and 16 up on Saturdays. There were through carriages to and from Waterloo on Summer Saturdays, and a return late train from Seaton Junction to Seaton at 21.42 on Fridays and Saturdays only. There were nine branch trains each way on Sundays. But such lines were by now in serious decline and the Seaton branch was amongst those proposed for closure in the 'Reshaping Report' of 1963. This 4¼-mile branch was closed to all traffic on 7 March

1966. This line was definitely 'Southern', but it never had any chance of becoming 'electric'. Or did it?

That would have been the end of it, other than for a surprise benefactor. From 1954, Claude Lane had run a 2ft-gauge miniature tramway two-thirds of a mile along the front at Eastbourne. This could certainly be described as 'electric', but not 'Southern'. However, he knew that he would have to quit the site in East Sussex in 1969, as it was wanted for a housing development scheme. Searching for a new location, he came upon the Seaton branch.

This appeared to fit the bill admirably, and so in the end it proved. The Seaton station site had already been acquired by other interests, but as already mentioned, it was far from an ideal position. There was however enough to make an opposed but successful application for a Light Railway Order in 1969 worth while, and the line was purchased from British Rail Estates Department.

By the start of the 1971 season, approximately one mile of 2ft 9in-gauge track had been laid along the River Axe estuary from what had become the Riverside depot area in Seaton to what is known as Bobsworth Bridge — on account of the 1970 fare! All the tramcars needed regauging to this wider gauge. There were no passing loops and no overhead wire, so the service was limited to a single car powered by a battery which was charged up during part of the morning. It

transpired that the vital need was to increase the number of trams which could be operated simultaneously in order to increase revenue. This meant two things — the addition of passing loops and electrification.

The two intermediate loops (there are now six over the whole length of the tramway) were fitted with automatic spring-operated points, which ensured that trams coming from opposite directions always took the same route, usually the left-hand one. For the electrification, 79 traction poles were recovered from Eastbourne Corporation's Lighting Department as scrap, while the company installed its own diesel generator and a standby. Most of the overhead line fittings were purchased from Bradford Corporation who were then dismantling their trolleybus system, and others from Hamburg City Tramways who closed their system in 1978. The first passenger service car ran from Riverside depot to Colyford, 2.2 miles, using overhead collection powered at 120V dc on 23 September 1973.

However, accessibility for passengers was very poor, and the company decided that a high priority was to make use of the land purchased from local farmers in 1971 to construct a ½-mile route towards the town centre. Taking advantage of the light rail geometry which allows relatively fearsome curvature, the new route took the railway westwards in its approach to Seaton. This lay behind the holiday camp which was nearer the sea, after which the tramway regained a southerly course to its Harbour Road terminus close to the seafront and adjacent to the town centre main car park, as well as the tourist information office. Opened on 17 May 1975, this section immediately started to generate the much-needed extra revenue.

The target now was Colyton. To go beyond Colyford, a road had to be crossed on the level, just as the Seaton branch had done before it. This is now an automatic open crossing, locally monitored (AOCL). Monitoring is the responsibility of the tram driver. He or she stops, presses the activating button on a post, waits until the sequence of traffic lights and audio warning has operated, checks that the white light is exhibited to confirm that all is in order, and crosses when it is safe to do so.

The extension was completed to Colyton, 3.2 miles, which is now the northern terminus. A great deal of ballast had to be recovered from other parts of the line to replace that washed away in the 1968 floods, while another 35 traction standards had to be erected and a fourth generating station installed. Commercial operations to Colyton began on 3 April 1980 where the instantly

Below:
This sign may be seen alongside the Seaton Tramway terminus at Colyton. Photographed on 15 April 2000, it offers no doubts about the line being electrified. *Author*

recognisable ex-LSWR station is used. This also serves as a shop and tearooms. The trackbed beyond has been abandoned and the bridges dismantled.

The tramway is single track throughout, but with as many as six intermediate passing loops. There are presently 10 trams in the passenger fleet. Five of these are single deck, with three closed and two open vehicles. The five double-deck cars are all open-topped. There is also a works car. Most were built locally, based on designs such as the Llandudno & Colwyn Bay cars ex Bournemouth (Nos 6, 7 and 8 in the fleet), the Blackpool 'Open Boat' cars (No 4), the London Metropolitan Tramways Type A design (Nos 2 and 14), or the Manx Electric Railway 'toastrack' cars (No 17). Some are genuine oldies, as is the former Exeter Corporation Tramways 3ft 6in-gauge car of 1906 (No 19) which has been much rebuilt at Seaton.

The services provided run daily, every 20 minutes, during a season that lasts from April to the end of October. This is continued on Saturdays and Sundays until Christmas, the only variations during the seasons being the time of shutdown. Thus, the last tram arrives back at Seaton by 16.54 in the darker winter evenings, but this is as late as 21.34 in high summer. The first tram departure from Seaton is always at 10.00. Journey times are 23 minutes for the complete journey between Harbour Road

and Colyton. The line is operated by the Modern Electric Tramway Ltd, trading as Seaton & District Tramway Company.

Channel Tunnel

Opened in 1994, the Channel Tunnel is a major undertaking. The Anglo-French company of Eurotunnel is both owner and operator of a railway facility in its own right, and is also an infrastructure company which permits other railway operators to use the facility for the passage of their own trains. The tunnel is electrified at 25kV ac overhead. Services can be divided into two categories those of the shuttle services and the through railway operations.

The shuttles run only between the Folkestone terminal at Cheriton, and the Calais terminal at Coquelles. At each end of the 59km journey there are terminal loops on which are situated the loading and unloading bays. On the passenger shuttles, car and coach drivers drive the vehicles on to the shuttles themselves, and they and all passengers stay in their vehicles throughout the journey. For cars, the vehicles are double-deck. Toilets are provided in the shuttle vehicles, but no other facilities. Customs formalities are undertaken at the point of departure, which means that on arrival vehicles are free to drive away.

Similar arrangements apply to freight shuttles for heavy goods vehicles, except that here drivers can leave their vehicles and

and are 393.48 metres long. This is the equivalent of 19 Mk 1 coaches.

Eurostar services started on 14 November 1994 with the opening of Waterloo International station. Journey time from Waterloo to the British portal is 1 hour 10 minutes, with 21 minutes for tunnel transit, and 1 hour 24 minutes from the French portal to Paris Nord. This allows five minutes for one intermediate stop within an overall 3-hour 0-minute journey time. The time to Brussels, initially 3 hours 15 minutes, was reduced by 30 minutes or so by the completion of the TGV Belge line in Belgium in 1996.

The distance from Waterloo International to Continental Junction is 69m 11ch, with the fastest timing of 1 hour 7 minutes, but pathing difficulties can extend this to 1 hour 15 minutes. Waterloo International, with its five platforms, is designed to handle 6,000 passengers an hour. Train turnround in the platforms is 50 minutes. There are 21 ticket selling positions, although many passengers arrive with pre-purchased tickets. Entrance to

Far left:
This general view of the Folkestone Eurotunnel terminal sees one of the Brush-built Shuttle locomotives at the head of a train in May 1994.
John Chapman

Left:
The size of the Eurotunnel freight shuttles is emphasised by this HGV in one of the skeletal rail vehicles, seen here at the Calais terminal in May 1994. *John Chapman*

Below:
The spacious and airy Waterloo International terminus has five platforms, which seems more than adequate for the modest service levels offered. On the other side of the same station, five platforms are enough to dispatch 24 trains an hour, but this is not a suburban operation. Seen here is Platform 24 with unit No 3229, a French-owned set. The date is 4 July 1999. *Author*

proceed to a vehicle offering refreshments where they can relax. Again, all Customs work is completed before departure.

In both cases, the end-to-end journey time is about 35 minutes; the service is continuous throughout the day, with service frequencies varying to meet the anticipated traffic requirements.

This still leaves plenty of capacity for through trains, which consist of Eurostars between London and Paris or Brussels, or international freight from the former Railfreight Distribution business, which is now part of English, Welsh & Scottish Railway (EWS).

A fleet of 31 Trans Manche Super Train (TMST) sets of Class 373 rolling stock provide the Eurostar services. Of these sets, 11 are UK owned, 16 French and four Belgian. An operational set consists of two identical nine-coach half sets and a power car on each end. Sets are articulated within themselves. Trains contain 210 first class seats and 584 second class (not standard class) seats, totalling 794,

the security area is via gates which read the encoded information on the tickets. Passengers are advised to allow 20 minutes for checking in, reduced to 10 minutes for full-fare ticket holders. This includes Customs clearance. Passengers are called forward to their trains from a large lounge which has 16 shop units. There are separate levels for the trains (top), departing passengers (centre) and arriving passengers (bottom). There is also a short-stay car park in the basement with space for 140 cars.

A second set of international platforms (Nos 3 and 4) were built centrally at the existing Ashford station and opened on 8 January 1996. Platforms 1 and 2 cater mainly for domestic traffic towards London, and Platforms 5 and 6 for the domestic down services. All platforms, and indeed the through routes, are reversibly signalled.

Other supporting infrastructure for Eurostar services included the following:

- The new flyover west of Vauxhall for Eurostar access to the Chatham fast lines from Victoria
- The Stewarts Lane chord to give access from Waterloo to the West London line, and hence the new depot at North Pole.
- North Pole depot itself, and the electrification of the lines giving access from Waterloo.

Eurostar trains run from Waterloo International to Brussels Midi alternate hours on Mondays to Fridays, with the service increasing to hourly at the principal business times. Six of the 10 trains a day call at Ashford, and all serve Lille.

To Paris Nord, trains leave hourly, but extra services make it a half-hourly provision leaving Waterloo International between 16.23 and 17.48. There are 16 trains a day on Mondays to Fridays, of which nine stop at Ashford but

only four at Calais Fréthun. The timetables are those of Winter 2000/1. The frequencies are given only as a general guide, as the services are not as regularly timed as has been common on the Southern for many years.

Croydon Tramlink

What has become the Croydon Tramlink system had its origins in a 1986 study by London Transport covering London as a whole. This assessed the possibilities of light rail techniques for a number of locations, of which the Croydon area scored the highest.

The key problem was how to serve the central shopping and business districts, and this was to be a uni-directional clockwise loop using existing streets, some of which were closed to normal traffic. The most northerly part of the loop passed West Croydon station and the adjacent bus station. However, assuming the loop was a practicable idea, this still did not solve the problem of how to feed the centre of Croydon from the outlying areas.

The main components were three radiating routes. To the north west and Wimbledon lay the Wimbledon-West Croydon railway, or 'WimWon' to its friends. Latterly, this had only a basic service provided by one two-car EPB unit of a train every 45 minutes, which was not attractive, and patronage was not overwhelming. This was one candidate for conversion to light rail.

On the east side of central Croydon, the two parts of the loop come together to pass outside East Croydon station, a major interchange. Continuing to Sandilands, and more or less segregated from other traffic, the trams encounter the former Elmers End to Sanderstead railway where it passes underneath, with a road overbridge and cutting. Here, it was decided that a steep ramp down could enable trams to turn both left (north) and right (south).

The left turn takes them to the existing bay platform at Elmers End station, and although Beckenham Junction was a further objective, a spat with the planning authority meant that trams for that route would have to leave the Elmers End line of route before reaching the terminus. These trams thus turn to the left at the new Arena stop and pass over new territory before rising to run alongside the ex-Brighton branch from Crystal Palace, which they join a little to the west of Birkbeck station. This line remains operational on the single-track formation. A new terminal was built as close as possible, but outside the existing Beckenham Junction station.

Turning right at Sandilands Junction takes the trams through the old tunnels to the site of Coombe Road station, after which they leave the original railway formation and continue alongside a road to New Addington. This large housing area was until then the largest population in Greater London (25,000) to have no rail connection.

This left the problem of depot facilities, for which a site was found on the Wimbledon line at Therapia Lane. To connect this section to the loop required a flyover to be built over the West Croydon to Sutton railway line, and another was needed to bridge the railway at Mitcham Junction. Previously, the 'WimWon' trains had shared the same pair of platforms, but the new tram stop was now to be laid alongside. At Wimbledon, trams are allowed to use only the western end of Platform 10. Thameslink services now use the other half of the same island, Platform 9, in both directions.

A casualty of the Tramlink scheme was the section of the Addiscombe branch south of Woodside station, but the abandoned length is less than $^3/_4$ mile long and extra stops on Tramlink compensate to a large extent. On all lines, stops are placed considerably closer together than usual stations, as befits the type of service offered.

The Elmers End-Sanderstead service ceased in 1983, and to allow construction to proceed, the last Southern services ran both from Wimbledon to West Croydon and from Elmers End to Addiscombe on 31 May 1997.

Tramlink opened in three separate stages during May 2000 and services are provided by a fleet of 20 six-axle, articulated and 70% low floor trams; the traction motors are mounted in the pair of bogies at each end of the 30.1m vehicle. The trams have 70 seats and a total capacity, including standing, of

Left:
Avenue Road stop is on the Beckenham Junction spur of Croydon Tramlink; this view was taken looking towards Croydon on 30 September 2000. The Railtrack line was singled and can be seen on the right-hand side, while Tramlink was built, nominally, on the other trackbed. Fortunately, there was enough width available for this modest expansion. *Author*

about 200. They were built by Bombardier and most sport a smart red and white livery. Services are run on the following routes from around 05.30 to midnight, with later starts on Sundays.

Route 1   Wimbledon-Croydon-Elmers End
Route 2   Beckenham Junction-Croydon
Route 3   New Addington-Croydon

Service frequencies are around five per hour during the bulk of the day but dropping to two each hour at other times and on Sundays. In general, Route 3 runs at twice the frequency of the others.

On the former railway sections, there are now three more stops than there were stations between Sandilands and Elmers End, two more between Birkbeck and Beckenham Junction and six more on the Wimbledon branch. Power supplies are at 750V dc from overhead wiring. It could hardly be said that the loss of the old rail services imposed any real hardship for users

due to the minimal numbers, and the new operation offers great opportunities for the communities along the routes.

As an indication of the importance of the former railway alignments, of the 17.5 route miles of the present system, 10.6 miles (61%) were formerly British Rail, 1.9 miles (11%) are on-street, and a further 5.0 miles (28%) are off-street and completely new.

Services are operated by Tramlink (Croydon) Ltd.

Channel Tunnel Rail Link

Now under construction is Section 1 of the 25kV ac Channel Tunnel Rail Link. The opening of the Channel Tunnel in 1994 was only part of the story, at least as far as through trains were concerned. Eurostar and Railfreight Distribution trains were then faced with a long and relatively slow journey over a congested network to reach London. The Channel Tunnel Rail Link Act of 1996 authorised the construction of a specialised high speed link, which is being constructed in two sections.

Section 1 is the 70km from the Channel Tunnel to Southfleet Junction in North Kent, where the initial route diverges towards the Chatham main line which it reaches at Fawkham Junction, a little to the west of Longfield station. There is a freight connection from Dollands Moor Yard and a

major intermediate station at Ashford International, incorporating connections to and from the domestic network. Engineering features further west include the 3.2km North Downs Tunnel and then a spectacular 1.2km viaduct across the River Medway. The 4km link line from Southfleet Junction to Fawkham Junction utilises the formation of the old Gravesend West branch, and is designed to allow trains to serve Waterloo International.

The 39km of Section 2 from Southfleet Junction to St Pancras will have a station at Ebbsfleet, again international and domestic, with a connection to the North Kent line between Northfleet and Gravesend. The Rail Link is then to negotiate the 3km Thames Tunnel. On reaching Ripple Lane, Barking, there will be a connection for freight traffic to leave the link. The line will then enter the 19km London Tunnel to reach Stratford international and domestic station, and continue underground until reaching St Pancras as the London terminus, 109km from the Tunnel. There will be a connection to the West Coast main line via the North London line.

The new railway is being built under a private/public partnership contract between the Government and London & Continental Railways (LCR), and under a purchase agreement between Railtrack and LCR. On completion, Railtrack will purchase Section 1 from LCR, at cost. LCR has a contractual obligation to complete Section 2.

The total construction costs of the new railway infrastructure, including land purchase, at 1997 prices are:

	Private Sector	Public Sector	Total
Section 1	£890m	£780m	£1,670m
Section 2	£1,510m	£1,000m	£2,510m
Total	£2,400m	£1,780m	£4,180m

There are three stages in construction for Section 1, which is scheduled to be completed by 2003:

Civil engineering work
    Earth movement, bridges, tunnels, retaining walls £780m
Railtrack interfaces
    Dollands Moor, Ashford, Fawkham Junction £690m
Systems installation
    Track, overhead line equipment, signalling, communications...........£200m

Signalling for Section 1 will be controlled from Railtrack's Ashford IECC, with electrical control from Paddock Wood. There is a need to distinguish between the ordinary domestic railway, which is regulated, and the Rail Link, which is not.

When the Rail Link is complete, that is after Section 2 is commissioned, it will be able to take trains running at 300km/h (186mph). Over two-thirds of it is on curves, for which a radius of not less than 4km is desirable. It is however heavily graded, with sections of 1 in 40 and there are only two lengths of line which are 100% flat, totalling a mere 4km in distance. Through Ashford, speeds will be limited to 270km/h.

In terms of capacity, the completed railway will have train paths sufficient to run, in a specimen hour:

- 6 Eurostars to St Pancras (or north of London).
- 2 Eurostars to Waterloo.
- 4 peak domestic trains from Ashford to St Pancras.
- 4 peak domestic trains from Ebbsfleet to St Pancras.

Journey times will be decidedly short, that from Ashford to London being 37 minutes compared with the present 75 minutes, and from Ebbsfleet 15 minutes as opposed to 46 minutes from Northfleet. This benefit can be extended to locations on the existing railway; thus travellers from Margate could save 20 minutes, from Canterbury West 35 minutes, and from Dover 40 minutes. That however depends upon the provision of through services, using highly sophisticated and thus costly rolling stock, which will also need to be fitted with dual voltage equipment for ac overhead and third rail. Alternatively, cross-platform transfers to a Rail Link-dedicated fleet might be arranged at Ashford or, particularly, Ebbsfleet, where the potential time savings are that much less.

The line is being constructed to carry freight, with passing loops at Lenham, midway between Ashford and the Maidstone area, and at Singlewell, to the south of Gravesend, There will be no daytime paths for freight or for any other trains travelling at a mere 140km/h (87$\frac{1}{2}$mph), unless Eurostar gives up (a euphemism for 'sells') some of its contracted paths. There are prospects for 200km/h paths at night to and from the West and East Coast main lines as well as into Europe.

Maintenance will be a key requirement. It will be a new railway, and there is every intention to keep it in such condition. It is intended that night-time possessions be limited to six hours (Monday to Friday) and seven hours (weekends). Longer possessions will not be permitted. Crossovers between lines are placed roundly 15km apart, and the distance between track centres is as much as 4,500mm. Thus the traditional (if very approximate) 'six foot' between the outer edges of the running rails of adjacent tracks is expanded to something nearer 10ft. This will aid substantially the ability to undertake work on one track while traffic continues on the other, and it is hoped that the 15 minutes additional journey time will be allowed from 22.30 to 06.15. The line will use cab signalling, which will extend to everything that uses it, including track maintenance equipment. There may be a role here for vehicles which can operate on both roads and the railway.

However, there will be no old 2EPB sets going up and down at night on Sandite runs! Having said that, adhesion for heavy trains on 1 in 40 gradients under conditions of falling leaves or snow or ice may still be problematic, and this is a matter which will need to be addressed.

Administrative matters include the need to write a new rule book and electric lines instructions, the training of any staff who may come into contact with the new railway, and taking the message on the dangers of overhead electrification to the community, especially schools.

Section 1 work is in the budget to open on 28 September 2003, with Railtrack hoping to operate the complete railway. Section 2 is on target to open on 1 January 2007. The Channel Tunnel Rail Link will have a substantial effect on the traffic on the existing rail network, affecting travel demand as well as the number of train paths which become available. The Ebbsfleet domestic and international station is planned to have parking spaces for 9,000 cars, leading to the quip that walking from the far reaches of the car park to the station will take as long as the journey time to St Pancras! More seriously, though, where will the passengers here and at Ashford come from, and will there be a net gain or a net loss to franchise operator Connex SouthEastern? Either way, what further developments might follow?

Large scale change is not new. The Southern Railway's policy of electrification resulted in a huge expansion of traffic volumes and the suburbanisation of the Home Counties, with the benefits of what was perceived as their fresh, clean air. People were enticed to 'live in Kent and be content', in the advertising copy of what is becoming an increasingly remote period. Transport links shrink distances; will Ebbsfleet become a dormitory for Paris commuters as well as those of London? Alternatively, when Stratford International is open, might one live in Calais and commute to London Docklands in less time than it takes presently to commute from Margate? How feasible will it be to work for the EU in Brussels and travel daily from England?

Below:
Work on Section 1 of the Channel Tunnel Rail Link, which uses the old Gravesend West branch alignment in part, was progressing apace in early 2001. This is the bridge whereby the CTRL will cross the B260 road near Longfield, about $\frac{1}{4}$ mile short of the junction with the Chatham line at Fawkham Junction. The view was taken on 29 January 2001, looking north west. *Author*

12. The Modern Era

The Board was challenging the continued use of slam door compartment stock in the late 1960s. Tests on a mock-up constructed at Doncaster compared boarding and alighting times in a range of conditions of crowding for various types of door configurations and internal layout. The decision went in favour of developing a vehicle with sliding power-operated double doors, with open saloons and vestibules. The prototype vehicles appeared in 1971 and 1972.

Sliding Doors in the Suburbs

4PEP, 4001-2; 2PEP, 2001

The experimental trains were built at York. They were sent to the Southern, where they were employed primarily on the less busy South Western suburban services from 1973. Every axle was powered, which gave them a sprightly turn of speed. Rheostatic as well as electro-pneumatic braking also stopped them quickly. Forced draught ventilation used warm air created by the braking system in cold weather, with double glazing. The Scharfenberg couplers enabled the simultaneous achievement of electrical, brake and physical connections.

Ride quality was considerably better than that of the domestic stock. On the other hand, traction motors at one per axle were thought by the engineers to be excessive (there are an awful lot of axles on the Southern), bearing in mind that recent moves had been towards having one power car only in a four-car unit. In capacity terms, the inclusion of three sets of double doors per side in the two intermediate cars (the driving cars had two sets) did limit the seating space. The PEP units also had low-backed and relatively hard seats, which did not meet with approval universally. The new types of unit are set out in Fig 12.1. One of the later BR-series EPB units is also included, for comparative purposes.

Class 508 508001-43

Their development work over, the PEP trains were retired from the public eye in 1976. The first fruits of their pioneering work were not seen south of the Thames until 1979, with the delivery of the Class 508 stock. These were each formed of two driving motor cars with all axles motored and two unpowered trailers. The result was a considerably reduced maximum power output. One motor vehicle and its trailer were equipped with air

Above:
The two Rail Blue PEP prototypes ran generally as an eight-car unit, but with one of the unpainted cars from the two-car unit substituting. Here, No 4001 leads an up service from Hampton Court into Clapham Junction on 9 October 1976. In those days, sliding doors were downright revolutionary here! *Author*

compressors, which supplied air for the suspension, braking and door mechanisms, while the second motor vehicle had an alternator and battery. Underframes were steel. The car bodies were of integral construction, with an alloy skin riveted to a lightweight steel frame. All traction and auxiliary equipment, apart from the driving controls, was under the floor. Each set was internally gangwayed, but the end doors were for emergency use only.

The basic seat layout was 2+3, reduced to 2+2 at bulkheads and partitions. This managed to increase the seating by 14% compared with the PEP prototype. Another new feature was the door closure button, with which passengers could close individual doors themselves if they so wished. Tightlock couplers were fitted at the ends of the units with similar all-embracing qualities to the Scharfenberg couplers.

However, the Class 508s were not to stay on the Southern, and in five years they had departed for Merseyside. They left behind only one trailer from each of the 43 units, and this was incorporated in the Class 455/7 units then about to be delivered. Meanwhile, the Class 455/8 early versions had arrived, representing what the Southern really wanted.

Fig 12.1: New Wave SR Four-car Multiple-units

Year	No Series	Doors per Side	Seats	Length	Tonnes	Output	Couplers
1960	5301-55 (4EPB)	36 slam doors	392	77.7m	141.0	740kW	Buckeye
1971	4001-2 (4PEP)	10 pairs double	280	81.4m	139.8	1,184kW	Scharfenberg
1980	508001-43	8 pairs double	320	79.4m	125.0	660kW	Tightlock
1983	455801-74	8 pairs double	316	79.5m	131.7	740kW	Tightlock

In 1999, 12 of the now three-car Class 508 units returned from Merseyside to be leased for use on the South Eastern franchise, and have undergone facelift treatment at Eastleigh.

Class 455s and the 456 Version

The Class 455/8s were integral all-steel vehicles, without a separate underframe and were based on the Mk 3 coach with a shorter body. Total weight, which had fallen a little with the Class 508, was now back up again. They appeared from 1983 onwards.

They are made up of a driving trailer second, motor second, trailer second and driving trailer second. Only one vehicle carries the traction motors, which have reverted to the tried and trusted EE507s, exactly as used in the 4EPB stock and elsewhere. Performance is, again, correspondingly ponderous. The interiors are broadly similar to the Class 508s, although they are lacking in handrails – one of the identified faults with the original PEP train. Couplings are again Tightlock, but this time physically joining the vehicles only. Cables and hoses are once more hung on the outside of the cab, and the whole unit has a decidedly unattractive appearance, although subsequent deliveries of the Class 455/7 and Class 455/9 variants effected some small improvements in this respect. The fleets consisted of 43 Class 455/7, 74 Class 455/8 and 20 Class 455/9, and are shared between South West and South Central operations.

Above:
The contrasting front ends of the newcomer on the left, Class 455 No 5803, and the then incumbent No 508002, suggest that the design team took a holiday in between. They are at Waterloo on 13 April 1983, and will form the 17.34 to Shepperton and the 17.26 to Effingham Junction respectively. *Author*

Above right:
The Class 456s were the two-car versions of the Class 455, intended originally for the South Western lines but delivered to South Central. No 456024 is in Connex livery as it departs from Smitham with a train for Tattenham Corner on 9 February 1999. *Author*

The final essay in this direction for the Southern was the Class 456 two-car unit of 1991. This version was broadly similar, and the intention was that it would be used to vary the formations of the South Western fleet to match more nearly with the traffic on offer. However, the 24 units are now operated as part of the South Central franchise.

Hastings Electrification

Late in 1984, the Hastings line electrification was approved, to cover the 31 route miles from Tonbridge through to St Leonards, where the South Eastern line joins the Brighton's coastal route from Lewes. The project included work to eliminate the problems caused by the substandard tunnel dimensions, so that standard rolling stock could be used.

It was not just one tunnel, but three. These were Somerhill (410yd), Strawberry Hill (286yd) and Wadhurst (1,205yd), the total length of which was well over a mile. To undertake enlargement work of this magnitude on brick-lined tunnels would have been exceedingly costly, to say nothing of the revenue lost from the disruption this would cause to rail traffic over an extended period. The track through the 526yd Mountfield Tunnel between Robertsbridge and Battle had already been singled and laid on slab track in 1975, as there were then signs of impending tunnel collapse.

The preferred approach was to lay single track through all of them, on the basis that modern signalling would still allow adequate headways for the timetabled services. It did also, of course, avoid the need to build new stock, with the result that Hastings would see redeployed 4VEP or maybe 4CIG units. Why there should have been sufficient 'spare' trains is another matter, but this was in the early days of deliveries of large quantities of inner suburban electric units.

Apart from the tunnel work, this was a relatively simple exercise. Tunbridge Wells Central (as it then was) is a difficult station, wedged as it is on a curve between two tunnels. They are not quite a 12-car train length apart, which is a potential problem for formations of this length. Dispensation was obtained to ensure that this would not become a problem, as there is no alternative action which could be taken to lengthen the platforms. Both tracks in the station area at Tunbridge Wells have been reversibly signalled to give as much flexibility as possible to cope with terminating trains.

Slab track was installed in Grove Tunnel immediately to the south of Tunbridge Wells Central station, while substandard platform heights were raised at all 10 stations along the route. The elimination of Grove Junction itself, where the single track tunnelled link to the Brighton station at Tunbridge Wells West left the main Hastings line, became possible when the then Secretary of State, Nicholas Ridley, gave his consent to the closure of the Eridge service in 1985.

Four-aspect signalling was to be controlled from the existing signalboxes at Tonbridge, Robertsbridge and Bo-Peep Junction. For electrical supplies, use was made of the existing Paddock Wood Control Room which was to feed five new substations; there were seven track paralleling huts. A new departure was the use of an 11kV ring main rather than the more expensive and conventional 33kV ring main. This meant that stopping trains were limited to eight cars, but through empty stock trains of 12 cars were permitted. Conductor rail gaps were also introduced to cater for known badger runs.

The work was completed and the new services implemented on 6 May 1986. This offered a two-trains-per-hour service for the standard off-peak frequency, as shown in Fig 12.2.

Progress is rarely made at a uniform rate. Even so, it was now 19 years since the previous Southern electrification scheme had been completed, which was that to Bournemouth. The Southern Railway had made enormous progress in the interwar years up to and including 1939. Even with the intervention of World War 2, it was only 20 years before the next major scheme, Phase 1 of the Kent Coast electrification, which was completed in 1959.

The Hastings electrification was followed by a number of others which collectively almost – but not quite – completed the electrification of all surviving parts of the former Southern Railway, from the Bournemouth main line eastwards.

Next, however, was organisational change, for on 10 June 1986 Network SouthEast was created. For the first time ever, all the commuter railways of south east England within a radius of roundly 50 miles from central London, but including the whole of the

South Coast as far west as Weymouth, were to come under one unified management.

There had always been an element of a 'them and us' feeling between the 'real' railways north of the Thames and that 'tramway' in the south, as it was so often (unfairly) characterised. But when it came to moving vast numbers of people, the Southern had a thing or two to teach most of the others, if their commercial people could ever drum up enough custom. We digress. However, if the incipient plans to reactivate passenger links for local services through the Snow Hill Tunnel between Farringdon and Blackfriars, or via the West London line, were to come to anything, north and south would have to talk seriously with each other.

Another development of this period took place on 11 May 1987, when the term 'second class' was formally declared to be associated in the mind too much with second rate or second best. It was thus renamed standard class. Perhaps it was as well that third class had been abolished three decades earlier.

A rather subtler change took place in how the timetables were presented. The reader had been entitled to assume that all trains carried first and second class accommodation, unless informed otherwise. Thus there would be a symbolised figure 2 at the head of the column. Such trains were second class only. Henceforth, the assumption was to be that trains were standard class only, unless a figure 1 in a block appeared in that same position.

East Grinstead

The next electrification scheme was that to East Grinstead, where the same asbestos problems were occurring in the resident diesel-electric multiple-unit fleet. What is nowadays an 18-mile branch leaves the Brighton main line at South Croydon Junction and proceeds via eight intermediate stations to the terminus. It is double track throughout, save only for the station throat at East Grinstead which narrows to a single lead before diverging immediately to the two terminal platforms. At Oxted, there is a down side bay, which is used by the connecting DEMU trains for Uckfield. These follow the same route for the mile to Hurst Green station before diverging.

Electric trains ran as far as Sanderstead before, where they terminated, but this ceased in 1983 with the closure of the line from Elmers End. There was thus a gap of 30ch in the conductor rails between South Croydon and Selsdon Junctions. Historically,

Fig 12.2: Hourly Pattern of Charing Cross to Hastings Services – 1986 Inaugural Timetable		
xx15	Waterloo East, Sevenoaks, Tonbridge, High Brooms, Tunbridge Wells, Wadhurst, Battle, St Leonards Warrior Square, Hastings	84min
xx45	Waterloo East, London Bridge, Orpington, Sevenoaks, Tonbridge and all stations to Hastings	99min

the branch there became a joint Brighton and South Eastern line and this continued to the long defunct Crowhurst Junction, where it passed beneath the Redhill-Tonbridge line.

Thus, from the former Selsdon station site, the conductor rails already continued for half a mile or so to the crossover beyond Sanderstead station. After that there was nothing, but it was not strictly accurate to say that the whole branch was newly electrified in 1987. There were no civil works of any consequence. No new trains were constructed and the 4VEP units are the most frequent providers of services, although 4CIG units may also be seen.

This route and that to Uckfield are controlled from Oxted signalbox, which became the first solid state interlocking (SSI) installation on the Southern. Oxted fringes with the Three Bridges power box in the Upper Warlingham area.

Electric services were inaugurated on 26 September 1987, and the basic service operation is shown in Fig 12.3.

Weymouth Electrification

There has always been a question mark as to how far the Southern's electrification should extend westwards. The Alton branch was included in the 1939 scheme, which covered the main line to Pirbright Junction, a little beyond Brookwood. This is 29m 30ch from Waterloo. As we have seen, the decision to electrify to Bournemouth in 1964 (strictly, to Branksome for depot access), was carried out on the traditional third rail system.

Not to include Poole in the original scheme did seem to be a curious oversight; it is after all part of the combined Bournemouth and Poole linear development, and is a sizeable traffic centre

in its own right. The station is also well situated for the town centre, something which could never be claimed for Bournemouth despite its previous name of Bournemouth Central. Poole remained as a useful terminating point for the InterCity Cross-Country trains which originated from the North West or North East of England. Other trains west of Bournemouth were diesel-hauled to Weymouth.

From a railway business point of view, the problem with the route to Weymouth is the lack of sizeable towns. Major centres and traffic generators just do not exist. But it would have been inconceivable not to serve Poole by rail, although the population of the territory beyond is much more spread out

---

Fig 12.3: Hourly Pattern of London to East Grinstead Services – 1987 Inaugural Timetable

From Victoria

| xx36 | Clapham Junction, East Croydon and all stations to Oxted *(connection all stations to Uckfield)*, then all stations to East Grinstead | 52min |

From London Bridge

| xx07 | Norwood Junction, East Croydon and all stations to East Grinstead | 52min |

Below:
North of Croydon, four-track railways from both Victoria and London Bridge merge, and then separate towards the main Brighton line via East Croydon or to West Croydon and Sutton. Although there was a long-standing complex of flying junctions, they did not address the need to carry the slow lines to and from Victoria over the up and down local lines between Norwood Junction and West Croydon. This picture shows a new flyover under construction at Gloucester Road Junction on 18 March 1983, which was carried out as part of the Central Division rebuilding and modernisation. *Author*

geographically. With the ageing fleet of Class 33s, 4REPs and 4TC units with their second-hand components needing replacement, there was bound to be some change. Fortunately, the decision was made to continue with the 750V third rail through to Weymouth. Had Poole been the electric terminus chosen in 1967, the chances of a diesel unit shuttle between there and Weymouth would surely have been that much higher. To put the distances concerned into context, the mileages are given in Fig 12.4.

Poole retains an ability to reverse electric trains back towards Bournemouth, for which the up platform has been reversibly signalled. This avoids the need for passengers on an arriving terminator to cross the footbridge, as the train can then proceed into the sidings until it is next required. Wareham can and does also reverse normal service trains.

The five miles between Moreton (exclusive) to Dorchester South (exclusive) were singled. Beyond Branksome, signalboxes remained at Poole, Hamworthy, Wareham, Wool and Dorchester.

Dorchester South station underwent a badly needed rebuilding and was opened in its new form on 22 November 1986. The new station building is on the up side of the main line through Dorchester and this finally sorted out the ridiculous situation dating back to railway building days when Dorchester was a temporary terminus in the push westwards. Thwarted by the Great Western's route from Westbury which blocked its path, the South Western eventually joined forces by executing a sharp turn to the south and joined the GW's Weymouth branch at Dorchester Junction. However, the previous terminal remained, and until 1972 all up trains (but only the up trains) had to reverse into the former terminal platform if they wished to call there. The construction of a new platform on the curved main line eased the operation, but until now passengers had to use the old

station buildings and cross to the new platform via a wooden causeway.

The ticket office is now at the present station and the subway connection to the down platform has been closed and replaced by a new footbridge. The old station buildings were incorporated into the adjacent Eldridge Pope brewery.

Weymouth terminus was completely rebuilt, with new station buildings and the platforms reduced to three. There is a release crossover for locomotive-hauled trains. The Weymouth Harbour Tramway remains intact, but is no longer in use.

Electric services commenced on 16 May 1988, the basic service being shown in Fig 12.5.

Class 442, 2401-24, 5WES

This time, new trains were needed and a fleet of 24 five-car units was authorised. These were to be a substantial departure from previous practice; the basis was the 23m (75.5ft) Mk 3 bodyshell as opposed to the 20m (65.6ft) Mk 1. Hence the reduced number of vehicles; 5x23m is not quite as long as 6x20m, but the small reduction is offset by there being only four sets of intermediate gangway connections (which are

of little practical use in accommodating passengers) instead of five.

The specification of these Wessex units was rather different from what Southern customers had been used to. They were to be air-conditioned and featured power doors to the saloons inside and plug doors operated by push buttons to enter or leave the coach. These were then, and still remain, the only examples of the 23m InterCity type Mk 3 vehicles in Britain, as opposed to Ireland, to have such a feature.

The internal arrangement was for standard class to be in open saloons in three of the vehicles, but first class in one of the driving trailers was split into an unusual part open and part compartment arrangement. Originally, these were to be composites with only the first class in six compartments with 36 seats, but a quick upgrade by reupholstering the 14 seats in the open section provided a total of 50 first class seats instead. In the power car in the centre of the train, which houses a buffet counter, this was designed originally with a traditional amount of van space as well as a room for the guard. Consequently, seating was limited to accommodate a mere 14, but this was revised during construction. Later units had this altered to take 30, with commensurate reductions in the luggage or parcels areas. Earlier vehicles were subsequently rebuilt to match.

Overall, the seating changes, together with those already considered for the 4VEP units, are summarised in Fig 12.6 (overleaf). The comparison is made on the basis of full length trains, and demonstrates some of the changes which can be achieved within a similar total length of bodyshell.

The new units were fitted with public address and were also some of the earliest to make extensive provision for wheelchair access and carriage. In external appearance, they benefited substantially from the front end being cleaned up and an attempt made,

Fig 12.4: Waterloo to Weymouth Distances, by Section

Waterloo	Pirbright Junction	29m 30ch	20.6%	Electrified by 1937
Pirbright Junction	Bournemouth	78m 55ch	55.1%	Bournemouth 1967 scheme
Bournemouth	Branksome	2m 47ch	1.8%	Bournemouth 1967 scheme
Branksome	Poole	3m 10ch	2.2%	Weymouth 1988 scheme
Poole	Weymouth	29m 02ch	20.3%	Weymouth 1988 scheme

Fig 12.5: Hourly Pattern of Services and Times from Bournemouth Towards Weymouth – 1988 Inaugural Timetable

xx11	(From Waterloo, fast) Poole, Wareham, Wool, Moreton, Dorchester South, Upwey, Weymouth
xx25	(From Southampton) All stations to Wareham
xx51	(From Waterloo, semi-fast) All stations to Poole

Fig 12.6: Seating Capacities of Bournemouth Line Trains

Formation	First	Std	Total
REP + TC + TC	108	471	579
442 x 2 as originally built	72	528	600
442 x 2 composite modified	100	500	600
442 x 2 brake also modified	100	524	624
VEP x 3 as originally built	144	696	840
VEP x 3 downgrade first comp	108	744	852
VEP x 3 brake also modified	108	798	906

not altogether successfully, to hide the cluster of cables on the front of the driving trailers.

This electrification too was a minimum-cost scheme, and while new vehicles were authorised, budgets were tight. It was a distinct possibility at one stage that power cars from the REP units would be retained for use with new unpowered Mk 3 stock in a push-pull version like the REP+TC arrangement. The ultimate decision was to build completely new vehicles, but to recondition and then reuse the English Electric EE546 traction motors of 400hp each from the REP units.

The effects, though, were rather more complicated. At least some of the REP power

Below:
A Class 442 unit arrives in the up platform at Dorchester in March 1989 with a Weymouth-Waterloo service. The relatively sharp curve with its effect on train-to-platform distances is noticeable. *Author*

cars had to be withdrawn from service considerably in advance of the first of the new vehicles being ready. There were however plenty of trailing vehicles of one sort or another, and the mixed bag of Class 33 diesels, Class 73 electro-diesels and whatever multiple-unit or other stock that could be found were all pressed into service together. This was compounded by late deliveries of the new units from BREL, and by May 1988 when the new service was to be inaugurated, no more than a quarter of the Class 442s had been received.

Blackfriars and Farringdon

The Snow Hill link between Blackfriars and Farringdon was part of the Widened Lines system, which was used primarily for the transfer of freight traffic between north and south London railway networks. It had some little use for passenger services, but these were long discontinued by the time the whole

of the link was declared redundant. It was closed completely on 3 May 1971.

The introduction of the electric services from Bedford to Moorgate did however interest the Greater London Council as to what else might be possible. This would, inter alia, require the construction of dual voltage units which came about, and the Class 319s today monopolise the Thameslink services. They were delivered from 1987; although similar to their Class 317 ac only predecessors, they offered retention toilets and first class accommodation was provided on some units.

While the destinations north of the Thames are merely a matter of how far one proceeds towards Bedford, southwards there is a huge choice. However, select too many and the service frequency becomes unattractively low. To illustrate this, 1985 proposals were for a 5tph service, made up as follows:

- 2tph Bedford-Gatwick, alternate trains extended to Brighton.
- 2tph Luton-Sanderstead.
- 1tph West Hampstead-Orpington.

After ballast renewal, tracklaying and resignalling had been completed, full services were introduced on 16 May 1988.

That, however, was only the beginning. The short link between the Holborn Viaduct terminus and Blackfriars could be replaced

Above:

This busy scene is of a Thameslink service arriving at Farringdon from the Midland line, where the unit, No 319054, will change to third rail pick-up before proceeding. The date is 2 January 1998 and the platforms are crowded in both directions. Thameslink 2000 will expand capacity considerably. *Author*

very satisfactorily by the new Thameslink service and a station at St Paul's, later named City Thameslink. This depended upon a realignment scheme, which would be needed to drop the line at 1 in 29 as it left Blackfriars heading north, so that a level site could be prepared for a 12-car length platform at City Thameslink. This also required the lowering of the bridge across Queen Victoria Street by 300mm, but the prize was the demolition of the railway bridge over Ludgate Hill. Used for railway access to Holborn Viaduct, it would now be surplus to requirements. As it also blocked a fine view of St Paul's Cathedral, this was seen as a very positive planning gain.

Holborn Viaduct station was abandoned completely on 26 January 1990. A 17-day blockade of the Thameslink route was imposed to allow the new alignment to replace the old, and rail services were restored on 29 May. City Thameslink opened the same day, although it was known initially as St Paul's Thameslink, it being renamed on 6 November 1991. Immediately north of City Thameslink, some third rail sidings were commissioned to enable trains to be turned back.

Altogether 86 units were built, and the fleet is presently split four ways:

- Class 319/0. 13 units. As built. Leased by Connex SouthCentral, but two loaned to Thameslink on a daily basis. Standard class only.
- Class 319/2. Seven units. Third rail only. Leased by Connex SouthCentral, upgraded to Express status for the London-Brighton service.
- Class 319/3. 26 units. Leased by Thameslink, for the 'City Metro' Luton-Sutton service. Standard class only.
- Class 319/4. 40 units. Leased by Thameslink, upgraded for the 'City Flyer' Bedford-Gatwick Airport-Brighton service.

The basic service pattern through Snow Hill Tunnel in Winter 2000/01 is shown in Fig 12.7.

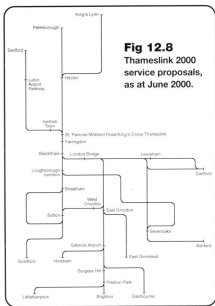

Fig 12.8
Thameslink 2000 service proposals, as at June 2000.

Fig 12.7: Thameslink Service Pattern 2000/1, Southbound, Times from Blackfriars	
xx04	London Bridge, East Croydon, Gatwick Airport, Three Bridges, Haywards Heath and all stations to Brighton
xx11	All stations to Sutton via Herne Hill, Wimbledon and St Helier.
xx19	London Bridge, East Croydon, Redhill, Gatwick Airport, Haywards Heath, Brighton.
xx26	All stations to Sutton via Herne Hill and Mitcham Junction.
xx34	London Bridge, East Croydon, Gatwick Airport and all stations to Brighton.
xx41	All stations to Sutton via Herne Hill, Wimbledon and St Helier.
xx49	London Bridge, East Croydon, Gatwick Airport, Haywards Heath, Brighton.
xx56	All stations to Sutton via Herne Hill and Mitcham Junction.

Above:
The Solent electrification saw the building of a station at Hedge End between Eastleigh and Botley to serve a new housing estate. It is staffed and the station was opened on 9 May 1990. 4CIG Class 421 unit No 1308 is seen arriving with the 08.38 Eastleigh-Portsmouth Harbour in March 1993. *Author*

As will be seen, the service provision is very different from that discussed 15 years previously. One of the difficulties, though, is the inability to run via London Bridge during peak periods. The problem is the lack of line capacity, which will be addressed by Railtrack's investment package for the route. The opportunities are however far wider, as Fig 12.8 (previous page) shows. This includes connection to the Great Northern line from King's Cross as well as the range of objectives south of the Thames.

It might be added that the Class 325 units built for the Royal Mail and dedicated to the carriage of the Post Office's York trolleys use the same basic Class 319 bodyshell and traction package. There are 16 of these units, which are non-gangwayed. They have dual 750V dc and 25kV ac capabilities.

Solent Electrification

The Southern Region, having completed the Bournemouth electrification in 1967, found itself with a piece of infilling to be done. The railway along the coast westwards from Portsmouth or Havant is not the straightest, having been forced inland by Portsmouth Harbour itself, followed by the need to bridge the River Hamble and then the Itchen, before joining the main line at St Denys and turning decisively towards Southampton. Nevertheless, this is densely populated territory with a growing local economy, and

includes the substantial town of Fareham. Not to be forgotten either is the rail link north west from Fareham to Botley and Eastleigh.

The same problem of ageing DEMU sets was to be found here. But there was also another factor, in that these link other interesting traffic alternatives. Services on the Portsmouth-Reading axis have a long history, but why not turn due east at Basingstoke and carry on to Waterloo? Likewise, traffic from east of Havant might find other outlets west of Southampton. Such routeings may have commercial advantages, but they also offer a range of ways of overcoming engineering blockades. The same services can of course be offered with diesel traction, but it seemed unlikely that the full benefits could be gained without electrification. One of the spin-offs would be an enhancement of the role of Fratton depot for servicing and cleaning (but no longer maintenance), and creative stock diagrams which could achieve more work with no more vehicles.

Local authorities and developers were also in favour and their contributions enabled a new station to be constructed at Hedge End, as well as the renovation of other stations along the line. A total of 61 route miles was to be newly electrified following the 1988 go-ahead. Where necessary, station platforms were extended to take eight cars.

Traction maintenance was centred at Eastleigh, which previously concentrated on

the DEMU fleet, locomotives, coaches and wagons. The Class 442 Wessex units remained at Bournemouth, but there was a general reallocation of stock between these depots and also Wimbledon.

Traction power control via the seven new substations was taken from the existing Eastleigh control room. New composite aluminium and steel conductor rail with superior conductivity properties was laid on the 4.5-mile single-track section between Botley and Fareham, which allowed the substation numbers to be reduced by one. At 1990 prices, the capital cost of substations was around £200,000 each, so this was a worthwhile economy. This followed an earlier non-energised trial installation at Upwey Wishing Well, north of Weymouth, to determine how well it would wear.

Following the experience of other recent schemes, 11kV ring mains were again used. In this case, it meant that pairs of Class 442 units on diversions would be allowed, but at the expense of reduced performance.

The entire area had already been resignalled, so track circuit immunisation was the only work needed here. The new services were inaugurated on 14 May 1990, with the basic service provision as shown in Fig 12.9. The times are shown on leaving Cosham, from which it can be seen that passengers could travel from Victoria to Waterloo via Cosham, only having to step down from one train and enter another from the same platform. While such an itinerary would have no real point, it does perhaps demonstrate the journey opportunities that were opened up by the offering of a range of longer-distance through services.

Upgrading Routes to the Channel Tunnel

For freight operations, the intention was to run trains via Redhill to Tonbridge and the tunnel. This required also:

- Electrification of the link between the West London line and Clapham Junction (south side).
- Electrification of Redhill-Tonbridge, which also benefited local passenger services.
- The construction and commissioning of Dollands Moor Yard, east of Saltwood Tunnel.

The other major requirement for freight was the provision of a dual voltage locomotive fleet. The result was the Class 92, of which

Fig 12.9: Hourly Train Service Pattern, Solent Electrification 1990 Inaugural Timetable; Times Leaving Cosham	
xx06	Portsmouth Harbour and all stations to Eastleigh, Winchester, Basingstoke, Woking and Waterloo.
xx23	From Victoria via Gatwick Airport. In area, calling at Havant, Cosham, Fareham, Swanwick and Southampton.
xx39	Portsmouth Harbour to Wareham, calling all stations.
Additional hourly diesel services operated by Regional Railways South Wales & West run from Portsmouth to Southampton, Salisbury and beyond	

46 were built by Brush Traction at Loughborough. The fleet of 4,000kW machines is owned by EWS (30), Eurostar (7) and SNCF, the French operator, (9).

In line capacity terms, there was much more to do. Four signalling centres control Eurostar trains between London and the tunnel. Wimbledon is in control from Waterloo to the Stewarts Lane chord, a section on which the international trains have been allocated only one track, to be used bi-directionally. Victoria takes over from there to Petts Wood, after which the new IECC at Ashford assumes control. The final change is to Eurotunnel control at Dollands Moor.

Below:

Unit No 319002 forms a Connex SouthCentral service from Gatwick Airport to Rugby as it uses the West London line on its approaches to Kensington Olympia. To the right is the District Line's Olympia branch, while a D stock train disappears in the direction of Hammersmith. The date is 17 December 1998. *Author*

Orpington, Chislehurst, Sevenoaks and Tonbridge boxes were abolished in 1993. As part of the resignalling, the line from Sevenoaks to the tunnel was given bi-directional signalling. On the crucial Ashford to Dollands Moor section, this is a comprehensive scheme allowing 100mph running in either direction, with signal spacing the same for the 'wrong' as well as the 'right' direction. This ensures that the capacity available can be exploited to the absolute maximum. It is not all good news, though. Passengers waiting for domestic services at local stations are very dependent upon accurate and timely indications of the platform at which their train will arrive. Otherwise, it can be a very quick scurry across the bridge. If this happens, it is the sort of thing which makes nonsense of efforts elsewhere to promote disabled access.

Between Ashford and Sevenoaks, simplified bi-directional signalling with just two-aspect signals and longer sections in the 'wrong'

direction has been installed. West of Ashford, there is of course the alternative route via Maidstone East available.

Comprehensive remodelling has been undertaken at four key points with the Ashford resignalling. A principal aim has been to separate out international and domestic flows of traffic. At Chislehurst Junction, the chord from Bickley towards Petts Wood is now double track instead of single. At Orpington, two extra 12-car terminating platforms have been provided and the existing ones lengthened. This is to ensure that local trains do not have to terminate on one of the through tracks, although the 12-car Networker project has yet to bear fruit.

At Sevenoaks, the up loop has become the up main, and vice versa, again keeping terminating local trains and international services as far away from each other as possible. At Tonbridge, another remodelling saw the speeds to and from the Redhill line raised from 15mph to 30mph and the up island platform made reversible. This has given the operators an opportunity to switch down Hastings services from the north side island to the south side, although the remarks about adequate passenger information apply equally here.

South of Sevenoaks, speeds of 100mph are permissible; the only lesser limits beyond are the 50mph on the Tonbridge curves, 90mph through pointwork at the London end of Ashford station, and 90mph on the curves through Sandling. New crossovers were installed to give more flexibility in routeing trains from one track to the other. Power supplies were upgraded, and track-paralleling huts which are used to equalise the voltage between the two running lines have been turned into feeder stations, putting more power into the third rail.

Through the 100yd Sandling Tunnel, concrete slab track was used to make sure that the clearance to roof level would be maintained. At Saltwood Tunnel (954yd) which follows very shortly afterwards, the trackbed was lowered but conventional ballasted track retained. Overhead catenary starts at the end of the tunnel, and drivers of Eurostar services are able to raise their pantographs in preparation for entering the tunnel itself. They will, however, have to reduce speed to $87\frac{1}{2}$mph for the tunnel itself.

Most freight trains will run via Redhill for clearance reasons, particularly those in Sevenoaks Tunnel, which at 1m 1,693yd is the longest on the Southern. This then gives them access via Clapham Junction to the West London line. A bi-directional loop has been built for freight use at Redhill itself; at Headcorn there are new loops on each side of the track, and again east of Ashford. The aim is to keep freights clear of passenger services if at all possible. While this is commendable in some ways, it speaks volumes for the attitude towards rail freight in that it should always

come second, after passenger traffic. This is a competitive world, and the conventional railway has to offer a saleable product. Eurostar has a 64% share of the London-Paris market, its customers are satisfied, and traffic grows steadily. This is not the case for cross-Channel rail freight which, with a 3% market share, has failed to secure a real position in a market dominated overwhelmingly by ship and truck transport.

A problem raised by the swap-body loading gauge is overbridge clearance, and 18 bridges have had to be completely rebuilt. Another 70 or so have needed altering, the most common requirement being at what might be termed the shoulders. This is where they might be hit by a high container load. Underbridges are another matter, and strengthening has been carried out on Chelsea Bridge over the Thames, so that two trains may now pass each other on the bridge. Elsewhere, 15 underbridges have needed their decks to be strengthened for heavy freight use. Again for freight, the short (78yd) Penshurst Tunnel has had slab track laid through it, while two short tunnels on the alternative route near Maidstone have been demolished completely and replaced with cuttings.

East of Continental Junction towards Dover, the railway is not what it was. The prestige trains had slowly withered away; first class Pullman cars could no longer sustain the 'Golden Arrow', and the 10.30 Victoria to Dover Marine became just that on Monday, 2 October 1972. Next to go was the 'Night Ferry', the only through passenger rail service to the Continent. Latterly, it had been loading to only four passenger vehicles and a few vans. Haulage was well within Class 33 capabilities, the last Class 71s having been withdrawn some time previously. This service ceased on 31 October 1980. Still 14 years before the Channel Tunnel opened, these withdrawals reflecting the then lessening attraction of travel by rail to the Continent.

The next casualty was Dover Western Docks station, formerly Marine, which was abandoned completely on 25 September 1994. It was then the turn of the feeder routes, as part of the Ashford resignalling. The reduction of the section between Folkestone West and Folkestone Central from four tracks to two tracks, using the outer pair only, made the 1960s showpiece station of Central look very forlorn. The Channel Tunnel has also rendered the Folkestone Harbour branch of little use, as well as the railway platform at Newhaven Marine.

Of the other electrification schemes in west London, the completion from Clapham Junction (north side) to Kensington Olympia in 1994 was a material help to the long established but, until relatively recent years, unadvertised service. This now runs throughout the day to Willesden Junction, which caused a return to diesel traction until

the electrification to North Pole Junction and the short section beyond was completed. This whole area is a complex mixture of third rail and overhead. For the record it should be stated that third rail runs as far as North Pole reception sidings, but trains continuing towards Willesden need to change to overhead pick-up once they have passed the A40(M) Westway bridge.

The local services between Clapham Junction and Willesden Junction are operated by Silverlink Metro using Class 313 units, and these call also at the new West Brompton station on the West London line which was opened on 30 May 1999. Other users of the West London are Connex SouthCentral with its Gatwick Airport to Rugby service, using dual voltage Class 319 stock.

Class 465/466 Networkers

The objective of the Networker development programme was to produce a train that would be up to 25% cheaper to run while offering significantly higher comfort standards. This was the reason to adopt a lightweight aluminium body, new low-cost ac traction motor technology and regenerative braking to improve energy efficiency. These trains feature three-phase drive. Compared with the steel body Class 455, it was expected to offer 24% lower operating costs, 16% more capacity, 10% improvement in journey times and 5% higher reliability.

A total of 147 four-car and 43 two-car Networkers took over the operation of the whole of the South Eastern inner suburban services, starting in 1993. They were supplied both by ABB and GEC Alsthom as follows:

465/0	ABB	50 4-car sets
465/1	ABB	47 4-car sets
465/2	GEC Alsthom	50 4-car sets
466	GEC Alsthom	43 2-car sets

Seating is 3+2, standard class throughout in the 20m vehicles. This gives a total of 348 seats, reduced to 168 in the Class 466s. There are sliding plug doors and on-board information screens giving the service stopping pattern. The ABB vehicles feature Brush traction motors; the GEC Alsthom ones are equipped with that company's own. The make-up of the Class 465 sets is driving motor, trailer, trailer and driving motor. In all cases, there are four motors in each of the driving motor vehicles, each producing 280kW. In the 466s, one driving vehicle is unpowered.

All are based at Slade Green, where maintenance is carried out. This includes all stores holding and facilities such as a Hegenscheidt underfloor wheel lathe. There are outbased stabling facilities at Orpington, also at Grove Park, which has a carriage washer,

Right:
A Gatwick Express Class 460 unit bound for Victoria begins to slow as it comes through Battersea Park on 19 January 2001. *Author*

Fig 12.10: Results of First Round of Franchising, as Let

Start	Train Operating Co	Period	Operator	Premium Payments	Passenger Miles, 99/00	Subsidy per pass mile, 99/00
4.2.96	South West Trains	7 years	Stagecoach	none	2,434.9m	2.4p
28.4.96	Gatwick Express	15 years	National	1996/7	117.9m	10.3p
26.5.96	Connex SthCentral	7 years	CGEA	none	1,569.0m	3.2p
13.10.96	Connex SthEastern	15 years	CGEA	2010/11	1,935.0m	3.3p
13.10.96	Island Line	5 years	Stagecoach	none	3.6m	52.8p
2.3.97	Thameslink Rail	7yr 1m	GOVIA	1998/9	754.2m	17.6p

and Gillingham. The whole of the Networker fleet is driver-only-operated (DOO).

Class 365

Orders for 16 of these units from ABB York for Kent Coast services were announced at the same time as a complementary order of 25 for Great Northern services from King's Cross. In both cases these are dual voltage units, the South Eastern ones being 750V dc but with 25kV ac capability, and the Great Northern ones the reverse. It remains to be seen when or where this ability to run on either electrification system will be used.

These vehicles, with aluminium alloy bodies, were built by ABB at York. The four-car units consist of a pair of driving motor composites with a pair of standard class trailers in between. There is seating for 24 first class and 239 standard class, with one wheelchair space and a lavatory in each of the trailers. The seating is of 2+2 arrangement and pressure ventilation is fitted. They entered service in 1996.

Franchising

The franchising regime was set up under the terms of the Railways Act, 1993. The then Office of Passenger Rail Franchising let contracts for the operation of the passenger railway, using divisions of the railway which were largely determined by reference to the former BR business units. Those relevant to electric operations on what was the Southern are listed in Fig 12.10. Missing are the Eurostar operations and those of Eurotunnel, both of which are commercial operations by private companies and outside the franchising arrangements.

In making their competitive bids, franchisees were allowed to include an element for Government support over the franchise period. As matters progressed, a typical result was seen to be a declining requirement for Government money as time went on, which in some cases turned into a premium payment to the Government in later years.

Contractually, franchise holders have to provide services which, at a minimum, are in accordance with a prescribed Passenger Service Requirement, and to do so to defined standards of punctuality, reliability, capacity, and so on. Train Operating Companies will usually obtain their rolling stock from a leasing company, and will need to pay Railtrack access charges for the use of the network. In the case of electric trains, this includes the cost of power supplies. Other TOC responsibilities are the staffing of all stations other than those for which Railtrack retain management control, and the crewing of trains and their day-to-day maintenance and cleaning. The principal fares charged are subject to laid down maxima, expressed in relation to changes in the Retail Price Index (RPI).

Above:
The 30 Class 458 4JOP units of South West Trains built by Alsthom are intended for the Reading services, although they are being run-in on the main line. No 458013 is seen inside Wimbledon depot on 2 November 2000, with Class 455 No 5708 alongside. *Author*

Franchising does not extend to Eurostar, Eurotunnel or any freight operations. In general, these companies own their assets outright, and in the case of Eurotunnel, they also own the system infrastructure.

The variations in the size of the undertakings as measured by the passenger miles made on each of them is huge, and the results in terms of the amounts of public money that they consume is equally variable. Of the operators listed, Thameslink does have the substantial proportion of around half its total operation north of the Thames, and to that extent is outside the electrified area considered in this volume.

As can be seen, the big three companies are South West Trains, Connex SouthEastern and Connex SouthCentral, in that order if measured in terms of usage, and between them they absorbed £171.5 million of Government subsidy in the 1999/2000 financial year. The contributions to the Government by Gatwick Express and Thameslink Rail combined were £27.9 million, while the tiny Island line, despite a very discouraging result when measured as support per passenger mile, absorbed a mere £1.9 million of Government funds. Even so, that amount of money would buy a considerable number of bus services in somewhere the size of the Isle of Wight.

The next round of franchising was under way as this book was being written. As at mid-2001, the situation was as shown in Fig 12.11:

New Trains

New trains for train operating companies are being procured as follows:

Class 375: Being built by Adtranz for Connex, there are 92 of these four-car units on order to replace the rest of the CEP fleet. These are air conditioned, and the first was accepted by Connex South Eastern in spring 2001.

Class 458: Built by Alstom for South West Trains. Intended for services to Reading, the first few four-car units were running experimentally between Waterloo and Alton in 2001.

Class 460: Built by Alstom for Gatwick Express. A small order of eight 8-car trains was running most of the services by June 2001.

Large scale procurement of additional vehicles to implement the Mk 1 rolling stock replacement programme is also anticipated.

Fig 12.11: Progress on Second Round of Franchising, as at Mid-2001	
Island Line	Present Stagecoach franchise extended by two years until September 2003, with an increased subsidy profile and various improvements to passenger benefits. A report on the provision of future rail services is to be prepared by consultants GIBB Rail.
Connex South Central	GOVIA named as preferred bidder to acquire the franchise from Connex at a date to be agreed, franchise end date 2021.
South West Trains	Stagecoach named as preferred bidder to retain franchise, end date 2021.
Thameslink Rail	Decision by the SRA on a short list awaited.
Connex South Eastern	Long-term Connex franchise until 2011, no change.
Gatwick Express	Long-term National Express franchise until 2011, no change.
OrbiRail	Possible new franchise to run Silverlink Metro services and those via the LUL East London line tunnel, presently intended to be projected to Wimbledon and to West Croydon. Unlikely before 2003/4.

13. Service Management and Operations

The market which the railway serves is never still; change is endemic. This section examines how services are organised, and how operations have been adapted over the years. Incident management is also covered. It starts with a simple branch line.

Servicing the Branches

The Sittingbourne-Sheerness branch is an interesting example of the limitations inherent in running the railway. Sittingbourne lies on the Chatham main line, roundly halfway between Gillingham and Faversham, and has three platforms, one of which is a down side loop.

Leaving in the London direction, trains reach the branch via the main line, which they use for half a mile to Eastern Junction. Here, they swing north to Middle Junction, where the spur from Western Junction comes in. (Quite clearly, there was no poetic licence in choosing the names for these junctions.) The double-track branch continues north to Kemsley, but becomes single just before reaching Swale. From this desolate spot, the railway rises to cross the King's Ferry lifting bridge over the River Swale, continuing to the passing loop at Queenborough. The single track continues to the two-platformed branch terminus at

Below:
Sheerness branch track layout, 1994.

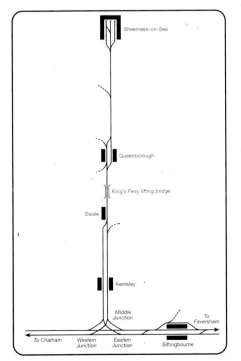

Fig 13.2: Sheerness Branch Connections at Sittingbourne, Mondays to Fridays Middle Day – 2000/1 Timetable	
xx12	Branch train arrives from Sheerness.
xx18	Up fast service Ramsgate/Dover to Victoria departs.
xx21	Up stopping service Faversham to Victoria departs.
xx25	Down stopping service Victoria to Faversham arrives.
xx33	Down fast service Victoria to Ramsgate/Dover arrives.
xx37	Branch train departs to Sheerness.

Sheerness. There is also access to numerous freight sidings, as shown in Fig 13.1.

Two Class 508 units provide branch services. With a single journey time for the eight-mile branch of 15 minutes, it irritatingly needs two trains to provide a half-hourly service. Nearly all the spare time in the diagrams is spent at the Sittingbourne end, where connections are offered for three trains in each direction in every half-hour. The connectional pattern is shown in Fig 13.2.

There are a number of very positive points about this service pattern:

- The best connections are between the branch and travel by the fast trains to and from the London direction.
- All passengers transferring between the branch and the up services must use the footbridge, and slightly longer connectional times are allowed for this movement.
- Connections to and from points further east are less good, but there is always a branch train waiting to receive passengers.
- Branch service patterns can be stepped up to offer a more frequent peak service.

The less positive points are:

- Branch timings have to recognise that conflicts with the main line occur over the first half-mile, and timings need to be adjusted to suit.
- The long single-track sections of the branch limit the variations in timings which can be accomplished, even with two trains operating.
- Freight paths are also required from time to time.
- Productivity is modest, with each train and train crew achieving no more than

16 miles of running (one return trip) in each hour.

- The occasional need to open the King's Ferry bridge for shipping is an unknown quantity.

The reality, of course, is that there are very many other constraints on service provision, and this example is given to show some of the difficulties in what is otherwise a fairly straightforward branch operation. The Southern has many far more complex situations with which to cope, but these are really outside the scope of a book of this nature. However, let us look briefly at other ways of offering a branch service.

The second is the Lymington branch from Brockenhurst where, since track remodelling was carried out around 1966, the branch is totally self-contained with its own platform at Brockenhurst. A single four-car unit provides a 2tph shuttle service over the $5\frac{1}{4}$ miles, which is accomplished in a single-journey running time of nine minutes.

The problem here is that in most hours there are, in each direction, three South West Trains services with which to connect at Brockenhurst, one Connex SouthCentral and (often) one Virgin CrossCountry. There is also a boat to connect with at Lymington Pier, for Yarmouth, Isle of Wight passengers. It is simply not possible to provide good connections with all of these, and the branch train's turnround times at the termini are, successively, four, five, six and nine minutes.

It is thus not realistic to hold a branch train for a late running main line service, however frustrating this might be to passengers, since this will result very quickly in further lost connections. Tight turnrounds are excellent news in terms of making railway assets work

Above:

Schools traffic lasts for around 190 days a year and can produce large numbers, albeit often for short distances and at half-fare only. Southbourne station, west of Chichester, is of basic construction; it sees the 15.32 Portsmouth Harbour-Brighton service approaching on 11 June 1981. The train is formed of a pair of 2HAP units with No 6030 leading. These were frequently used on the Coastway services at this time. *Author*

hard, but they are also very inflexible when things go wrong.

The third method is to incorporate the branch service into the main line operation, the example here being the Maidstone West service from the south. For many years, this ran as a shuttle between Paddock Wood and Strood, but more recently this was severed at Maidstone West to work in two halves. The logic of this was to make the best connections at either end for longer-distance journeys, given that the number of passengers travelling through Maidstone on this route was relatively low anyway.

However, Paddock Wood is hardly a natural terminal, many passengers wanting to go to the rather larger town of Tonbridge. And why stop there, when there is a newly electrified line to Redhill?

The upshot was the inauguration of a through London Bridge to Maidstone West service, via East Croydon, Redhill and Tonbridge, operated by Connex SouthEastern. It may be recalled that this route goes right back to the early days of the South Eastern Railway, and was available (although not of course electrified) as early as 1844. It is not the fastest of journeys, and few are likely to travel from end to end other than out of curiosity, the longest journey possible lasting nearly two hours. The rolling stock used is again the Class 508 units which, it is perhaps pertinent to note, do not have toilets. However, the service does offer a whole new range of point-to-point journey opportunities, all of which are available without the perceived fuss of changing trains and wondering if the connection will be kept.

For the record, comparisons between the alternative routes, fastest first, are shown in Fig 13.3.

As an aside, it does perhaps indicate how vulnerable the South Eastern Railway was, for some destinations, to competition from the London, Chatham & Dover Railway, with a more direct line of route.

Coastway Services

The South Coast is characterised by a line running parallel to the coastline, but which has a number of intervening dead-end termini. To add to the complication of train service provision, there are also several radial lines from London reaching the coast at intervals. Fig 13.4 shows the general layout.

As can be seen, several junctions are restricted in that trains can proceed only in a limited number of directions. Even where the arrangements are comprehensive, as for instance at Littlehampton, it still takes time for

a through train to arrive, the driver to change ends, and for it to depart again. The Littlehampton branch is about 1³/₄ miles long, and to call there would add not less than 10 minutes to a through journey from Brighton to Portsmouth. This is irritating to passengers who have no interest in Littlehampton, but on the other hand it seems perverse to omit calls at such a major centre of population.

Notably, the following movements *cannot* be made:

Fig 13.3: London to Maidstone Journey Times, 2000/1 Timetable

Route	Notes	Time	Distance	Frequency
London Cannon St-Maidstone East	direct	49min	37³/₄ miles	hourly
London Victoria-Maidstone East	direct	54min	40 miles	hourly
London Charing X-Maidstone West	change at Strood	89min	44 miles	half-hourly
London Bridge-Maidstone West	direct	101min	55³/₄ miles	hourly

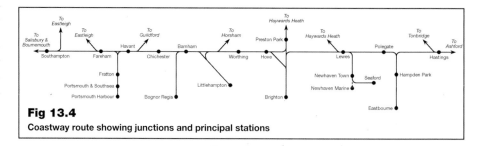

Fig 13.4
Coastway route showing junctions and principal stations

Time	Type	Train Details	Co	Refreshments	Notes
Fig 13.6: Haywards Heath, Summer 1963. Down Trains in Sample Hour, 11.00-11.59 Mondays to Fridays					
11.14	fast	10.25 Victoria-Littlehampton	BR	Pullman conveyed	
11.23	semi-fast	10.28 Victoria-Brighton	BR	none	
11.24	stopping	11.16 Horsted Keynes-Seaford	BR	none	train departs 11.35
11.28	semi-fast	10.16 London Bridge-Brighton	BR	none	
11.33	fast	10.45 Victoria-Eastbourne-Ore	BR	Pullman conveyed	
11.35	stopping	11.16 Horsted Keynes-Seaford	BR	none	train arrives 11.24
11.45	nonstop	11.00 Victoria-Brighton 'Brighton Belle'	BR	Pullman cars only	
11.58	stopping	10.47 Victoria-Brighton	BR	none	

- Between London Waterloo (via Guildford) and Chichester.
- Between Bognor Regis and Chichester
- Between Arundel and Worthing
- Between Seaford and Eastbourne
- Between London Charing Cross (via Tonbridge) and Eastbourne

In addition, it is not possible to omit calling at either Brighton or Eastbourne and reversing, since there is no avoiding route.

The above place considerable restrictions on the train services which can be offered. While the coastal strip is not completely built up, there are nevertheless many reasonably sized centres of population. All the main routes shown in this diagram carry a minimum of two trains per hour, which expands to as many as seven between Hove and West Worthing and six between Havant and Portsmouth Harbour. There is a need to balance longer-distance, or in other words London, traffic and the local coastway journeys. However, it should be noted that some of the latter may be of considerable length. From Hastings to Portsmouth Harbour is 85½ miles and there are 44 intermediate stations on the most direct route. Some limited stop services would clearly be desirable.

This is not a treatise on operations, but the above discussion is aimed at illuminating some of the contradictory elements which the

timetable planners have to address. What is true of the Coastway services can be multiplied many times over in the very busy inner-suburban areas, but a more detailed example is confined to the stretch of railway east of Brighton. The standard Monday to Friday off-peak service interval for eastbound services is shown in Fig 13.5 for the 2000/01 winter timetable.

The immediate target here is the urban stretch through Falmer, for which 4tph is deemed necessary. Services leave Brighton at 11, 24, 41 and 54 minutes past each hour. At Lewes, the twice-hourly London service joins for the run to Eastbourne, but two of the local services divert to the Seaford branch, leaving Lewes at 27 and 57. Careful scheduling means that departures from Lewes for Eastbourne are more or less evenly spaced at 09, 23 (ex London), 39 and 53 (ex London), but ensuring that the local train which also stops at Glynde, Berwick and Hampden Park precedes the fast from Victoria which terminates at Eastbourne; the three Eastbourne to Hastings services leave Eastbourne at 03, 17 and 39 past the hour. Again, careful adjustment of stopping patterns produces well-spaced arrival times in Hastings at 27, 48 and 10 minutes respectively. Note that passengers from London to Seaford also have good connections at Lewes. These should be maintained easily, as the branch train has to follow the departing main line service for the first mile to Southerham Junction.

This diagram does not however show the whole story; for instance, any passengers

from Seaford wanting to travel towards Eastbourne will be dependent upon a different set of connections at Lewes. In fact, they will have either eight or nine minutes for their connections, for which the minimum allowance recommended is four minutes.

All timetables have to allow for junction conflicts, and every junction in the area under review is, without exception, flat. There are no flyovers or diveunders which can make the operator's life easier. The timetables which result are never perfect and there may be all manner of constraints originating elsewhere on the system, but it is hoped that this example does show some of the inherent problems and the professionalism involved in coming to an acceptable result.

Haywards Heath

The changes in Southern operations over time can also be evaluated in terms of what an observer might see at the same location at the same times, many years apart. Haywards Heath on the Brighton main line has been chosen for this, as it is a relatively uncomplicated location where most trains stop. The tables show the service in the down direction between 11.00 and 11.59, Mondays to Fridays, during Summer 1963, Fig.13.6, Summer 1985, Fig13.7 and Summer 2000, Fig 13.8. Timings are derived from the public timetables, and the passing times of the few nonstop trains (shown in italics) are estimated (top).

The Summer 1963 timetable was very much the traditional Southern one, and shows remarkably little change from that of the immediate postwar years. The long-standing hourly services from Victoria to Littlehampton and to Eastbourne and Ore are there, and the nonstop to Brighton in this particular hour was the 'Brighton Belle'. Travel in any of the Brighton line Pullmans carried a supplementary charge which was then 3s 0d first class or 2s 0d second class. To this was added the ordinary fare of 19s 0d first class or 12s 9d second class. The cost of the Pullman supplement was thus a noticeable proportion of the fare, bearing in mind that this was the equivalent of a reservation fee and that 'meals and light refreshments' were charged as incurred.

Haywards Heath then had three trains in the hour to Brighton, one of which originated from London Bridge. There was also the

Below:
Brighton-Eastbourne-Hastings, hourly eastbound services, Mondays to Fridays, 2000/01.

Fig 13.5

Fig 13.7: Haywards Heath, Summer 1985. Down Trains in Sample Hour, 11.00-11.59 Mondays to Fridays

Time	Type	Train Details	Co	Refreshments	Notes
11.07	fast	10.20 Victoria-Littlehampton/Portsmouth Harbour	BR	buffet service	train divides Hove
11.12	stopping	10.08 Victoria-Brighton	BR	none	
11.22	semi-fast	10.32 Victoria-Brighton	BR	buffet service	
11.37	fast	10.50 Victoria-Eastbourne-Hastings	BR	buffet service	
11.45	nonstop	11.02 Victoria-Brighton	BR	buffet service	East Croydon only
11.47	stopping	11.47 Haywards Heath-Brighton	BR	none	

moribund service from Horsted Keynes, which in the event was to close on 28 October that year, together with the off-peak service thence as far as Lewes. For the time being, though, it used the twin island platform layout at Haywards Heath to stand for 11 minutes and make some potentially useful connections.

By 1985, Haywards Heath was experiencing a rather less full service, although the Littlehampton train has acquired a Portsmouth Harbour section. There were still three trains to Brighton in the hour, one of which started there, but none from London Bridge. The replacement of the 6PULs by CIG/BIG formations had extended the availability of refreshment facilities, albeit only a buffet car, but this was available on all but the stopping trains (above).

A much fuller timetable was offered in 2000 (below). There were now four Thameslink trains an hour from London Bridge, which has become a more accessible station with the advent of the Jubilee Line extension opened in 1999. Haywards Heath itself had become a dividing point for the longer-distance trains, and this happened twice an hour. Portsmouth Harbour was replaced by Bournemouth as the furthest point west that could be reached directly, while Eastbourne services were increased from one to two. These were the only trains stopping at Haywards Heath which originated from Victoria. Trains to Brighton were now five an hour, of which only the Rugby service was operated by Connex.

Noticeable, though, was the removal of all the buffet facilities. A trolley service was all that

was left, and this was available only on the two Connex fast Brighton services, which did not call at Haywards Heath. As far as Thameslink was concerned, the timetable entry for catering on trains read, quite simply, 'none'.

The timetables have thus been anything but static, and the overall result seems to have been a greater range of destinations, including some in central London and stations to Bedford, and also to places like Watford, Milton Keynes and Northampton. Service provision overall has also increased, and to have nine southbound departures an hour constitutes a very substantial service level, which is rather better than the other snapshots offered of earlier years. Train catering, though, seems to have moved from occasional Pullman luxury, to a near universal buffet, and now nothing.

Summer Saturdays

Next to be considered are the holiday services. The rush to the coast at bank holidays and at weekends during the 1930s and again in the postwar years is a recurring theme. It was the era of the British seaside resort and the railways, which through their services had helped create these attractions, were rewarded with huge numbers taking advantage of the facilities. Or, perhaps reward is not the right word.

They certainly perplexed Dr Beeching. As he established in his 1963 Reshaping Report, out of a fleet of 18,500 coaches on British Railways, 2,000 were required on only 18 occasions a year, a further 2,000 on 14, and the last 2,000 on a mere 10 occasions. Their provision costs were put at seven times their

earnings. This was not a traffic which he was inclined to sustain.

Fig 13.9 shows the situation, as far as Margate was concerned, in four different years.

In 1955, these were entirely steam-hauled services, before the disruption of electrification began. To have required 27 trains over a five-hour period, traffics must have been very buoyant. Of note are the services starting elsewhere in Greater London; it was not assumed automatically that all trains should start in central London.

Eight years later, in the year of the Reshaping Report, the number of trains was a little lower, but by now there was a well-established electric service. A train formed CEP+BEP+CEP would have more capacity than the steam services it had replaced, so the real change was probably negligible. But quite apart from Dr Beeching's feelings, change was afoot in the market. The era of the cheap package holiday by air was all but with us, while car ownership was increasing fast. If you had to go to the cold and wet British resort, you might as well drive there, so you could then use the car for touring in the area. By 1979, the rail service had all but halved,

Fig 13.8: Haywards Heath, Summer 2000. Down Trains in Sample Hour, 11.00-11.59 Mondays to Fridays

Time	Type	Train Details	Co	Refreshments	Notes
11.05	fast	10.17 Victoria-Bournemouth/Eastbourne	CSC	none	front Bournemouth
11.07	fast	The above train divides at Haywards Heath	CSC	none	rear Eastbourne
11.08	fast	09.12 Bedford-Brighton	TLK	none	via London Bridge
11.16	stopping	08.50 Rugby-Brighton	CSC	none	via Clapham Jnc
11.19	nonstop	10.38 Victoria-Brighton	CSC	trolley service	East Croydon only
11.25	semi-fast	09.27 Bedford-Brighton	TLK	none	via London Bridge
11.35	fast	10.47 Victoria-Hastings/Littlehampton	CSC	none	front Hastings
11.37	fast	The above train divides at Haywards Heath	CSC	none	rear Littlehampton
11.38	fast	09.42 Bedford-Brighton	TLK	none	via London Bridge
11.49	nonstop	11.08 Victoria-Brighton	CSC	trolley service	East Croydon only
11.55	stopping	09.57 Bedford-Brighton	TLK	none	via London Bridge

CSC refers to Connex SouthCentral; TLK Thameslink.

Fig 13.10 (overleaf)

coming down to a basic service with just modest enhancements. To what extent this was due to shortcomings on the railways' part, or whether they were victims of circumstances beyond their control, is another matter. Perhaps by now they did not want the traffic, anyway.

Twenty years on, to the present day, there is a respectable two trains per hour, with no enhancements at all in their numbers. Some judicious strengthening of formations may take place.

Stock Utilisation

The productive use of railway assets has always been a worthwhile goal, and the Southern seems to have been alive to this. Fig 13.10 (overleaf) sets out a roster for a suburban set on a weekday in 1939, from 05.00 to 00.40 the following day. During this time, the train covered about 400 miles and in the process visited most parts of the Eastern Section which were then electrified.

This is a complex diagram; readers may wish to ponder how not just one but a whole series of such diagrams is compiled, to run the entire service with efficiency, economy and within the available resources. Is this a duty for a single electric unit, or does it need strengthening to two units at certain times? If so, where does the second unit come from, and where is it to be coupled up? What happens to the second set of crew when two trains become one? The staff rosters have to be compiled with appropriate allowances being made for meal breaks and the length of the duties. Are all the drivers conversant with all the routes? Also, staff tend to want to end up back where they signed on, unlike the trains which, as in this example, may be less fussy. On the other hand, trains need cleaning and maybe some maintenance and fault rectification. This is not a text book on such matters, and the example is given merely to show some of the difficult issues involved.

Station Control Rooms

Coupled with the regulation and running of trains is the need to inform both passengers and staff of what is happening and any changes which are necessary to the timetabled plans. The Southern had commissioned station control rooms at its major London termini in the 1960s, the aim of which was to centralise and improve communications all round. Using Charing Cross as an example, the control room overlooked the station concourse, with a clear view of all platforms. It housed the duty inspector and the station announcer; the inspector had loudspeaker communication with the guards and motive power foremen, and to the Waterloo East station inspector. There were also direct telephone lines to the box, London Bridge inspectors, Dartford inspectors (for alterations to stock rostering) and line control.

Fig 13.9: Summer Saturday Peak Service, London to Margate via Faversham

Departure Times From:	07.00-07.59	08.00-08.59	09.00-09.59	10.00-10.59	11.00-11.59	Total Trains
Victoria	2	6	4	5	5	22
Charing Cross	1	1				
Other suburban*	1	2	1	4		
Total 1955	3	7	6	6	5	27
Victoria	2	4	4	4	4	18
Charing Cross	1	1	1	1	1	5
Catford	1	1				
Total 1963	3	5	5	6	5	24
Victoria	2	2	2	2	2	10
Charing Cross	1	1	1		3	
Total 1979	2	3	3	3	2	13
Victoria	1	2	2	2	2	9
Total 2000	1	2	2	2	2	9

*These trains originated at Gravesend, Blackheath, Bromley South and Herne Hill respectively.

Fig 13.10: Stock Utilisation for a Suburban Set, 1939

05.00	Herne Hill sidings	Blackfriars (empty)		17.03	Sevenoaks	Cannon Street
05.28	Blackfriars	Dartford		17.53	Cannon Street	Bromley North
06.18	Dartford	Cannon Street		18.28	Bromley North	Charing Cross
07.05	Cannon Street	Gravesend		18.59	Charing Cross	Bromley North
08.05	Gravesend	Charing Cross		19.35	Bromley North	Cannon Street
09.10	Charing Cross	Sevenoaks		20.06	Cannon Street	Dartford
10.08	Sevenoaks	Cannon Street		20.57	Dartford	Charing Cross
11.02	Cannon Street	Orpington		21.48	Charing Cross	Bromley North
11.45	Orpington	Holborn Viaduct		22.18	Bromley North	Charing Cross
12.31	Holborn Viaduct	Sevenoaks		22.48	Charing Cross	Bromley North
13.46	Sevenoaks	Holborn Viaduct		23.20	Bromley North	Charing Cross
14.55	Holborn Viaduct	Herne Hill		23.53	Charing Cross	Dartford
15.12	Herne Hill	Holborn Viaduct		00.40	Dartford	Slade Green (empty)
15.31	Holborn Viaduct	Sevenoaks				

The major problem with Charing Cross is the very restricted concourse, and the inspector was responsible for taking regulating decisions when necessary. Trains in the evening peak were kept to their booked platforms wherever possible, to avoid large movements of passengers and the consequent congestion when changes were made at short notice. The morning peak was less of a difficulty, as those arriving would usually leave the concourse area as quickly as they could. Some trains were booked for five- to six-minute turnrounds with the same crew, or 3½-4 minutes with a changeover crew in the evening peak. In the morning peak, turnrounds might need to be slightly longer, since with the concentrated surge of passengers the incoming driver might not be able to leave his cab for anything up to three minutes. This was of course in the days with the universal use of slam door stock, when many of the doors would be open and passengers alighting before the train had come to a stand. Undesirable it may have been, but there was no way of stopping it. Power doors do at least give the train crew some control.

The station announcer also looked after the departure indicator. As many announcements as possible were taped, 64 tapes covering the regular interval main line departures and specified peak services. Alternative tapes allowed for announcements when formations varied or if multiple-portion trains were formed in reverse order. (Trying to make unambiguous announcements which avoid total chaos amongst the passengers in such circumstances is not easy!) Suburban trains were not usually announced except in the case of platform alterations. The train departure indicator was operated from punched cards for each train. Dials were also available in the set-up equipment to provide a manually determined display if needed. The departure indicator control desk also had repeaters showing when the platform starting signal was clear and when the 'train ready to start' indication had been given by the platform staff to the signalman.

Right:
Level crossings are points of intermodal conflict, which are undesirable but, in many cases, unavoidable. In this view of Newhaven Town station, the well-patronised Southdown bus could use the flyover in the background, thereby missing the station and the town centre — and what would be the point of that? Level crossings are something to be managed as best they can, for safety but also to cause minimum delay to both modes. This view shows 2HAP No 6022 at the head of a Brighton-Seaford service on 5 September 1981. *Author*

Service Comparisons

The railways comprising what used to be the Southern are sometimes thought to offer slow services. This series of tables (below and right) takes a number of journeys on the Southern and makes comparisons with the situation elsewhere. How well, all things considered, does the Southern work? The approach used is to set out a number of bases for comparison, and evaluate them using the Summer 2000 timetables (Figs 13.11–13).

Fig 13.11: What are the Overall Speeds for Longer Distance Journeys?

Distance miles	From (Origin)	To (Destination)	Fastest mins	TOC	Av Speed mph	Notes
63	Charing Cross	Hastings	88	CSE	42.6	
62	Victoria	Canterbury East	83	CSE	44.6	
66	Victoria	Eastbourne	85	CSC	46.6	
74	Victoria	Margate	95	CSE	46.6	
75	Waterloo	Portsmouth Harbour	89	SWT	50.2	via Guildford
115	Liverpool St	Norwich	96	AR	71.9	

Evaluation: Many traditional Southern services struggle to reach an average 50mph. The Southern is unlike many other railways in that nearly all longer-distance services need to make a number of intermediate stops. Whatever benefits result, it does add to the overall times. However, it was perhaps surprising to find Anglia Railways to be substantially superior in speed.

Fig 13.12: What Journeys Can be Completed in About Half an Hour?

Distance miles	From (Origin)	To (Destination)	Fastest mins	TOC	Av Speed mph	Notes
27	London Bridge	Gatwick Airport	29	TLK	54.8	
27	Victoria	Gatwick Airport	30	GEX	53.5	
28	Marylebone	High Wycombe	30	CT	55.5	
19	Waterloo	Staines	31	SWT	36.8	
30	Waterloo	Guildford	32	SWT	56.7	via Woking

Evaluation: A distance of almost 30 miles seems to be the norm in a half-hour journey; only Staines has noticeably slower services. Chiltern Trains' performance to High Wycombe was directly comparable.

Fig 13.13: Do Average Speeds Vary for Middle-distance Journeys?

Distance miles	From (Origin)	To (Destination)	Fastest mins	TOC	Av speed mph
22	Waterloo	Dorking	40	SWT	33.0
30	Victoria	East Grinstead	52	CSC	34.9
38	Cannon Street	Maidstone East	49	CSE	46.2
51	Victoria	Brighton	49	CSC	62.4
67	Waterloo	Winchester	52	SWT	76.7
77	Paddington	Swindon	52	FGW	89.1

Evaluation: The sample chosen suggests that average speeds increase as distances rise. Premier destinations such as Brighton and Winchester do best, but nothing like as well as Swindon.

Fig 13.14: Does it Make any Difference Living on the Other Side of the Thames?

Distance miles	From (Origin)	To (Destination)	Fastest mins	TOC	Av speed mph
36	Fenchurch St	Southend Cen	45	c2c	47.0
36	Victoria	Gillingham, Kent	46	CSE	47.0

Evaluation: These are similar in respect of both services and areas served, and those similarities extend to the service speeds.

Fig 13.15: Are There Quicker Ways of Reaching Destinations Served by the Southern?

Distance miles	From (Origin)	To (Destination)	Fastest mins	TOC	Av speed mph
44	Waterloo	Reading	71	SWT	36.8
36	Paddington	Reading	25	FGW	86.4

Evaluation: This is perhaps the main route for which there is an alternative, but others include Heathrow (from Waterloo via Feltham with bus), Windsor, Basingstoke and even Weymouth. For Reading, the Waterloo trains call at many intermediate stations, as well as having a longer route.

Fig 13.16: Can the Southern Long-distance Trains Match Those Elsewhere for Speed?

Distance miles	From (Origin)	To (Destination)	Fastest mins	TOC	Av speed mph
143	Waterloo	Weymouth	159	SWT	53.9
269	King's Cross	Newcastle	155	GNER	103.9

Evaluation: No, the longest journey on the Southern is the 143 miles to Weymouth. Newcastle by GNER is four minutes quicker than Weymouth, but at 269 miles is nearly twice as far!

The abbreviations used in the tables are as follows:		CT	Chiltern Trains
		FGW	First Great Western
AR	Anglia Railways	GEX	Gatwick Express
c2c	London, Tilbury & Southend	GNER	Great North Eastern Railway
CSC	Connex SouthCentral	SWT	South West Trains
CSE	Connex SouthEastern	TLK	Thameslink Rail

There are clearly more attractive journey times to be had elsewhere, but that does not make the Southern wrong. As the discussion on the services at Haywards Heath shows, frequencies are often very commendable. The most important element is to provide the service which is right for the market; to run from Waterloo to Weymouth with only one or perhaps two intermediate stops does not sound like a viable business proposition!

Mishaps

Railways, like any other industrial organisations, are bound to have mishaps. This word is used, rather than accident, to cover a broad range of events. It is, in any case, not intended to pursue more than a few illustrative events here; the aim is to show a variety of types of incident and not just to list all such happenings. The involvement of electric trains is in many cases only incidental. One of the most destructive events on the Southern, that of the Hither Green derailment in 1967, did not involve an electric train at all. Indeed, incidents need not even involve trains. The Cannon Street signalbox fire of 1957 is one example; the disruptive effects upon the train services were severe and lasted for an extended period, but this was neither a train nor a movements accident.

It must not be assumed, either, that movement incidents which do not result in injury or loss of life may be disregarded. What is important is the potential for serious consequences; was the absence of such a result due more to good luck than anything else? These events also deserve careful analysis of cause and remedies that could or should be undertaken to avoid a recurrence. Next time, the company might not be so lucky.

The issue of the cost of preventive measures is also important, to which should be coupled the likelihood of the event occurring – or re-occurring. Another issue is how serious the result is likely to be, if the event does happen. Prioritisation is always necessary; crudely, there is little point in spending huge sums if the potential for injury or damage is small and the event is statistically unlikely. The argument is not that one should avoid spending money on safety measures, but that such spending should be properly focused and concentrated on areas where it can have the maximum beneficial effect.

Operator Error
Purley Oaks, 24 October 1947

On 24 October 1947, at about 08.37 in thick fog, the 07.33 Haywards Heath–London Bridge, running on the up main, was held by signals at Purley Oaks for about eight minutes. It then continued slowly and was running at about 15/20mph when the 08.04 from Tattenham Corner travelling at about 40mph ran into the back of it. The accident happened near South Croydon Junction. The rear motor coach of the 07.33 and the leading motor coach of the 08.04am were very badly damaged, the controls in the motorman's cab being so broken and scattered that it was impossible to tell whether the motorman had applied the brakes or not. The motorman of the 08.04 and 31 passengers were killed, and 58 persons injured. Due to the fog, both trains were crowded, the 7.33 carrying about 800 passengers and the other about 1,000. Both main lines were badly damaged and the local lines blocked by debris. The latter were clear by 16.00 and all lines were available by 10.30 the following morning.

Although the porter-signalman at Purley Oaks had worked there for four months, it was the first time that he had experienced thick fog. At the ensuing inquiry, he admitted his responsibility for the accident. The exact sequence of events proved difficult to establish, but it appeared that he overlooked that the Haywards Heath train was standing in the station (it was out of sight in the fog) and gave 2-1 'out of section' for it after a telephone enquiry from Purley North box. He was then offered the Tattenham Corner train and, assuming that the Sykes lock-and-block instrument had failed, accepted it by using his release key. When South Croydon Junction accepted the Haywards Heath train, he then thought this acceptance applied to the train from Tattenham Corner, although he had never, in fact, offered it to that box, and pulled off all his signals. As the Haywards Heath train left, its passage over a rail treadle correctly altered the indication on the Sykes instrument from 'free' to 'locked', but he again assumed there had been a failure and manipulated the instrument irregularly to restore its previous indication. Two trains were therefore running in the same block section, and the collision occurred.

The Inspecting Officer found that the primary cause of the accident was the porter-signalman's forgetfulness and irregular working, and he suggested that the man had been given such responsible duties too soon after being passed for signalling work. The accident would not have happened if colour-light signalling had been installed.

Motspur Park, 6 November 1947

On 6 November 1947, and again in dense fog, the 16.45 Holmwood-Waterloo ran into the second coach of the 17.46 Waterloo-Chessington South as it was crossing to the Chessington line at Motspur Park. Four passengers were killed and 12 injured. When the inquiry was held, the motorman of the 16.45 (who was severely injured) said that as the Motspur Park outer and inner distant signals were at caution, he approached the outer home signal cautiously. He could not see that signal but he saw the fogman showing a green light. He did not see the lights of the Chessington train and the collision took him completely by surprise. The fogman admitted

Above:
In May 1987, a 4CIG formation headed by No 7379 emerges from the tunnel to the south of Haywards Heath station and will come to a halt in the up side island platform. *Author*

that he could not see the signal and he relied on the sound of its rise or fall to take up or put down his detonators, and he did not go up the signal ladder to check the position of the arm.

The Inspecting Officer found the cause of the collision to be the fogman's failure to observe the signalling rules; it might not have occurred if the signal had been repeated on the ground or fitted with a co-acting detonator placer.

New Cross, 4 December 1957

A very serious and remarkable accident occurred near St Johns at about 18.20 on 4 December 1957. It was a foggy day, turned dense by dusk, especially in the cutting between New Cross and St Johns. A fog service was not in force, and trains were running late and out of turn. Misapprehension about the description of the 17.25 Charing Cross-Hastings diesel unit led the signalman at Parks Bridge Junction to stop it by signal in the belief that it was the 17.18 electric from Charing Cross to Hayes via the Ladywell loop. The situation was not cleared up when the true 17.18 stopped at the signal in the rear of the 17.25.

The 17.18 was a 10-coach train, carrying about 1,500 passengers, and while it was standing on the up gradient with the brakes full on, the 16.56 Cannon Street-Ramsgate via Faversham – a Bulleid 4-6-2 with 11 corridors, carrying about 700 passengers – ran into it at about 30mph. The eighth coach of the 17.18 was destroyed when the ninth coach was forced through it. The tender and the front coach of the 16.56 were crushed together and thrown left, bringing down one of the steel stanchions of the overbridge carrying the Nunhead-Lewisham loop, two of the lattice girders falling on to the leading coaches.

Two minutes later, the eight-coach 17.22 Holborn Viaduct-Dartford electric was

approaching the bridge cautiously when the motorman saw a girder at an angle and promptly stopped the train. There was no derailment or damage, but one coach was tilted.

Heavy short circuits cut power off all lines except the down Nunhead. Current was cut off this line by the control room. The North Kent lines through Lewisham were closed and deprived of power for rescue work. Ambulances were called from a house by the line at about 18.22. They arrived promptly and all the injured were removed by 22.30. Five breakdown gangs, with four heavy steam cranes, arrived from 23.30 onwards and by early next day the undamaged coaches of the colliding trains were withdrawn. The fallen girders had to be shored up to prevent further settlement, but the engine of the 16.56 with the rest of the wreckage was removed by late on 6 December.

From 06.10 on 5 December, an emergency electric suburban service ran via Lewisham, main line trains being diverted to Victoria. Freight services over the Lewisham-Nunhead loop were completely disorganised and many were cancelled. The fallen bridge girders and flooring were so distorted that it was decided to cut them up with oxy-acetylene jets. Although more shoring up was needed, the work was finished by midday on 9 December. The site of the accident was cleared, permanent way made good, and normal services resumed on the main lines at 05.00 on 12 December.

Traffic over the Nunhead line was suspended until a temporary bridge of steel joists on steel trestling on concrete foundations was opened on 13 January 1958. Meanwhile, passengers on the peak-hour Holborn Viaduct-Dartford services had to use already heavily loaded trains from Charing Cross and Cannon Street, freight trains being diverted elsewhere.

Casualties were 88 passengers and the guard of the 17.18 killed, 109 passengers seriously injured (one of whom died later) and 67 slightly injured. The driver of the

16.56 was badly shocked and his fireman seriously injured.

In his report on the accident, the Chief Inspecting Officer pointed out that the four lines from New Cross to St Johns were one of the busiest sections in the world, with 990 passenger trains on a normal weekday and 81 in the busiest evening hour. No previous fatal accident had occurred since four-aspect colour-light signalling was installed in 1929. The train describers used were of old design, but very reliable and familiar to the signalmen. He blamed the driver of the 16.56 for the accident; although he passed two caution signals after New Cross he made no attempt to stop until he came suddenly on a stop signal at St Johns. The accident could have been prevented by the use of automatic warning control giving audible warning of a restrictive signal aspect, but lines equipped with multi-aspect colour-light signalling did not rank high for the installation of AWS and he saw no reason to alter the order of priority. The provision of magazine train describers and revised signal-to-signalbox telephone circuits was already under review.

The steam locomotive driver was prosecuted for manslaughter of the guard of the 17.18, but when he appeared at the Central Criminal Court on 23 April 1958 the jury failed to agree. At the next sessions the prosecution offered no evidence in view of his mental and physical state and he was formally acquitted.

Roundstone Crossing, 22 September 1965

In thick fog on 22 September 1965, the 08.47 Brighton-Portsmouth Harbour, running at about 50mph passed the distant signal for Roundstone Crossing, between Goring-by-Sea and Angmering. It was at clear, but when the home signal came into sight the motorman saw that it was at danger. Although he made an emergency brake application, the train ran through the gates and into a double-deck bus which was using the crossing. The bus was pushed in front of the train for 54yd and then burst into flames, three of its passengers being killed and eight injured. The leading coach of the train was partly derailed and damaged by fire.

At the inquiry, the crossing keeper said that a line of road traffic was waiting to use the crossing. He overheard a telephone conversation between signalmen which led him to assume that the section was clear, although the block indicators in his cabin showed 'train on line'. He put his signals to

danger and opened the gates, the bus being the first vehicle to cross.

The Inspecting Officer considered that the crossing keeper became confused because trains were running late and road traffic was waiting. He could have tested his hasty assumption that the section was clear by telephoning either of the signalmen, or waiting before he opened the gates. The accident would have been avoided if automatic half barriers (AHBs) with track-circuit control were in use and he suggested that they should be installed. That was done subsequently, and they are monitored by CCTV.

Marden, 4 January 1969

At about 20.42 on 4 January 1969, the 20.00 Charing Cross-Ramsgate (2x4CEP) ran into the rear of the 19.18 diesel-hauled London Bridge-Dover Priory parcels train of eight

vans, at Marden. The driver and three passengers were killed and 11 others injured. The three leading coaches of the 20.00 and the three rear vans of the parcels train were derailed and badly damaged.

It was stated at the inquiry that the 19.18 was preceded by a ballast train, which was stopped by signal at Marden. When the second man telephoned the Ashford signalman, he was told there had been a track-circuit failure, but it had been cleared and the train could proceed on signal indication. The parcels train had also been stopped by signal, and proceeded when it cleared. However, it had only reached a speed of 10/15mph when the collision occurred.

In his report, the Inspecting Officer said he was certain that the signals were operating correctly as the time of the accident. After passing Paddock Wood under clear signals, the

Right:
Low tide on the River Swale sees a pair of 2HAP units from Sittingbourne crossing the King's Ferry lifting bridge on the Sheerness branch, en route for the terminus. The road is on the far side of the single-track railway, which accounts for the lamps attached to the bridge pillars. The date is 25 March 1981. *Author*

driver of the 20.00 thought the line ahead would be clear and relaxed his vigilance. In thickening fog, he failed to see a signal at caution and another at stop. When he saw the next signal at caution, he cut off current and braked, and when he saw the tail lamp of the parcels train he made a full emergency brake application and tried to escape from the cab. AWS would have prevented the accident, but the Southern's policy was to give higher priority to replacing semaphores with colour lights. The Inspecting Officer supported the Southern's priorities.

Wimbledon, 12 October 1972

A freight train, made up of an electro-diesel locomotive, 22 wagons and brake van, ran into the rear of the 19.05 Holborn Viaduct–Sutton (4EPB) as it was standing in Platform 10 at Wimbledon on 12 October 1972. The driver and 11 passengers were injured. The locomotive, rear coach of the 19.05 and the station platform were all damaged, and repairs were not completed until 15 October.

The Inspecting Officer held the driver of the freight train responsible for not controlling his train properly. He may have dozed or allowed his concentration to wander, and was probably brought to his senses by the passing of an up train. By then, it was too late to avert the collision.

Around this time, trials were undertaken of a new automatic warning system, Signal Repeating Automatic Warning System

Below:
Embankment slips are a hazard which careful monitoring should manage to avoid, but if they occur repairs can be costly and take a considerable amount of time. This anonymous photograph is thought to be in the vicinity of Hook on the South Western main line, an area which has suffered on more than one occasion. This view shows the extent of work which may be involved, a corollary of which is the interruption to rail traffic in the meantime. *Ian Allan Library*

(SRAWS). This consisted of lineside and track apparatus, with a panel in the driving cab containing push-button replicas of double yellow, single yellow and red signals. If the driver did not acknowledge the indications by pressing the corresponding buttons, the brakes were applied. A green signal aspect was also provided but did not require acknowledgement.

SRAWS was installed west of Totton in 1972 and also between Raynes Park and Esher, but it was not pursued.

Eltham, 11 June 1973

Monday, 11 June 1973 saw a destructive accident at Eltham. A diesel-hauled special due to leave Margate at 20.05 for its return journey to Kentish Town on the Midland was routed via Chatham, Dartford and the Bexleyheath line. It approached Eltham Well Hall station, where there was a speed limit of 20mph over a sharp curve, at high speed. It was derailed extensively, the driver and three passengers were killed and 126 persons injured.

Interviewed by the media in hospital soon after the event, the second man alleged that the brakes failed when the driver tried to slow down. At the formal inquiry, it was stated that the brakes on the locomotive and the train were in good order but showed no sign of having been applied. A pathologist stated that when samples were taken 18 hours after the driver's death it was found that the amount of alcohol in his blood was three times the legal limit allowed for motorists. Other evidence indicated that the driver had been drinking heavily before he took the train over.

The Inspecting Officer found that the derailment was caused by the driver's failure to brake on the steeply falling gradient before Eltham Well Hall in readiness for the speed limit, and he estimated the speed at 65mph. He exonerated the guard, who made two partial brake applications to attract the

driver's attention, but the second man was guilty, on his own admission, of breaking the rule that employees must not consume intoxicating liquor while on duty. He considered that the present rules about drinking were sensible and sufficient, and did not advise any alteration. He expressed disgust at the conduct of sightseers who crowded to the scene of the accident and hampered relief work.

Following this accident, warning discs with orange figures on a black background and lit at night were installed in advance of places where a speed limit was in force. Much later, the Transport & Works Act, 1992 formalised the consumption of drugs or alcohol above certain limits as an offence. This applied to transport employees concerned with operations or maintenance. The British Railways Board effectively reduced the limits to zero and extended the requirement to all staff.

Equipment or Infrastructure Fault
Cannon Street, 5 April 1957

The station at Cannon Street had a huge semicircular overall roof, which had been damaged by high explosive bombs and incendiaries during an air raid on 10/11 May 1941. Subsequently, the roof was stripped of its glass and so performed little useful purpose. As a Modernisation Plan scheme, the old roof was to be removed and replaced by a new one at a lower level. The platforms would be lengthened to take 10 cars, and a new concourse built.

The work was carried out in a number of stages and on 4 April 1957 five of the lengthened platforms came into service. In rush hours, 22 10-coach trains arrived in the morning and 21 left in the evening.

In the early hours on the morning of 5 April, the signalman on duty discovered a fire, and although the fire brigade arrived within four minutes, a strong wind fanned the flames and more than half the box was burnt out before the fire was brought under control. The cause was thought to have been a cable fault resulting in severe arcing. That morning there were no power operated points or signals in use, and a hastily rigged-up telephone line was the only communication between the station and the outside world. Hand signalling was set up and a skeleton suburban service began on 8 April. Main line steam services were diverted to Charing Cross, Holborn Viaduct or Victoria, none of which was very popular with those whose offices were within a short distance of Cannon Street. Special buses were laid on from London Bridge, which was a considerable improvement on the circumstances in 1926 when the station was closed for over three weeks for track layout redesign and resignalling. Then, passengers had to walk from London Bridge, and like it!

Right:
The Cannon Street signalbox fire was a devastating event, and all credit was due to the signal and telecoms department for restoring matters as quickly as they did. This view shows the utilitarian external view of the new box on 15 December 1957. *Author's collection*

Bottom:
Internally, the new Cannon Street box had a 167-lever Westinghouse frame. It controlled Cannon Street station area only, and as the nearest signalling diagram shows, the conflicts at Borough Market Junction (top right) were considerable. This view dates from 15 December 1957. *Author's collection*

On the day of the fire, the London Midland Region offered to supply a 225-lever power frame in store at Crewe. This was gladly accepted, and sent off that same day by special train to the signal works at Wimbledon. Part of this was made into a 47-lever frame, installed in the reconditioned staff rooms of the Cannon Street box and brought into use on 5 May. This enabled six of the eight platforms to be used. From the next day, a full suburban service operated. Steam services remained a problem, not least because of the number of locomotive movements to be made. Only a fortnight after the fire, erection of a new signal cabin began.

The full 10-car scheme came into force with the summer service on 17 June 1957 as intended, with temporary arrangements being made at Cannon Street. This included fast electric trains to Gillingham to connect there with steam-hauled services, and the use of the brand-new Hastings DEMU sets.

Normality was restored with the opening of the new Cannon Street box on 16 December 1957. While the station was partly closed, Platforms 6 and 8 were lengthened and the new layout of the approach lines completed.

Borough Market Junction, 12 August 1958

Borough Market Junction is one of the worst places at which one can have a derailment, although trains are not moving fast at that point. On 12 August 1958, the 10-car 06.52 Sanderstead-Cannon Street was passing over the junction when the last two cars derailed.

The end vehicle was torn from its bogies and overturned across the lines leading to Charing Cross. Fortunately, only six passengers were hurt, but the lines into Charing Cross were blocked until 16.35 and those into Cannon Street until 20.25. The Inspecting Officer found that the derailment was caused by badly worn switches at the junction and blamed the supervising officer concerned for not arranging for earlier renewal.

Clapham Junction, 10 May 1965

At 08.40 on 10 May 1965, the height of the morning peak, the northern end of one of the girders carrying the 'A' signalbox across the Western Section lines at Clapham Junction partly collapsed and all trains to and from Waterloo were suspended for the rest of that day. Immediate steps were taken to support the northern end of the cabin by steel trestling. Full main line services ran on the following morning, but only a restricted service ran on the Windsor lines until 16.00.

The Inspecting Officer found that an end diagonal member in a girder failed because of heavy corrosion, causing the girder to fall about 4ft and foul some of the tracks below. Examination of other similar bridges was made at once, and it was found that some of the girders carrying the nearby West London Junction box were also in a precarious condition. He considered that both cases were due partly to lax examination, errors of judgement and faulty office organisation. Both boxes had been roofed over with steel sheeting during the war as an air raid precaution measure, but after the collapse of Clapham Junction 'A' this was removed.

Hither Green, 5 November 1967

The 19.43 Hastings-Charing Cross formed of two six-car Hastings diesel-electric units, was comprehensively derailed at Hither Green on 5 November 1967. The train was running under clear signals on the up fast line at approximately 70mph. The leading pair of wheels of the third coach struck a small wedge-shaped piece of steel which had broken away from the end of a running rail. The train became derailed towards the down fast line. It continued in this condition for about a quarter of a mile when the derailed wheels struck a crossover lead of a diamond crossing. This caused the third coach, the coach ahead and all the coaches to the rear to become completely derailed. The second to the fifth coaches turned on to their sides before they stopped, some 250yd further on. The coupling broke behind the leading coach, which was not derailed, and ran forward to stop about 220yd beyond the second coach. The overturned coaches were damaged severely and, with the train well filled, 49 passengers were killed and 78 injured. Examination of the train showed no defect that could have caused the accident, but a small piece of rail was found to have broken away from the running-on end of a rail joint near the scene of initial derailment.

The Chief Inspecting Officer concluded that the rail joint had been worn excessively, due to shortcomings in the way that maintenance and repairs to the track had been carried out. The result was a brittle fracture of the rail and fishplate, which caused the derailment.

He did not hold anybody responsible for the fracture which could not reasonably have been foreseen. However, the accident brought to light a generally unsatisfactory and disturbing state of track maintenance in the area, and the conclusion that the fast lines were not in sufficiently good condition for train speeds of 90mph. In the Chief Inspecting Officer's view, both the staff on the ground and the Southern Region's management were prepared to accept too low a standard of maintenance.

Strictly, perhaps, this was not a Southern Electric incident, but as the foregoing makes clear, the same fate could have befallen any train which passed over that section of track at speed.

Clapham Junction, 12 December 1988

Travelling between Earlsfield and Clapham Junction on 12 December 1988, the driver of the 07.18 Basingstoke-Waterloo, a 12-car VEP formation, saw signal WF138 change from green to red as he approached it at about 65-70mph. He made a full emergency brake application and reported the incident by phone at the next signal, WF47. Told by the signalman that there was no indication in the signalbox that there was anything wrong, he was returning to his train when it was struck by the 06.14 Poole-Waterloo, a 12-car REP/TC combination. Although braking heavily, the second train was estimated to have been travelling at 35-45mph at the time of impact. An empty stock train was passing in the other direction, and was struck also. The 06.53 Waterloo-Waterloo via Chertsey was stopped 50yd short of the Poole train, the driver having seen a single yellow on signal WF138, but sighting the obstruction when about 250yd from the signal. A total of 35 people, train crew and passengers, died.

A Public Inquiry was ordered by the Secretary of State, and this was conducted by (Sir) Anthony Hidden QC. This was only the fourth time that the procedure under the Regulation of Railways Act, 1871 had been invoked; the first was the Tay Bridge disaster of 1879. Mr Hidden's report said that the direct responsibility was placed with the technicians, supervisors and managers responsible for the signalling work before the accident, as part of the Waterloo Area Resignalling Scheme.

The system failed because, during alterations to the signalling system on 27 November, a wire which should have been removed both from the relay feeding it and the fuse it fed was removed only from the relay and not cut back or secured out of the way. When a new relay was installed adjacently on 11 December, the old wire was disturbed. Once again it made contact with its old terminal, and could therefore deliver feed current into a new circuit which should, because of the presence of a train, have been dead. This prevented signal WF138 from then turning to red. While this was the primary cause of the accident, many other shortcomings in the way that the work was carried out were identified.

The report blamed not only the individuals concerned, but also 'those who allowed an originally sensible and workable system to

Left:
The partial collapse of Clapham Junction 'A' box in 1965 caused major problems for the South Western Division. It is seen here on 23 August 1976, with a 4EPB set passing below. *Author*

degenerate into an incompetent, inept and potentially disastrous way of working'.

Recommendations by Mr Hidden included the rigorous implementation of good installation practice and testing, better monitoring of wrong side failures (signals indicating the line is clear when it is not), introduction of train recorders and train radio, financial appraisals to include safety, research into rolling stock structural integrity, and emergency plans to be prepared by area and station management.

Had the trains been overloaded, the report says, passengers standing as a result would not have been placed at extra risk, but attention to loading criteria was recommended to minimise casualties.

Bad Practices
Waddon, 4 November 1942

On 4 November 1942, in blackout conditions and dense fog, the 06.15 West Croydon-Holborn Viaduct ran into the 05.34 London Bridge-Epsom as it was standing in Waddon station. The 05.34 could not be accepted by the next signalbox at Wallington, where shunting was going on, and was held at Waddon so long that the guard went to the signalbox in accordance with the rules. While he was there, the 06.15 was heard approaching, but nothing could be done to avert the collision and the motorman of this train and a passenger were killed. At the ensuing inquiry, the signalman at West Croydon South box said that he received 'line clear' on the Sykes lock-and-block instrument from Waddon and it was suggested that the signalman there had freed the instrument

with his 'release key' in the mistaken belief that the 05.34 had left, but he denied doing so. The Inspecting Officer suggested that the company should consider installing a release system by which the two signalmen concerned would have to co-operate.

Longfield-Farningham Road, 10 September 1963

The 11.20 freight from Dover Marine to Hither Green Continental Depot on 10 September 1963, consisting of an electric locomotive, 24 Continental vans and a bogie brake, was running at about 60mph on a down grade of 1 in 100 between Longfield and Farningham Road. The couplings parted between the first and second wagons and 18 of the remaining wagons were derailed. The locomotive and one of the wagons ran on for over a mile before the driver realised what had happened. Many of the wagons were badly damaged, as was the track. It took the breakdown gangs 60 hours to clear the line and normal working was not resumed until 13 September.

The Inspecting Officer could find no definite cause for the derailment, although excessive axle play could have led to oscillation. The train was fitted with the vacuum brake, but it did not act on the locomotive when the train parted due to a technical fault.

Although not able to prevent the incident from happening, the failure of the braking system to act as intended may have worsened the result. If the driver had been aware of the incident as soon as it happened, he could have stopped and acted to minimise the possibility of a collision caused by an approaching train

from the other direction. Fortunately, it would appear that there was none.

Raynes Park, 28 November 1967

On 28 November 1967, the 03.47 Waterloo-Guildford parcels train was derailed at Raynes Park. Five vans, including a short-wheelbase four-wheeler, left the road, demolished Raynes Park station footbridge, and blocked all four lines. Portsmouth services were diverted from Guildford via Effingham Junction and Epsom to Victoria, while Bournemouth trains ran via Richmond and Staines.

The train was formed of 19 vans and hauled by an electro-diesel locomotive. It was on the down local line and travelling at just under 60mph. A lightly loaded short-wheelbase van, marshalled 15th in the train, derailed on plain track. On reaching the facing connection to the Epsom line, the van became deflected to the left and came into violent contact with the footbridge supports. This led to the derailment of the four following vehicles and caused extensive damage to the track as well.

The Inspecting Officer cited three causes: partly the derailment occurred because of minor track irregularities; also because the train was coasting at the time; and thirdly due to excessive speed. Short-wheelbase vans were by then restricted to 45mph, but the guard did not tell the driver, as it was his duty to do, and the driver, although he walked the length of the train before departure, did not notice the van. He was thus entitled to run at the overall line speed, which was 60mph at that point, and 75mph thereafter. The train had departed from Waterloo five minutes late.

After the accident, the availability of suitable vans had improved and there was no longer any need to include four-wheelers in the formation. This incident demonstrated another common feature, in that there were several elements which were unsatisfactory, but it was all three occurring together which produced the result that it did. However, the Inspecting Officer added that if it had not occurred then, the accident would have almost certainly happened later when the train accelerated to 75mph.

Third Parties

On 15 July 1970, an empty 4BEP from Ramsgate to Ashford ran into a lorry on an occupation crossing between Chartham and Chilham, killing the lorry driver and the train guard. At the subsequent inquiry, it was stated that as the crossing was used by lorries to and from a nearby quarry, a gatekeeper was provided, who should obtain permission from the signalman at Chartham by telephone before opening the gates. After a lorry crossed, the gatekeeper told the signalman that both gates were closed, but in fact he had left one open. When a second lorry came, it was driven on to the line and was hit by the train.

The Inspecting Officer considered that the arrangements for operating the crossing were satisfactory and held the gatekeeper responsible for the accident. It might be added that a road vehicle should not enter a railway crossing unless the exit is clear, which is why box junction markings are applied today at all automatic crossings.

In the latter part of 1960, there were three remarkable cases of mail robbery from electric trains. On 16 August as the 14.25 nonstop from Brighton to Victoria approached Haywards Heath, three hooded men went to the guard's compartment, bound, gagged and blindfolded the guard, and opened a number of mail bags, stealing registered letters said to contain £8,000. After securing the doors in the guard's compartment, the thieves returned to the passenger part of the train and were thought to have left it separately at Victoria.

On 20 September, the 21.28 Victoria-Brighton was stopped by signal between Hassocks and Preston Park. Three masked men entered the guard's compartment, overpowered the guard, threw out mail bags and ran with them to a waiting car. The signal cleared and the train went on to Preston Park, where the robbery was discovered. It

was found that one of the gang had tampered with a track circuit, putting a colour-light signal to danger.

Another robbery on precisely the same lines occurred on 29 November, when the 19.00 Ore-Victoria (6PUL No 3008) was stopped by signal south of Quarry Tunnel. No arrests were made for any of these robberies.

Then, on 21 January 1961, there was yet another mail robbery from an electric train. When the 21.47 Waterloo-Teddington stopped at Clapham Junction, a passenger was waiting with an 'invalid' in a wheelchair. The guard helped to load the wheelchair into his compartment, and the passenger entered a compartment nearby. As the train approached Earlsfield, it was stopped by signal, the 'invalid' jumped from his chair, overpowered the guard and threw out four mail bags. He and his accomplice leapt from the train, picking up the bags, and fled with them through an adjoining cemetery to a waiting car. They were chased by a passenger, but he failed to catch them. Like the previous cases, the stop was caused by one of the gang tampering with a track circuit.

The first occasion of a terrorist bomb was recorded on 8 September 1973, when a railman reported to the police that a suspicious package had been left in the season ticket office at Victoria. Prompt action to clear

Below:
Nobody could accuse Southease & Rodmell Halt, later plain Southease as being overgenerous in the facilities offered to passengers. As the old name implies, the halt was within a mile of both settlements, but close to neither. People avoid building houses in river flood plains, in this case that of the River Ouse. Station usage could only be described as exceedingly modest, but Southease still enjoys an hourly service, daily, with extra train calls at peak. Such are the benefits of living on the Southern's electrified network, as many over the years have discovered to their advantage. There is no evening service after 20.00. Here, a 2HAP formation headed by unit No 6016 arrives with a Brighton-Seaford working on 5 September 1981. *Author*

the area was taken, but the bomb exploded, injuring five people and causing much damage. No more explosions occurred at Southern termini, but there were many reports of bombs at other stations in the next few days, some at least being hoaxes. These delayed trains while stations were closed and searched.

Flood Disruption

Third rail electrification does have some drawbacks, as in the case of flooding. The following account relates to matters which took place at Lewes in November 1960.

On the morning of Thursday, 3 November, floodwater rose over the conductor rails in Platforms 1 to 3 of Lewes station and the electric service to London had to be shut down. During the day, conditions worsened quickly. For example, a 2-6-0 steam locomotive on the Uckfield line suddenly encountered floodwater high enough to enter its ashpan and extinguish its fire – and which remained at this level until lock gates up-river at Barcombe gave way and a tidal wave rolled down the valley meeting head on a spring tide rolling up from the coast. This put Lewes station completely out of action. A foot of water now covered the Brighton lines, while parts of the London platforms themselves were under water. North of the tunnel, all traces of the railway seemed lost to view. From that night until mid-morning on Sunday, 6 November, the station was unusable by any electric trains and the Brighton-Eastbourne service was maintained by two six-car Hastings diesel units.

The Lewes signalman had to row out to work on the morning of Friday, 4 November. The service was somewhat irregular but throughout Saturday the booked half-hourly departures at 12 and 44 minutes past the hour from Brighton and 21 and 51 past the hour from Eastbourne were maintained. The steam trains could not adhere strictly to the electric units' point-to-point schedules and some late running occurred, but the arrangements were

a credit to the resource of the operating authorities. This even included the use of some condemned coaches stored at Horsted Keynes, and a goodly selection of steam locomotives, but particularly the then almost ubiquitous Standard Class 4 2-6-2 tank.

Class M7 0-4-4Ts were brought out for the Seaford branch, but not before the Brighton Works 'Terrier' 0-6-0T had made one experimental sortie at the head of a single coach. Electric traction was able to resume operations the next week to Brighton, Eastbourne and Seaford, but the damage on the Lewes-London line was much more severe.

Snow-drifts and Blizzards

Planning a service is one thing, operating it is another. The necessary resources need to be available and in place, the staff organised, safety systems fully operational, and the conductor rail live. In the normal course of events this will happen as intended, and the whole becomes a 'non-event' — until, that is, something goes wrong.

If there is one thing which tends to defeat the third rail operations, it is the weather. Snow and ice are particularly difficult, not only of course for the loss of shoe contact with the conductor rail, but all the other items which may also get frozen. What follows is a much-abridged version of an account by Michael Woods, to whom I am indebted. He was the Area Manager BR Dartford, and he tells of the events of mid-January 1987.

Sunday, 11 January

11.30   Snow very heavy. Weather deteriorates during the afternoon.

20.00   Weather very poor. Heavy delays in Medway area. Several trains are being locomotive hauled and some 20-car formations are being run to try to give the best chance of picking up power from the conductor rail.

Monday, 12 January

02.00   Snow continuing. Line reported blocked beyond Gillingham, also Sheerness branch closed as snow there is up to platform level.

06.00   On duty at Gravesend. Large numbers of passengers at station despite warnings from BBC Radio Kent. First up train of the morning leaves at 0650, all stations via Bexleyheath.

07.30   Second up train leaves at 07.36. Huge queues at ticket office — make tea for staff there and unfreeze a little.

09.20   Last night's 1951 Faversham-Victoria comes through Dartford, formed 8CEP. It had been stranded all night.

14.30   Telephone conference. Loco-hauling on Maidstone East line and between Gillingham and Faversham. The forecast is bad — snow, and worse tomorrow.

17.10   There is a broken rail inside Blackheath Tunnel — all up trains diverted via Greenwich.

Tuesday, 13 January

05.30   Speak to box. Ghost trains had run over all routes during night, but Gillingham depot completely frozen in so a large proportion of morning peak service would not be available.

06.00   At Gravesend today we manage eight up trains before 09.30, an improvement on yesterday. Unfortunately, there is a long gap from 06.24 to 07.23. Platform 1 is packed from end to end. Several 'hopeful' announcements made, and passengers seem very good-humoured.

Medway Towns are virtually cut off by blizzard.

12.00   We abandon the booked train service and start operating on an 'out and back' basis. Tremendous co-operation from train crews. I hear that all the country routes in Kent are running loco-hauled services only.

14.30 There is an 8EPB in Gravesend up platform with burnt-out motors, also one failed on the up loop line around Bexley.

16.00 2L10 has taken two hours to struggle past Northfleet to get from Gravesend to Dartford.

19.30 Considering all things, we run a pretty frequent shuttle service and everyone gets home.

21.00 Manage to crew up a special to Gravesend. We get stopped at Swanscombe. Signalman tells me that we cannot get into down platform as Gravesend 429 points won't budge. We are to back in from the country end. Stop at Northfleet and walk down the platform to warn passengers. Move carried out without difficulty. Connection made into Strood train which was waiting on up side. Weren't those passengers pleased!

Wednesday, 14 January

06.00 At 06.15 a loco – No 33202 – succeeds in pulling an 8EPB back into the up side at Gravesend after it fails to get to Northfleet. All crewed up and ready to go in behind another failure – just by Hoo Junction. We set off. Conditions are terrible – you can't tell where the conductor rail is, so walking around is dangerous. The crew have difficulty in freeing the buffers on the frozen EMU, but eventually we reach the safety of Higham Tunnels and run down into Strood.

08.00 We decide to use the loco to run a hauled shuttle Strood to Dartford. Reports down the Medway are that snow is at platform height so we have to abandon the Paddock Wood branch – reluctantly – for the time being.

08.45 Stopped outside Gravesend waiting for 425 points to be freed. A PW gang get off the train and walk forward to help. After 10 minutes we pull forward into the up platform and form up: 8EPB+33202+8EPB. When we are all coupled up, we pull forward to detrain the passengers from the back and concentrate them all in the front portion. Arrive Dartford 0930. First train through today.

09.50 Reports flooding in. Failed train at Bexley, another going to push. Deep frozen points at North Kent Junction. Another loco found and 33+10EPB goes into the Strood shuttle.

11.00 Council of war. Medway Valley line now inaccessible. Strood- Dartford diesel shuttle to run for as long as we can get it through.

12.00 Message that there are four tank wagons of loco fuel stuck at Hoo Junction. Essential that we get them out for Chart Leacon, Ashford, or

loco hauling will cease. We get a Class 47 down to Strood to pick up a gang of men to dig the tanks out.

15.30 Regional telephone conference set up to plan our way out of this together.

15.55 Special tank wagons leave Hoo Junction. Conference looks at overnight de-icing programme, staff availability, the problem of paying wages to staff cut off, the attitude of the media. The fuel tanks are en route up the Sidcup loop.

20.00 Conference looks at stock availability, ploughing the main lines, running ghost trains and de-icers everywhere, and where all the diesel locomotives are. The fuel has arrived at Chart Leacon, after running round at Charing Cross!

Thursday, 15 January

06.45 Situation stabilised. No further snow, just very cold indeed, and high winds causing drifts all over the place. We plan our priorities.

09.00 We've managed to run five locomotive hauled trains up from Strood to Dartford, including one EMU on the juice. There's a panic on for point salt – there may be some at Hoo Junction.

11.10 Conference. Suburban services are beginning to settle down, but the country areas are getting worse. Eight-foot drifts are blocking Faversham-Dover, and reports of a snowplough stuck on the Sole Street line near Longfield. Conditions are dreadful. Apparently, there's a phone in a nearby farmhouse, and messages are being sent by waving a blanket out of the upstairs window. There's a large tree on the line too, and it is decided to seek military assistance. Meanwhile, I suggest running the Medway-Victoria services via Dartford if the Thanet area can free Rochester Bridge Junction. There's a problem with the King's Ferry Bridge – it won't budge, and there's a ship trying to get through.

15.00 We manage to get a half-hourly service on all routes from Dartford to London.

16.00 Next conference. There's a helicopter landing next to the snowplough, but at Lenham there's another one stuck. A Class 47 is on its way.

17.00 I discuss with one of my Eltham commuters how we can cope with increased loadings tomorrow on the Bexleyheath and Sidcup lines. We are going to try to increase the level of service.

Friday, 16 January

09.00 Success! We've managed a half-hourly service on all our lines this morning except the Medway Valley.

11.00 Our conference reviewed the snowplough, where a rescue train with a JCB was trying to get through. The Army was still in evidence, two of their tracked vehicles were reported en route. Our priorities were to progressively return to electric traction as each line east of Dartford became clear. Staff at Slade Green were to work right through the weekend repairing burnt-out motors, frozen brakes, wheelflats and the like.

14.00 Things are beginning to look better. Electric trains are now working through to Strood, but the Victoria-Faversham service is still loco-hauled and running via Dartford. Still some odd combinations around – No 56001+4EPB, and No 56082 with 2x4CEP. After the evening peak, No 56001 gets stuck at Gillingham after struggling through from Dartford.

20.00 I hear on the radio of widespread power cuts in Thanet. At 21.00 the lights go out in Gravesend too – not for long, but enough to create more problems for the trains – signals and lights out everywhere.

The Weekend

Slade Green and other depots worked like wartime munitions factories in trying to ensure that we had something like a normal number of units for Monday morning's peak. In the Thanet area, the Sheerness branch was the last to reopen. A train with three passengers and two Brutes full of milk did get through on the Friday, but it was late morning on the Saturday before things really got moving again.

My colleagues in the Orpington area continued to have problems with Sole Street bank because of lineside drifts collapsing back on the track. Stopping trains would be loco-hauled on the bank, but the through services were to be diverted via Dartford – if paths could be found.

A suggestion that diggers might be available for hire to clear station car parks was taken up and during the night about a dozen car parks were freed.

Many lessons were learned from this week of crisis management, particularly the importance of a good communication system, including conference and radio phones. You have to keep it simple when trying to run a service in the teeth of the elements.

There was also a range of technical matters; these included more effective point heaters, snowploughs and snowblowers, de-icer units, the availability of carriage washing machines in cold weather, and the best use of manpower in a crisis.

At least the railways in Kent kept running every day, when roads were blocked, buses and coaches immobilised, and towns and villages cut off completely.

14. The Southern's Customers

As discussed earlier, the Southern Electric was born as a counter to the spread of road competition in the form of electric tramcars. By electrifying, the railway was able to offer the benefits of speedy, clean and frequent train services, whose low operating costs offset the amount of capital investment required. For this, one proviso was necessary, in that the traffic had to be sufficiently dense to justify the company offering high service frequencies to its customers.

In some ways, this is a circular argument. It can be argued that the provision of high quality service in itself generates custom, and that this is reinforced by further service expansion to generate yet more custom. Few would disagree with the desirability of such a 'virtuous circle' of events. The problem is that journeys by rail are, in the main, not taken for their intrinsic benefits. People make journeys as a necessary part of wider goals, the principal one of which is employment. Whether one thoroughly enjoys one's work or not, it is an economic necessity for most of us. Central London has for long been a major employment centre; the electric railway was one of the elements which made the separation of work and home that much more possible.

A growing desire to live in the developing suburbs was apparent in the early years of the 20th century and accelerated in the interwar years. Concerns about urban sprawl came later, and were not misplaced. Between 1921 and 1961, the population of the City and County of London decreased by 1.25 million, while those resident in the so-called Outer Ring grew by two million. Practical steps to create a Green Belt of open country, mostly in a range of between 13 and 20 miles from Central London, began in 1935. Meanwhile, the Southern Electric did all it could to cater for and nurture the suburban growth, since at the same time it provided the railway with a growing source of business.

Today's commuting, it may be observed, does however stretch way beyond that 20-mile radius. Indeed stations such as Tunbridge Wells (34 miles from Charing Cross), Haslemere (42 miles from Waterloo), and Lewes (50 miles from London Bridge) are well within what many consider to be daily travel possibilities to London. Indeed, it can be argued convincingly that virtually the whole of the network electrified by the Southern and its successors, with origins from the Kent Coast in the east round to Bournemouth/Poole in the west, and perhaps even beyond, is commutable territory. Margate is 74 miles from Victoria, while Poole is a very substantial 113 miles from Waterloo.

Other Commuter Centres

Commuting, however, is not confined to those with destinations at London termini, and established towns in the area, including many of those mentioned already, will attract their own traffics. In none of these cases should it be assumed that commuting is the only or major traffic; many are important

Right:
This was the image of first class travel in a 4CEP unit for the Kent Coast electrification, although for some reason the armrests have not been lowered. The umbrella rack below the main luggage rack may be seen, while the view looks more like snow on moorland than somewhere in deepest Kent. The photograph is dated 28 August 1958. *Ian Allan Library*

regional shopping or entertainment centres in their own right. High in the list is Gatwick, which has its own specialised traffics. The most important destination stations in the area served by the Southern, as measured by those from which passengers return in the evening peak, are as follows. London terminals are excluded from this list, and in descending order of the number of users, the top 20 are:

1. East Croydon
2. Reading
3. Wimbledon
4. Gatwick Airport
5. Clapham Junction
6. Guildford
7. Brighton
8. West Croydon
9. Haywards Heath
10. Southampton
11. Tonbridge
12. Redhill
13. Bromley South
14. Kingston
15. Balham
16. Sutton
17. Basingstoke
18. Chatham
19. Portsmouth & Southsea
20. Woking

Balham, and to some extent Wimbledon, are likely to include substantial numbers interchanging from London Underground. The number of Reading passengers will also be overstated as it will include many who are not using electric services.

Above:
Queues for tickets are perhaps inevitable, but the number of windows provided and open at any one time can regulate the length of queues to an acceptable level. This is the ticket office at Victoria at 08.40 on 13 September 1983. The provision of ticket machines for passengers to serve themselves can help considerably. *Author*

Commuting is not in itself likely to be popular with the travelling public. It is carried out as part of an overall package in which the commuters see some advantage to themselves. More pleasant and spacious lifestyles may be matched with more affordable housing, to be set against a perhaps substantial expenditure on a season ticket and a train service which will vary in comfort, levels of crowding, reliability, quality including cleanliness, frequency and speed. Much here depends on the route and journey chosen. Those who travel from stations on relatively obscure secondary lines will lose out on frequency, with last trains often running earlier in the evening, but their trains may be rather less crowded and seats easier to obtain.

Station access at the residential end may or may not be convenient, while there may be a car to be parked. Crucially, access to the work destination at the London end must be reasonably satisfactory.

The Railway Businesses

The Department of Transport shed an interesting light on the Southern's businesses. The source is their guide issued in 1992, when the services were to be franchised. It may be noted that the Network SouthEast divisions are not aligned precisely with those

later to be franchised. In particular, what became the Island Line between Ryde and Shanklin was then part of the South Western Division of British Rail. Eurostar was not then operational, and was not to be included in the franchising arrangements.

In what follows, references to any non-electrified services and to Thameslink services north of London have been omitted. They are however included in the statistical analysis.

South Eastern

The market comprises the well-developed commuting suburbs in south east London, as well as a number of more prosperous commuting towns with a high element of first class travel. A number of towns (Canterbury, Greenwich, Thanet resorts) are important tourist attractions in their own right.

The South Eastern is the largest division on Network SouthEast by passenger journeys, and the second largest by income. It comprises a dense network of suburban services and a number of main lines serving all the principal towns in Kent as well as the Channel ports. It uses five London termini, at Charing Cross, London Bridge, Cannon Street, Victoria and Blackfriars.

The service pattern reflects its role in the major short-distance commuter market and also as a provider of longer-distance travel, although journey speeds on these are relatively low. This is partly because of congestion on the approaches to London and partly because of the infrastructure and rolling stock available. Electrification started in 1925, with Victoria/Holborn Viaduct to Orpington via Herne Hill and the Catford Loop.

This is an intensive network of suburban and inter-urban services south of London, based around the main lines from London to the Kent Coast via Tonbridge and via Gillingham. Major catchments are around the Medway towns (Chatham, Gillingham and Rochester), Maidstone, Canterbury, the Thanet Coast, Tonbridge and Hastings. Suburban services catchment areas extend to Orpington, Bromley, Dartford, Gravesend, Bexleyheath and Woolwich.

All services are operated at least hourly, and many as frequently as every 15 minutes. Where these are combined, inner areas such as Lewisham and New Cross have a train every few minutes into central London. A number of local services in Kent and East/West Sussex are operated as well, notably between Sittingbourne and Sheerness, Strood and Maidstone, and Maidstone and Three Bridges. All services are electrically operated throughout.

South Central

The commuting market is well established. There are a few particularly prosperous commuting towns such as East Grinstead and Haywards Heath. Brighton and the other coastal resorts are major tourist and leisure destinations in their own right. South Central serves Gatwick directly from Victoria, offering six trains per hour during most of the day, with just over half an hour's travelling time.

South Central serves the eastern part of Surrey and Sussex. It comprises a main line connecting London and Brighton, to Eastbourne and Chichester, the 'Coastway' route parallel to the Channel coast from Portsmouth to Hastings and a dense network of suburban lines in south London. All major towns in the area are served. It operates into three London termini at London Bridge, Victoria and Charing Cross.

The service pattern reflects the area served, with high-frequency services on most of the long-distance routes and also the inner-suburban routes. There is an intensive network of suburban and inter-urban services south of London, based around the main lines from Victoria and London Bridge to Brighton, and the branches. Major catchment areas are around East Croydon, Sutton, Crawley/Gatwick, Haywards Heath, Eastbourne, Worthing and Bognor Regis. Much of this is prime commuting territory, and not only into London.

All services are operated at least hourly, and many as frequently as every 15 minutes. Where these are combined, inner areas such as Balham and Clapham Junction have a train every few minutes into central London. Connex SouthCentral provide 4tph with only one or two intermediate stops between Victoria and Gatwick Airport in a journey time of 33/36 minutes. The services along the Sussex coast interlock to produce a mixture of stopping and semi-fast services, which provide not less than 2tph between most points, and frequently more.

South Western

South Western serves a mature and prosperous market. Both its inner and its longer-distance commuting services serve a predominantly professional and skilled clerical (ABC1) market, and it includes stations such as Haslemere with the highest number of first class season ticket holders in the country. The main lines have some of the characteristics of typical long-distance services, with substantial business and leisure demand. A number of major companies in the financial services sector have relocated part of their operations to Bournemouth and Southampton. South

Below:
It has now turned 10.00 and the first of the off-peak crowds are beginning to arrive at Waterloo on 21 April 1984. The volume, though, is nothing like that of the peak operation, to which the business is principally geared. *Author*

Western's area includes many tourist destinations such as the New Forest, Portsmouth, Winchester and Weymouth. Major shopping centres include Kingston, Guildford, Southampton and Richmond.

This is the second largest NSE division by number of journeys and the largest by income. It serves west Surrey, Hampshire and parts of Dorset and Berkshire. There are shipping links to the Isle of Wight at Portsmouth, Southampton and Lymington. It comprises a network of medium and shorter distance commuting lines as well as main lines to Portsmouth and the Solent. All lines radiate from Waterloo.

The service pattern comprises frequent trains throughout the day to medium-distance destinations such as Guildford, Woking and Surbiton with rather less frequent services on inner-suburban lines to Chessington, Staines and Hounslow. The main lines are served by a mixture of fast and semi-fast services.

An intensive network of suburban and inter-urban services to the south west of London is based on the main lines from London to Portsmouth, London to Southampton/Bournemouth and London to Reading via Staines. Other major catchment areas are around Aldershot, Basingstoke, Bournemouth, Guildford, Poole, Salisbury, Winchester and Woking.

Most services are operated at least hourly, and many as frequently as every 15 minutes. Where these are combined, inner areas such as Wimbledon and Clapham Junction have a train into London every few minutes.

Gatwick Express

Gatwick Express plays an important role in establishing Gatwick as a London airport. The total rail share of all passengers using Gatwick is approximately 25%. The market share of journeys to and from London is however much higher, reaching 80% for the West End and core boroughs. Business travel represents 22% of airport usage and this is closely reflected by Gatwick Express users.

The service commences at 04.30 from Victoria and runs every 15 minutes throughout most of the day, and half-hourly from 21.00 until 23.00. The service takes 30 minutes and a refreshment trolley is provided on most trains.

Thameslink

Markets have developed with the opening of through services between north and south London, offering a whole host of journey possibilities without the need to change trains or use the Underground. Thameslink connects Gatwick Airport with the City and provides services to major business destinations such as Croydon. Brighton is an important generator of off-peak leisure travel.

Thameslink provides a mixture of fast, semi-fast and all-stations services, but there are severe limitations in peak provision because of capacity constraints in the London Bridge area.

The relevant importance of the various British Rail divisions as they were a decade ago is demonstrated, as is also the imbalance between peak and off-peak operations. It should be stressed that this is people arriving at London stations; those travelling counter-peak or making other journeys on the network altogether are excluded.

Even so, there are approaching half a million passengers daily in this group, and over two-thirds of them have elected to be carried in three out of the 19 hours or thereabouts of the operating day. This puts enormous strain on the resources of people, equipment and infrastructure over that period, compared with which the off-peak is relatively quiet. The whole flow of course reverses itself in the late afternoon.

Onward Travel

Having arrived in London, how do people continue their journeys? London termini vary as to their nearness to workplaces, and often the peak-hour traveller has a further journey to his destination after arrival. For those arriving at the Southern termini, the average division of modes for the onward journey is: walking 53%, Underground or DLR 33%, and bus 13%. The remainder use taxi or cycle, or are picked up by car.

Averages always hide what can be quite wide variations. Perhaps unsurprisingly, 75% of Cannon Street passengers walk to their final destination, and the proportions are similarly large at London Bridge. On the other hand, walking is at its least popular at Waterloo main line and at Victoria. The alternatives are, presumably, too attractive! Passengers arriving at Waterloo head in large numbers for the Underground (32%) and the Waterloo & City line (14%). At Victoria, the Underground carries 45% of those arriving, but there is also a bus station immediately outside the station building with 18% of rail passengers using a bus – more than at any other main line station.

As many as 43% of passengers arriving at Vauxhall make straight for the Victoria Line. Stations from which the use of buses is very low are Blackfriars, Vauxhall and Cannon Street, while few transfer to the Underground at Cannon Street or London Bridge. The situation at the latter may change following the opening of the Jubilee Line extension in 1999.

Economics of Commuter Travel

The problem for the operator of the Southern Electric system is that commuter traffic is not unambiguously profitable. It requires a large resource commitment, whether in the infrastructure itself, the trains to provide the service, or the staff to run and maintain the system. Unfortunately, many of the resources needed for the few morning and evening hours in the Monday to Friday peaks are redundant outside those hours. The differences can be seen in the train services timetabled: 15

trains leave Dartford in the up direction between 07.30 and 08.29 Mondays to Fridays, but this diminishes to 10 during the day and on Saturdays, and to eight on Sundays. Outside the peaks, trains are also likely to be reduced from eight or 10 cars to four.

While this gives a valuable opportunity for trains to be maintained and cleaned during the normal working day, it is inescapable that this part of the fleet is not earning any revenue when it is not in use carrying passengers. Rolling stock leasing charges however continue unabated, as do the costs of train crews for whom no alternative work can be found. On the infrastructure side, the view southwards from the ends of Platforms 3 and 4 at London Bridge can be impressively busy at the height of the peak. Seven parallel lines on the South Eastern side are matched with four on the Brighton side, making 11 in all. This continues for as far as the eye can see; in practice the lines begin to separate after a mile or so. Nothing like this level of provision would be needed were off-peak service levels to be offered at all times.

Such provision has to be paid for, and it is a reasonable principle that costs should be borne by charges to those whose actions require them to be incurred. From this stems the adoption of charging systems which exact, in relative terms, a premium payment from the peak traveller – a standard fare. Regular travellers can obtain some relief by the purchase of season tickets; small discounts when compared with daily fares are commonplace for weekly tickets, while longer period tickets of a month or more give progressively larger discounts. An annual ticket is available for 40 times the weekly rate, but it must be remembered that this includes validity during annual holidays, bank holidays and for any periods of sickness or when travel is not required.

Off-peak and other promotional fares, which are usually available only outside the designated peak hours, are offered at considerable discounts.

Commuters' Charter

While considerable efforts have been made by railway operators over the years to meet peak demands for travel, the results have not been wholly satisfactory. Volumes vary over time, and the strength of the economy during the late 1990s led to a substantial surge in demand. This may or may not be sustained; the last boom peaked for travel demand around 1990, to be followed by several years of decline. Railway business planners can and do make assessments of where present trends might lead in the years to come, but it is not an easy decision to either find or commit extensive resources for a traffic which is at best only marginally profitable. Also, even if the moneys are made available, from whatever source, project implementation can never be instantaneous.

Fig 14.1:	Passengers Arriving in London, Typical Weekday, 1991			
NSE Division/ IC Gatwick	Peak Period 07.00-09.59	Off-peak All other times	Total	Notes
South Eastern	130,637	37,343	167,980	
South Central	67,338	37,635	104,973	
South Western	92,628	49,986	142,614	
Thameslink (south)	9,100	5,890	14,990	
Gatwick Express	7,000	6,000	13,000	peak/off-peak split estimated
Totals	306,703	136,854	443,557	
%	69%	31%	100%	
Source: Department of Transport, October 1992				

There has thus been a long-term trend to match service provision with the minimum realistic requirements, taking into account guidelines such as the maximum time for which it is reasonable to expect customers to stand and the ratio of standing to seated passengers on trains. Both were set out in the British Railways Board's document *The Commuters' Charter*, published in 1981.

The published document first set out the results of the Board's research into what their customers wanted. They appear to be in descending order of importance, although this was not stated explicitly. The attributes were:

- Punctuality and reliability.
- A reasonable chance of a seat on trips lasting more than 15-20 minutes.
- Information and advice when services are disrupted.
- Clean, comfortable, well-run stations.
- Open carriages for security and to reduce vandalism.

It then came to the crunch point, as to what (if anything) the Board intended to do about it. This was set out in a series of specific points, many of which have since found their way into the quality issues in today's franchising regime. This was then still 15 years away. Of the issues that perhaps now might seem noticeable by their absence are the provision of accurate and timely information, the importance or otherwise of staffing levels both at stations and on trains, and issues relating to personal security. The following are the standards that the Board set themselves:

- Ensure that 95% of trains depart on time.
- Ensure that 95% of services arrive at final destination on time, or less than five minutes late.
- Keep timetable cancellations to a maximum of 1% a year and spread them to avoid excessive disruption to any one service.
- Run clean, bright, open coaches, brushed and swept daily. Long-distance trains travelling more than about 20 miles should all have toilets. Graffiti should be removed as quickly as practicable.
- Improve standards of ventilation and ride, and install public address systems on trains.
- Seat 70% of short-distance passengers and virtually all long-distance passengers.
- Improve stations to give better weather protection, heating where appropriate, toilets at more important centres, more pay phones, better communications and loudspeakers, and easier interchange with buses, taxis and cars.
- Shorten journey times by reducing intermediate stops.
- Maintain service frequency as long as demand warrants it.

Cynics might say that this was, at its heart, a money-grabbing exercise, but Sir Peter Parker as the then BRB Chairman was quite forthright in his introduction. If more resources are needed he said, 'the question still to be answered is what contribution should come from those other than commuters who benefit from the services provided, and how that contribution should be made'.

Readers must judge for themselves as to how well the British Railways Board performed, but, as ever, performance was patchy. Travelling more than 20 miles on a train with no toilet depends very much on the journey one makes, and what does one conclude if there is just one toilet but it is not in working order? Such issues are at the heart of performance regimes, especially when they attract financial penalties if they are not achieved, or maybe bonuses if they are exceeded. The precise wording becomes very important, and the employment of a whole bevy of inspectors to monitor the situation has its drawbacks.

Standards have featured strongly in the contractual documents between what is now the Strategic Rail Authority and Train Operating Companies. Through such means, acronyms such as PIXC (passengers in excess of capacity) have become more widely known.

As with all such measures, though, they become that much more difficult to achieve when services are disrupted from any cause. Also, while they can reflect the general provision, guidelines tend to go by the board for such short journeys as those between Charing Cross and Waterloo East. This journey is much favoured by those in that part of the West End whose train home leaves from Waterloo, and is less onerous than using the Underground for short distances. If this means 'uncomfortable travelling conditions for two minutes', 'so what?' might be considered a reasonable reaction.

These are the easy cases; more problematic is a conclusion that passengers trying to join London-bound trains at East Croydon, for instance, have great difficulty in boarding a whole succession of trains due to their all being uncomfortably full. To the extent that this can be substantiated, there is cause for management action to be taken. First, though, it needs to be established that such trains are indeed very full on a regular basis, and also that this is not purely a phenomenon

at the front of London-bound trains. For those willing to take a few extra minutes to walk up the platform at Victoria, the rear of the same train can be surprisingly empty.

Overall, the conditions relating to peak travel and its role as an evil necessity of modern life do not make for the happiest of relationships between the providers and their customers. The former are at pains to keep costs within bounds and to operate as best they can a service which is all the time pushing at the limits of what is realistically feasible. The latter, who often think that they have to pay more than they should for a service which is not without its shortcomings, are wont to complain vociferously. They may feel, with some justification, that they are a captive market whose choice of alternatives is effectively non-existent.

Liveries

Finally, the question of rolling stock appearance and its livery. This may be considered a minor matter, but the Southern's way of presenting itself over the years did the railway little favours. A dull green utilitarian finish to often somewhat elderly boxes on wheels, with a hole cut in the end so that the driver could see out, was not something to inspire the interest and imagination of the customers – or potential customers. Even the Class 455s of the 1980s did not offer much in the way of improvement, although the Class 442 Wessex Electrics and the new offerings

coming on stream in 2001 are altogether more presentable.

All Southern Region passenger vehicles from the 1948 nationalisation until 1965 were painted what over the years needs to be described as varying shades of unlined green. Apart from the number 1 to indicate first class on doors and other lettering requirements, this was offset only by the 'cycling lion' British Railways emblem on the sides of powered vehicles, later replaced by the 'lion and wheel'. However, the colour coding below the cantrail of yellow indicated to passengers that the accommodation in that area was first class, and red indicated catering facilities. These were European designations, and remained unchanged for the rest of the life of the nationalised railway.

The small front end yellow warning panel, applied to make trains more visible to staff working on the track, made its appearance in 1964, and in 1966 the 'Rail Blue all over' livery began to be applied. This was associated with the double arrow symbol, which was displayed, in relief, on cab sides.

The all-yellow end appeared in 1967, replacing the small panels, and the overall result, if not actually depressing, earned the organisation which now wished to be known as British Rail few plaudits. Part of the problem was the use of the plain blue livery, which quickly lost any gloss it had, for all the Southern's rolling stock. The problem was that the services on which it ran did not fit

the newly created InterCity image. Even the 'new' stock for the Bournemouth electrification in 1967 was condemned to unrelieved blue, still with small warning panels when it was first delivered. For InterCity services, Rail Blue gave way to Rail Grey in a band from just above to just below the window areas. With the blue and grey livery, the BR symbol was only painted on and not displayed in relief.

Slowly, blue and grey was applied to the main line stock, and gradually spread until it became the universal British Rail passenger livery. It was carried even on the EPB suburban units, perhaps as low as one could go in the Southern's rolling stock pecking order. However, the 4SUB units which were by then reaching the end of their operational lives, always retained all-over blue.

The next move, in 1984, was the adoption of the replacement InterCity livery for Gatwick Express of grey and red, while in 1985 the London & South East sector introduced what turned out to be a short-lived colour scheme for application to express stock. This was a restrained dark brown around the windows, with an orange stripe below. The lower panels were painted in a lighter brown. Sadly, it quickly acquired the epithet of 'Jaffa cake' livery, but one could see why. This latter was overtaken by the creation of the Network SouthEast business sector on 10 June 1986. The colour scheme for this was a red line below the cantrail followed by white. The window surround was blue, and then the above colours were reversed in order. Lower body panels were grey, but the application was varied to suit the vehicles concerned. Some more modern vehicles had additional white replacing the grey band.

In the privatised railway, each Train Operating Company has adopted its own colour scheme. These are as follows:

- Connex: White, with yellow lower body and blue solebars
- South West Trains: Similar to Network SouthEast, but with an additional orange stripe below the lower red stripe. On newer stock, a blue window surround, and an otherwise white body with red doors, set off by orange and red flashes.
- Thameslink: Dark blue with a broad yellow stripe below window level lined in white, with an additional narrow white stripe at cantrail level
- Gatwick Express: Red, including the roof, and grey.
- Eurostar: Two-tone grey.

Left:
Clapham Junction station is nearly always busy, especially for services to Victoria. This is Platform 16 on a wet morning in December 1981, with 4SUB No 4692 arriving with a service from Horsham. Besides those entering the station from the street, large numbers transfer both from and to Waterloo services here. *Author*

15. Conclusions

'Things have a way of coming right if you think about them.'

Sir Herbert Ashcombe Walker

The Southern Railway, its predecessors and its successors, are both the beneficiaries and losers from the situation which they tried so hard to create. South east England is not, and never will be, the source of great industrial wealth. Natural resources are modest, and a railway has to rely first and foremost on the carriage of people for its revenues.

This is not the territory for long-distance traffic, other than in association with Eurotunnel. With the main South Coast towns like Southampton no more than 80 miles away from London, the emphasis has to be on many people making shorter journeys to bring in the revenue.

How, then, to make a successful business out of it? With trams nibbling away at the traffic in inner suburbs and overall housing shortages, there was a clear pointer to moving the population outwards and developing the hinterland. But the centres of employment remained largely in place, so the fortunates who took the hint 'to live in Surrey, free from worry' still needed to be brought back into town for their employment. They would need to make this journey twice a day, and in those days six days a week.

There was the source of revenue, but it had to be carried profitably. Operating costs needed to be contained to an affordable level, and the steam locomotive was at a disadvantage straight away as it needed two

Below:

Thameslink is likely to be expanded greatly when the upgrading of the line between Farringdon and Blackfriars, plus other infrastructure work in the London Bridge area, is completed. However, while the situation north of the Thames is relatively simple, there remains a huge selection of routes which could be taken south of the river. This is Herne Hill on 30 September 2000, with No 319381 approaching from Blackfriars forming a 'City Metro' train for the Wimbledon Loop. *Author*

crewmen, as well as the lighters up and those who had the ash to dispose of etc. The Southern needed an economical and clean source of traction power, and as quick and frequent turnrounds would be necessary at each end of the journey, electricity had huge attractions. The use of the multiple-unit was the key, as the necessary movements at the termini were only those of arrival and departure.

The scene was set for a programme of electrification under the Southern's General Manager Sir Herbert Walker and the able managers whom he gathered around him. The choice of the third rail system had its drawbacks, *but it did work*. This was the tried and tested technology, and available at relatively short notice. The suburban railway was electrified by 1930, and the push to the coast was already well advanced before it was

Above:
Folkestone was once busy with cross-channel shipping, but that which remains after the opening of the Channel Tunnel has been concentrated on Dover. Consequently, the Folkestone Harbour branch is little used. In happier days, in June 1984, a 4CEP unit leaves the station and begins the climb up to the main line. *Author*

curtailed by the 1939–45 war, and indeed Walker's retirement in 1937. It is perhaps reasonable to conclude that all Kent and perhaps even Bournemouth and Salisbury would have seen electric trains by about 1950 had circumstances not changed so drastically.

The postwar world was more difficult. The shortening of the working day brought an ever more concentrated peak, while the five day week cut revenues by one sixth. It was not merely a question of expanding capacity to meet demand; that was a financial impossibility, and in some cases a technical one as well. Some very worthwhile schemes were carried out, the rebuilding of Borough Market Junction being the outstanding example, but there were others too numerous to cover in a book of this size. Signalling schemes too controlled larger and larger areas, and although opinions differed on the most suitable size of area to be covered, multiple-aspect signalling was an essential component of a very busy railway.

How happy the customers were is another matter. Kidner may have been right to claim that by 1939 'the Southern was Britain's brightest and best run line', but a general mistrust of the railway and its management seemed to be prevalent in the postwar period

and certainly by the 1960s. The user may hear what he is told about the problems of the peak, but he nevertheless expects them to be solved so that he can at least enjoy a tolerable journey. It was perhaps such thoughts which led to the 'Commuters' Charter'. One thing, though, that was achieved was a general updating of the rolling stock and a slow, almost reluctant, giving way by the then Government to allow further electrification to take place. To be fair, it was only public money that was going to make this happen, and corners were cut to achieve this in the best Southern traditions. In the Network SouthEast of 1986, the railway found a new champion.

A new and perhaps more understanding era opened up in the 1990s, a major event being the construction of the Channel Tunnel. Here there were two distinct aspects – the tunnel itself and the traffic it would carry – and the rail (and road) routes leading to it. From the

Southern's point of view there was also the effect on the ferries and the traditional rail traffic. With the Channel Tunnel Rail Link now under construction, this will offer a whole new era for the railway in Kent and south east London when it opens.

Finally, the railway is no longer a single public industry, but divided between a number of private interests. The whole is overseen by the Strategic Rail Authority and the Rail Regulator. There is a need to regain momentum; sustained investment is a key requirement. Will the present structure be able to deliver what both the general public as a whole and the paying public as passengers want? Will those who are asked to pay the bill, be they passengers, private companies or taxpayers, find the package acceptable?

The Southern Electric has served the railways south of the Thames well, and it is almost a century since the Brighton company inaugurated electric train services between Victoria and London Bridge. This is a large undertaking upon which London has considerable dependence. It needs vision as well as tactics to find the way forward for the next century. What, one might wonder, will the Southern Electric look like in another hundred years' time?

Appendix 1: Electrification Dates

Table 1: Electrification, ac Overhead System, London, Brighton & South Coast Railway, Including the Subsequent Work by the Southern Railway

9 Dec 1909	Victoria-London Bridge, South London line
12 May 1911	Victoria-Crystal Palace LL via Streatham Hill
3 March 1912	Peckham Rye-Tulse Hill-Crystal Palace/Streatham Hill, Crystal Palace-Norwood Junction-Selhurst depot
1 April 1925	Balham-Selhurst-East Croydon-Coulsdon North, Selhurst-West Croydon-Sutton, Tulse Hill-Streatham Common

All ac overhead equipment was disused by 1928/29, when removal commenced.

Table 2: Electrification, Third Rail, London & South Western Railway/Western Section, 1923–47

July/August 1905	District Railway electrified fourth rail to Putney Bridge and Wimbledon over LSWR tracks
25 Oct 1915	Waterloo-Clapham Junction-East Putney
30 Jan 1916	Waterloo and Kingston Loop, Shepperton branch
12 March 1916	Hounslow Loop
18 June 1916	New Malden-Surbiton-Hampton Court
20 Nov 1916	Surbiton-Claygate
12 July 1925	Raynes Park-Dorking, also Guildford via Leatherhead, Claygate-Effingham Junction
6 July 1930	Hounslow Loop-Staines-Windsor & Eton Riverside
3 Jan 1937	Surbiton-Woking-Guildford, Staines-Weybridge, Woking-Farnham
4 July 1937	Guildford-Haslemere-Portsmouth Harbour, Farnham-Alton
29 May 1938	Motspur Park-Malden Manor-Tolworth (new line)
28 May 1939	Tolworth-Chessington North-Chessington South (new line)
2 July 1939	Virginia Water-Ascot-Reading, Ascot-Ash Vale, Aldershot-Guildford, Frimley-Brookwood via Sturt Lane Junction

Table 3: Electrification, Third Rail, London, Brighton & South Coast Railway/Central Section, 1923–47

25 March 1928	London Bridge-Forest Hill-East Croydon-Purley-Caterham/Tattenham Corner, Sydenham-Crystal Palace LL
17 June 1928	London Bridge-Denmark Hill-Victoria, Peckham Rye-Tulse Hill-Crystal Palace LL/Streatham Hill/Streatham Common, Sutton-Epsom Downs
3 March 1929	Victoria-Crystal Palace LL via Selhurst and Streatham Hill, Crystal Palace LL-Beckenham Junction, Streatham-Sutton-Epsom, Streatham-Haydons Road-Wimbledon
22 Sept 1929	Selhurst-Sutton, Purley-Coulsdon North
7 July 1929	Wimbledon-Wimbledon Chase-South Merton (new line)
5 Jany 1930	South Merton-Morden South-St Helier-Sutton Common-West Sutton-Sutton (new line)
6 July 1930	Wimbledon-West Croydon via Mitcham
17 July 1932	Purley-Redhill-Three Bridges/Reigate, and via Quarry line
1 Jan 1933	Three Bridges-Brighton, Brighton/Preston Park-Hove-West Worthing
7 July 1935	Brighton-Lewes-Eastbourne-Ore, Wivelsfield-Lewes-Newhaven-Seaford, Haywards Heath-Horsted Keynes
3 July 1938	Three Bridges-Horsham-Arundel-Ford, West Worthing-Ford-Havant, Ford-Littlehampton, Barnham-Bognor Regis, Dorking-Horsham
16 July 1947	Newhaven Marine branch

Table 4: Electrification, Third Rail, Eastern Section 1925–47

12 July 1925	Victoria-Herne Hill-Beckenham Junction-Orpington, Holborn Viaduct-Herne Hill, Brixton/Loughborough Junction-Nunhead-Catford-Shortlands, Nunhead-Crystal Palace HL
21 Sept 1925	Elmers End-Hayes
28 Feb 1926	Charing Cross/Cannon Street-London Bridge-Ladywell-Elmers End-Addiscombe, New Cross-Grove Park-Orpington, Grove Park-Bromley North, New Beckenham-Beckenham Junction
19 July 1926	Charing Cross/Cannon Street-Dartford via all four routes (Greenwich, North Kent, Bexleyheath, and Dartford Loop)
6 July 1930	Dartford-Gravesend
16 July 1933	Lewisham-Hither Green
1 May 1934	Bickley/Chislehurst-St Mary Cray
6 January 1935	Orpington-Sevenoaks, St Mary Cray-Otford-Sevenoaks
30 Sept 1935	Woodside-Sanderstead, Nunhead-Hither Green via Lewisham Loop
30 Sept 1935	Nunhead-Lewisham
2 July 1939	Gravesend-Strood-Maidstone West, Swanley-Gillingham, Otford-Maidstone East
11 Oct 1942	Crayford spur, new line giving access between the North Kent and Dartford Loop

Table 5: Sections of Line Which Have Been Electrified Since 1948

15 June 1959	Kent Coast Phase 1. Gillingham-Faversham-Ramsgate, also Faversham-Dover Marine via Canterbury East and Sittingbourne-Sheerness
10 August 1960	Sheerness branch diverted to use new King's Ferry Bridge across River Swale
18 June 1962	Kent Coast Phase 2. Sevenoaks-Tonbridge-Ashford-Folkestone-Dover-Ramsgate, also via Canterbury West to Minster, Maidstone East-Ashford, Paddock Wood-Maidstone West, and Folkestone Harbour branch
2 January 1967	Bournemouth electrification. Brookwood Pirbright Junction-Basingstoke, Lymington branch
20 March 1967	Isle of Wight electrification. Ryde Pier Head-Shanklin
10 July 1967	Bournemouth electrification. Basingstoke-Southampton-Bournemouth-Branksome
23 September 1973	Seaton Tramway, 120v dc overhead. Seaton Riverside depot-Colyford
25 May 1975	Seaton Tramway, 120v dc overhead. Seaton Riverside depot-Seaton Harbour Road terminus
3 April 1980	Seaton Tramway, 120v dc overhead. Colyford-Colyton
6 May 1986	Hastings electrification. Tonbridge-St Leonards Bo-Peep Junction
26 September 1987	East Grinstead electrification. South Croydon-East Grinstead
16 May 1988	Blackfriars-Farringdon. Link previously closed completely on 3 May 1971.
16 May 1988	Weymouth electrification. Branksome-Weymouth
9 May 1990	Solent electrification. Eastleigh-Fareham, St Denys-Farlington/Portcreek Junctions
November 1992	Stewarts Lane chord. New flyover west of Vauxhall for Eurostar access.
26 July 1993	Clapham Junction (north side)-Kensington Olympia
6 March 1994	Redhill-Tonbridge, to provide for electrically hauled Channel Tunnel freight
6 May 1994	Channel Tunnel and associated works. 25kV ac, Eurotunnel
29 May 1994	Clapham Junction (south side) for services from Brighton line to West London line, Olympia-North Pole, and Sheepcote Lane chord for Eurostar depot access
10 May 2000	Croydon Tramlink, 750V dc overhead. Croydon-New Addington
23 May 2000	Croydon Tramlink, 750V dc overhead. Sandilands-Beckenham Junction
30 May 2000	Croydon Tramlink, 750V dc overhead. Wimbledon-Croydon, Arena-Elmers End
In progress	Channel Tunnel Rail Link, Section 1. 25kV ac, London & Continental

Below:

Nowadays, Newhaven Maritime is also devoid of passenger vessels for what could never be described as a short sea crossing to Dieppe. The 07.50 boat train from Victoria arrives at the basic station on 5 September 1981 with 4CIG No 7372 in the lead. These trains were advertised only in the continental timetables, but local passengers still used them as they made intermediate calls en route. *Author*

Table 6: Yards and Sidings Electrified on Overhead dc System

In 1941 for the new No CC1 locomotive and its later class members:

Balcombe	Brighton	

In 1959 for the E5000, later Class 71, locomotives:

Angerstein Wharf	Dover Town	Maidstone West
Betteshanger Colliery	Faversham	Plumstead
Bricklayers Arms	Hither Green Goods	Sittingbourne
Deal	Hoo Junction	Snowdown Colliery

All dc overhead equipment was disused by 1975, when removal commenced.

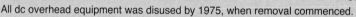

Appendix 2:
New Stations Opened

Table 1: New Stations Opened in Conjunction with Electrification, or Subsequently

Stations which were new or resited long before electrification are not recorded. For instance, Hurst Green station replaced a halt of the same name on a new site north of the road overbridge on 12 June 1961, but the line was not electrified until 1987. Where station names have been changed, in general the present name is used. 'New' stations which were previously designated as halts are not normally recorded.

Date	Station	Notes
12 March 1916	Barnes Bridge	New suburban station.
3 May 1925	Nunhead	Rebuilt on a new site.
12 July 1925	Motspur Park	New suburban station.
19 July 1926	Deptford	Previously closed on 15 March 1915.
10 July 1927	Leatherhead	Ex-LSWR station abandoned.
10 July 1927	Sunnymeads	New suburban station.
17 June 1928	South Bermondsey	Rebuilt on a new site.
9 July 1928	Petts Wood	New suburban station.
3 March 1929	Epsom	Ex-LSWR station totally rebuilt to serve both LBSCR and LSWR lines, ex-LBSCR station closed.
9 December 1929	New Hythe	New station for works access.
2 March 1930	Birkbeck	New suburban station.
6 July 1930	Chestfield & Swalecliffe	New station for works access.
6 July 1930	North Sheen	New suburban station.
6 July 1930	Swanscombe	Rebuilt on a new site $^1/_2$ mile further east.
6 July 1930	Waddon Marsh	New suburban station, now on Croydon Tramlink alignment.
6 July 1930	Whitton	New suburban station.
20 October 1930	Hinchley Wood	New suburban station.
5 July 1931	Syon Lane	New suburban station.
17 July 1932	Salfords	Workmen's platform brought into general use.
17 July 1932	Stoneleigh	New suburban station.
17 July 1932	Woodmansterne	New suburban station.
16 October 1933	Berrylands	New suburban station.
7 July 1935	Albany Park	New suburban station.
30 September 1935	Bingham Road	Reopened on electrification – now on Croydon Tramlink alignment at Addiscombe stop.
30 September 1935	Tinsley Green	Renamed Gatwick Airport, 1 June 1936, closed 27 May 1958.
1 January 1936	Falconwood	New suburban station.
28 September 1936	Hersham	New suburban station.
4 July 1937	Durrington-on-Sea	New suburban station.
26 September 1938	Bishopstone	Effectively replaced Bishopstone Beach Halt, closed 1 January 1942.
16 April 1939	Swanley	Replaced Swanley Junction on new site, $^1/_4$ mile west on London side.
2 November 1941	Hilsea	Opened October 1937, then restricted to workers only.
21 September 1942	Longcross	Opened c1940, then restricted to Army use only.
1 May 1944	Upper Halliford	New suburban station.
28 May 1958	Gatwick Airport	Formerly the rarely used 1891 Gatwick Racecourse station, totally rebuilt for a new role.
20 April 1960	Swale	Replaced 1913 halt on new alignment, after King's Ferry lifting bridge built.
18 April 1966	Soton Airport Parkway	Originally for airport access, its targeted usage has been extended.
15 May 1980	Moulsecoomb	Provides access to University of Sussex.
17 March 1985	Eltham	Replaced Eltham Well Hall and Eltham Park, relief road construction.
12 May 1986	Winnersh Triangle	Serves new housing estate and commercial developments.
25 May 1986	Polegate	Moved $^1/_2$ mile west nearer town, as Hailsham line now closed.
11 May 1987	Lake	Serves housing area.
3 October 1988	Martins Heron	Serves new housing estate.
9 May 1990	Hedge End	Serves new housing estate.
29 May 1990	City Thameslink	Associated with a new alignment from Blackfriars to Farringdon.
20 July 1991	Smallbrook Junction	No public access, available only for interchange with IoW Steam Railway.
14 November 1994	Waterloo International	For Eurostar services only.
8 January 1996	Ashford International	For Eurostar services only.
30 May 1999	West Brompton	Gives access to Underground and Earl's Court Exhibition Centre.

Appendix 3:
Electrified Line and Station Closures

Table 1: Sections of Line From Which Third Rail Electrified Passenger Services Have Been Withdrawn

This list does not include the closure of individual stations on an otherwise operational line (see below). Also, it does not take into account any reductions in the number of running lines, as when double track is converted to single.

Date	Line	Notes
5 May 1941	Wandsworth Town-Wimbledon	Retained for ecs workings; passenger services provided by London Underground southwards from East Putney.
18 September 1954	Nunhead-Crystal Palace HL branch	Branch abandoned completely.
28 October 1963	Haywards Heath-Horsted Keynes	Branch retained to Ardingly only, for ARC roadstone traffic.
4 September 1965	Reading Southern and approaches.	Services withdrawn and diverted to Reading General.
26 June 1966	Virginia Water west curve	Electrified but not used by regular services.
21 July 1966	Staines west curve	Electrified but not used by regular services.
21 July 1966	Frimley Junction-Sturt Lane Junction	Spur abandoned completely.
5 January 1969	Polegate-Stone Cross Junction	Eastbourne avoiding line, abandoned completely.
17 May 1983	Woodside-Sanderstead	Section north from former Coombe Road station area subsequently resuscitated for the construction of Croydon Tramlink.
26 January 1990	Holborn Viaduct-Blackfriars	Abandoned completely and replaced by City Thameslink on new alignment.
25 September 1994	Dover Western Docks and approaches	Formerly Dover Marine station, now abandoned completely.
31 May 1997	Elmers End-Addiscombe	Section south to former Woodside Junction used for Croydon Tramlink construction, remainder of Addiscombe branch abandoned.
31 May 1997	Wimbledon-West Croydon	Used almost in its entirety for Croydon Tramlink.

Table 2: Electrified Sections of Line Which are no Longer in Regular Use

Newhaven Marine branch
Folkestone Harbour branch

Table 3: Station Closures Since 1948 on Electrified Lines

This list does not include stations where the line has been closed in its entirety (see Table 1 above). Also excluded are those 'stations' which were not for public use, for instance Ampress Works Halt on the Lymington branch, which was always restricted to use by employees only.

Date	Station
7 May 1956	Holland Road Halt
6 September 1965	Folkestone East
3 January 1966	Grove Ferry
6 January 1976	East Brixton
10 July 1967	St Leonards West Marina
4 October 1971	Chislet Colliery
3 October 1983	Coulsdon North
16 March 1985	Eltham Well Hall
16 March 1985	Eltham Park

Table 4: Station Which Never Opened

Lullingstone, between Swanley and Eynsford, was completed on 2 April 1939 and even appeared in the summer 1939 timetable. However, the station was never opened. The surrounding land was being sold by the Hart Dyke estates and was intended for housing. This was never built, primarily because of the general concern about consuming ever more countryside on urban borders with yet more houses. This was the basis of what later became the Green Belt legislation.

There was also a proposal to build an airport at Lullingstone, fed by a new spur line off the railway. The site was agreed as suitable by the Southern Railway, Imperial Airways and the Air Ministry, but with World War 2 impending, the Government failed to buy the land. This proposal was never carried out. Subsequently, Lullingstone station was partly demolished, but little remains today.

Hastings signalbox at the east end of the station still exists as a traditional semaphore operation, a pair of which on a rail-built post are seen here in this view of 1 February 2001. *Author*

Appendix 4: Boundaries

Table 1: Railtrack: Boundaries of Southern Zone

Traditional third rail Southern passenger trains operate entirely within the bounds of Railtrack's Southern Zone. There is a single exception in that the railway infrastructure on the Isle of Wight between Ryde Pier Head and Shanklin is leased from Railtrack by the train operator. To that extent, the Isle of Wight is a vertically integrated railway.

Dual voltage trains as used on Silverlink Metro services between Richmond and North Woolwich run entirely within East Anglia Zone, while Silverlink and Connex SouthCentral trains on the West London line (WLL) enter Midlands Zone north of Kensington Olympia, at Mitre Bridge Junction. By this point, the WLL is 25kV only.

Thameslink services north of Blackfriars enter Midlands Zone just prior to Farringdon Junction, where the line joins the Moorgate branch, itself electrified at 25kV ac. Third rail electrification ends in Farringdon platforms, where the changeover takes place.

Immediately to the east of Saltwood Tunnel, at Saltwood Junction for Dollands Moor freight yard, 25kV electrification starts. It also continues on the adjacent Dover line for the short distance to Continental Junction, which is used by Eurostar trains. Shortly beyond these points, the railway leaves Railtrack Southern Zone and enters Eurotunnel property.

There are no other connections with adjacent zones where the lines are electrified both sides of the boundary.

Table 2: Extensions of Third Rail Beyond the Territory of the Old Southern Railway, but Reached Directly From its Lines

Clapham Junction-North Pole Junction.
Blackfriars-Farringdon.
North London line from Richmond to North Woolwich (formerly to Broad Street), although the third rail section between Acton Central and Camden Road has since been removed and is electrified at 25kV ac only.
Euston-Watford Junction dc electric line via Watford High Street and branch to Croxley Green. The latter (only) is presently disused, and its future is unclear.

Table 3: Fourth Rail Sections

Sections of the former Southern which are also used by the Underground's District Line are equipped with the fourth rail system. Here, the negative (centre) rail is earthed where the line is used also by third rail services. These sections are Richmond-Gunnersbury and Wimbledon-East Putney.

For many years, the North London and the Euston-Watford dc lines were fourth rail, but the services were converted to third rail on 2 August 1970, other than for the section between Queen's Park and Harrow & Wealdstone. This is shared with the Bakerloo line services, and again the fourth rail is earthed. Elsewhere, the fourth rail has been removed.

There is no other scope for through running with the Underground from third rail territory, as all remaining physical connections between the two systems have long since been removed. Compatibility issues will arise again, however, as and when the East London Line of the Underground is connected to the Railtrack network. It remains to be seen how these will be addressed, but one option is that future services will be provided exclusively by a Train Operating Company.

Table 4: Services on the Southern for Which Dual Voltage Electric Trains are Required for Operational Reasons

Eurostar services	Waterloo to Brussels/Paris, including access to North Pole depot.
Connex SouthCentral services	Gatwick Airport to Rugby via Clapham Junction.
Thameslink Rail services	Bedford to Brighton and Luton to Wimbledon/Sutton, both via Blackfriars
Silverlink Metro services	Clapham Junction and Willesden Junction
Silverlink Metro services	Richmond and North Woolwich

Connex SouthCentral also uses dual voltage Class 319 units on some of their Victoria-Brighton services, but there is no technical requirement to do so. Potentially, the Connex SouthEastern fleet of Class 365 units have dual voltage capabilities, but the necessary additional equipment for ac operation is not fitted at present.

Table 5: Sections of the Former Southern Railway Over Which Regular Passenger Trains Run in 2001, But Which Have Never Been Electrified. Preserved Railways are Excluded

- All lines west of Worting Junction (Basingstoke), west of Eastleigh and north west of Redbridge (Southampton), both towards Romsey. The lines north of Dorchester Junction and between Basingstoke and Reading are both parts of the former Great Western.
- Hurst Green Junction-Uckfield.
- Wokingham-Aldershot South Junction and Shalford Junction (Guildford)-Reigate.
- Ashford International-Ore (Hastings).

It may be noted that this does not preclude diesel operation elsewhere, notably the longer-distance services of Virgin CrossCountry and Wales & West. Also, West of England services run through to Waterloo, including via Southampton, while Uckfield trains run at peak times to Victoria and London Bridge. There are many other examples, including new services such as Brighton to Reading via Basingstoke (South West Trains) and Ipswich to Basingstoke via Feltham (Anglia Railways).

Appendix 5:
Rolling Stock as at February 1961

This shows the volume of stock and the types which were in operation at that time.

Year Intro'd	Type code	No Series	Total Units	Total Vehicles	Set Length	Seats per Unit 1st	2nd	Total Seats	Seats per car	Notes
1935	2BIL	2001-2152	148	296	125ft 0in	24	84	108	54	Brighton stock for stopping services
1939	2HAL	2601-2700	98	196	125ft 0in	18	110	128	64	Kent suburban stock
1931	4LAV	2921-2955	35	140	249ft 0in	30	234	264	66	Brighton stock for main line locals
1932	6PUL	3001-3020	20	120	383ft 6in	72	280	352	59	Brighton stock with Pullman car
1935	6PAN	3021-3037	16	96	376ft 6in	72	240	312	52	Brighton stock with pantry car
1932	6PUL	3041-3043	3	18	370ft 0in	72	252	324	54	Converted from former 6CITY stock, with higher 1st/2nd class seating ratios
1932	5BEL	3051-3053	3	15	330ft 0in	40	152	192	38	'Brighton Belle' stock
1937	4RES	3054-3072	16	64	254ft 0in	42	140	182	46	Portsmouth stock with restaurant car
1937	4BUF	3073-3085	13	52	254ft 0in	30	154	184	46	Portsmouth stock with buffet car
1937	4COR	3101-3158	58	232	254ft 0in	30	196	226	56	Portsmouth stock
1949	4DD	4001-4002	2	8	249ft 0in	0	552	552	138	Double-deck suburban stock
1948	4SUB	4101-4754	251	1004	249ft 0in	0	386	386	96	Early batches included vehicles converted from pre-1923 coaching stock
1951	4EPB	5001-5260	210	840	249ft 0in	0	386	386	96	SR design
1960	4EPB	5301-5356	56	224	254ft 11in	0	388	388	97	BR design, another 14 sets constructed later
1957	2HAP	5601-5636	36	72	125ft 0in	18	120	138	69	SR design on 2NOL underframes
1959	2NOP	5651-5684	34	68	125ft 0in	0	178	178	89	SR design on 2NOL underframes
1953	2EPB	5701-5800	79	158	127ft 11in	0	186	186	93	BR design, includes ex-Tyneside units
1957	2HAP	6001-6105	105	210	127ft 11in	19	134	153	76	BR design
1956	4BEP	7001-7022	22	88	258ft 0in	46	157	203	51	Kent Coast stock with buffet car
1956	4CEP	7101-7204	104	416	258ft 0in	24	200	224	56	Kent Coast stock
1959	MLV	S68001-06	6	6	64ft 6in	0	0	0	0	A further four vehicles were constructed later
Totals			1,315	4,323						

A cold morning at Wimbledon in January 1996 sees a Class 455 unit arriving in Platform 5 with an inner-suburban service for Waterloo. The platform edges have been cleared of snow and services are running normally. *Author*

Index

Cover captions

Front, right:
The view from Preston Park looking towards Brighton on 23 June 1968. In the foreground are a couple of 'Brighton Belle' sets and a pair of 4LAV units, while London Road viaduct carrying the line from Brighton to Lewes may be seen in the middle distance. *Colour-Rail*

Front cover, upper:
930007 is a Gillingham-based Sandite unit in Railtrack green and blue livery. This is the nearest that can be seen to a Southern green at present. It has been converted from two old 4SUB Driving Motors. The unit is seen here heading east through Eltham on 27 January 2001. *Author*

Front, left middle:
The Gatwick Express Class 460 8-car Alstom Juniper units entered service in 2001. On 27 January 2001, one of these units is seen passing Wandsworth Common with the 14.30 departure from Victoria to Gatwick Airport non-stop. *Author*

Front, left lower:
The Class 442 Wessex Electrics have been repainted strikingly by Stagecoach-owned South West Trains, and units Nos 2403 and 2404 were photographed coupled head to head at Surbiton on 8 July 1999. *Author*

Back upper:
Connex South Eastern have leased 12 Class 508 units, which were previously with Merseyrail Electrics. This is 508204 arriving at Queenborough with a Sheerness-on-Sea to Sittingbourne service on 29 January 2001. Patronage is a little thin. *Author*

Back, middle:
The most powerful electro-diesels in the fleet were the 10 members of Class 74, which were converted from the Class 71 straight electrics. No E6106 was photographed at Stewarts Lane on 18 July 1968. *Author*

Back, lower:
'Live in Kent and be content' was one of a series of posters commissioned during the mid-1920s by (Sir) John Elliot, then in charge of the Southern Public Relations and Advertising. 'Evenings by the Sea' seemed an appropriate way for Southern Electric to promote the results of its push to the coast in the mid-1930s, while the attractive third poster trumpeted the completion of electrification to Reading in 1939. *Author's collection, courtesy Dalkeith Picture Postcards (all)*

End papers:
These system maps of the Southern Region are derived from those in the 1963 public timetable. All lines are shown, as opposed to those electrified only, but it is hoped that readers will find this a useful source of reference to a complex system. *John Chapman collection*

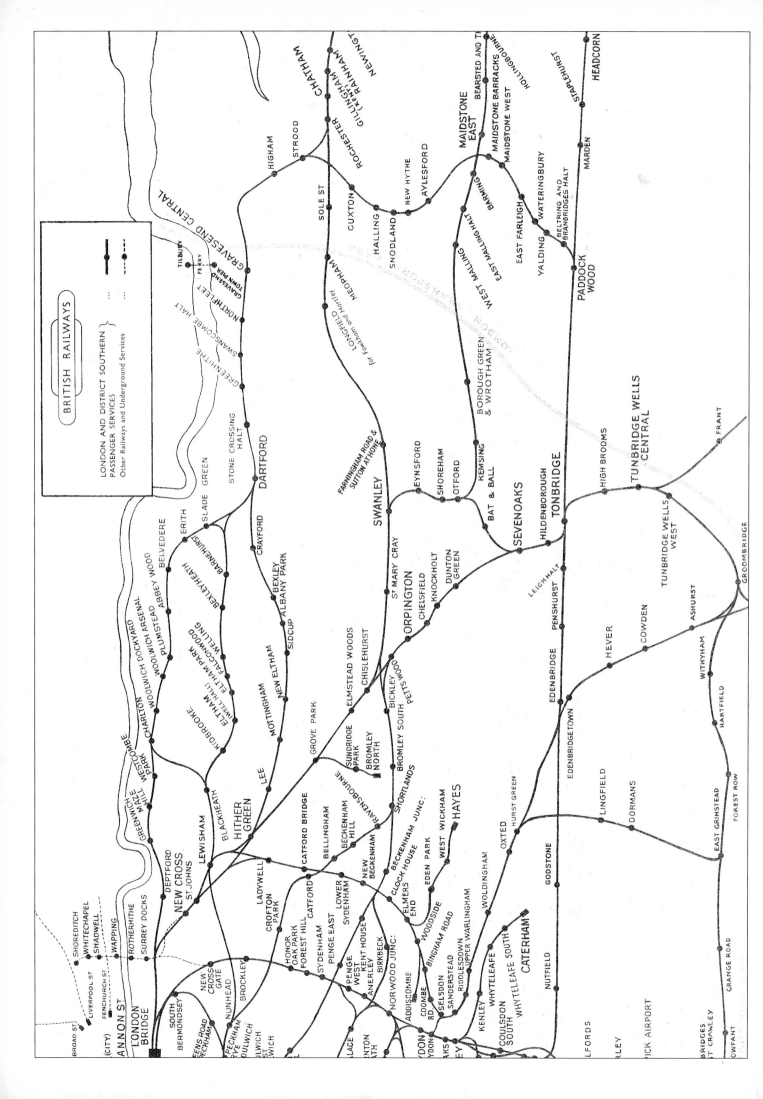